SYNERGY

SYNERGY

A Theoretical Model of Canada's
Comprehensive Approach

Eric Dion, CD, MBA, PhD

SYNERGY
A Theoretical Model of Canada's Comprehensive Approach

iUniverse books may be ordered through booksellers or by contacting:

iUniverse
1663 Liberty Drive
Bloomington, IN 47403
www.iuniverse.com
1-800-Authors (1-800-288-4677)

ISBN: 978-1-5320-3057-4 (sc)
ISBN: 978-1-5320-3058-1 (e)

Library of Congress Control Number: 2017915312

Print information available on the last page.

iUniverse rev. date: 12/12/2017

Contents

List of Figures

List of Tables

Foreword

Since 2001, the Comprehensive Approach has been a key emerging phenomenon within the field of national security and defence. On August 22, 2001, then United Nations Secretary-General Kofi Annan suggested in a report that the UN adopt a "Comprehensive Approach to ending Afghanistan conflict."[1] This was before the tragic attacks of September 11, which saw the launch of the global war on terrorism by the United States. Not long after, Canadian Special Forces were being engaged on the ground in Afghanistan (Horn and Balasevicius 2007, 13–14). This was to be the start of Canada's engagement in Afghanistan, which lasted close to 10 years in its combat and comprehensive form until July 2011 and finally ended completely in its training form in July 2014, thus providing a circumvented background.

This engagement saw the emergence of new constructs for the management of organisations and operations, such as the three *D*s of defence, diplomacy and development, as well as the whole of government and the joint, integrated, multinational and public. Particularly from 2006 onward, the comprehensive approach emerged as key construct, but it was not supported by a framework, a model or a theory. It has been found through a systematic review of the literature on this subject that in fact the "Comprehensive approach is a *philosophy*," according to CF Land Ops (2008, 5–14). And according to former NATO Secretary General Rasmussen: "The comprehensive approach not only makes sense—it is necessary."[2]

---

[1] UNSC, *Comprehensive Approach Needed to End Afghanistan Conflict*, speech, Secretary General Kofi Annan, August 22, 2001, http://www.un.org/apps/news/storyAr.asp?NewsID=1165&Cr=Afghanistan&Cr1

[2] NATO, 2010, http://www.nato.int/cps/en/natohq/opinions_66727.htm (accessed January 16, 2016)

Indeed, the military alone is unable to solve the root causes of conflicts, which then calls upon the other elements of national and international power to collaborate more closely. The aim of this research is therefore to propose a theoretical model for this new approach. What would be an applicable decision-making model of the comprehensive approach? Where, when, who and with whom, what, how, why and to what effect can such a model of the comprehensive approach be employed? This book aims to answer these questions.

The comprehensive approach can be defined as "commonly understood principles and collaborative processes that enhance the likelihood of favourable and enduring outcomes within a particular situation."[3] From a management perspective, it appears possible to propose a much more integrated theoretical model in order to support executive-level thinking in regard to future engagements. Such a model is thus constructed of six management dimensions: the situational context, the socioculture, the organisation structure, the strategic policies, the systemic processes and the synergy dynamics. Together, these dimensions fundamentally represent what would be the basic constructs for a more integrated theoretical model of the comprehensive approach. By employing the principles of grounded theory as a research design, iterating between documentation review, content analysis and a meta-analysis, such triangulating methodology employing qualitative and quantitative methods provided the reflexivity required to construct an executive-decision support model. Such a model could be employed in Canada's future engagements or even for the United Nations' own engagements.

The original contribution of this research lies in its ability to propose an integrated theoretical model of Canada's comprehensive approach, which up to now seems not to exist. Such a theoretical model could namely assist academics in analysing future engagements; it could also assist practitioners with their own executive decision making within these same engagements. Moreover, taking a strategic management perspective on the comprehensive approach proposes to open new perspectives within the field of national security and defence, a field traditionally dominated by

---

[3] UK, 2010, p. 9, http://www.publications.parliament.uk/pa/cm200910/cmselect/cmdfence/224/224.pdf (accessed January 16, 2016).

political science and more specifically international relations. In the end, it is found that synergy appears to better explain the complex dynamics at play within the comprehensive approach. Thus, basic constructs for a more comprehensive theory are proposed in <u>Annex A</u>, which would account for a more synergistic perspective.

Préface

Depuis 2001, *l'Approche Compréhensive* a émergée comme un phénomène important au sein des études de Sécurité Nationale & Défense. Le 22 août 2001, Kofi Annan, alors Secrétaire-général de l'Organisation des Nations Unies (ONU), suggérait dans un rapport que l'ONU adopte « une *Approche Compréhensive* pour mettre fin au conflit en Afghanistan[4] ». Or ceci était avant les évènements tragiques du 11 septembre 2001 qui menèrent au lancement d'une guerre globale contre le terrorisme par les États-Unis. Peu de temps après, des opérateurs des Forces Spéciales Canadiennes étaient engagés sur le terrain en Afghanistan (Horn & Balasevicius, (2007), p. 13-14). Et ceci marqua le début de *l'Engagement du Canada en Afghanistan* qui dura près de 10 ans dans sa forme de combat / compréhensive jusqu'en juillet 2011 et se termina finalement complètement dans sa forme d'entraînement, en juillet 2014.

Tout au long, cet engagement vit l'émergence de nouvelles idées pour le management des organisations et des opérations, telles que les 3D de la Défense, Diplomatie et Développement, de même que l'approche pangouvernementale et l'approche interarmées, inter-agences, multinationale et publique. En particulier à partir de 2006 *l'Approche Compréhensive* a émergée comme une idée maîtresse qui cependant n'était pas supportée par un cadre de référence, un modèle ou une théorie. Or nous avons trouvé, suite à une revue systématique de la littérature exhaustive sur le sujet, qu'en fait «*l'Approche Compréhensive* est une **philosophie**», selon le CF Land Ops (2008), p. 5-14, qui apparait comme nécessaire. De plus, selon Rasmussen, l'ancien secrétaire-général de l'OTAN:

---

[4]   UN, 2001, http://www.un.org/press/en/2001/sc7130.doc.htm and http://www. afghanistannewscenter.com/news/2001/august/aug23h2001.html and http:// reliefweb.int/report/afghanistan/annan-suggests-un-adopt-comprehensive-approach-ending-afghanistan-conflict (accessed January 16, 2016).

The Comprehensive Approach not only makes sense—it is necessary.[5] En effet, les militaires seuls sont incapables de résoudre les causes fondamentales des conflits, ce qui interpelle alors les autres éléments de pouvoirs nationaux et internationaux à collaborer plus étroitement. Le but de cette recherche est ainsi de proposer un modèle théorique intégré de cette nouvelle approche. Quelle serait un modèle de prise de décision applicable de *l'Approche Compréhensive*? Où et quand, qui, avec qui, quoi, comment, pourquoi et alors à quel effet un tel modèle de l'Approche Compréhensive peut être utilisé? Ce livre propose de répondre à ces questions.

L'Approche Compréhensive peut être définie comme : « des principes généralement compris et des processus collaboratifs qui augmentent la probabilité d'un résultat favorable et durable dans une situation particulière (traduction libre)[6] ». Dans une perspective managériale, il apparait possible de proposer un modèle bien plus intégré pour supporter la réflexivité au niveau exécutif en regard des engagements futurs. Un tel modèle est construit à partir de six dimensions du management : le contexte situationnel, la socio-culture, la structure organisationnelle, les politiques stratégiques, les processus systémiques et la dynamique synergique. Ensemble, ces dimensions fondamentales représentent ce que seraient les assises de base pour un modèle théorique plus intégré de *l'Approche Compréhensive*. Employant les principes de la théorisation enracinée comme devis de recherche, alternant entre la revue de la documentation, l'analyse du contenu et une méta-analyse, une telle méthodologie triangulée employant des méthodes qualitatives et quantitatives, fournira la réflexivité requise pour construire un modèle de prise de décision. Ce modèle pourrait être employé pour les engagements futurs du Canada de même que pour ceux des Nations Unies.

L'apport original de cette recherche est de proposer un modèle décisionnel intégré de *l'Approche Compréhensive* du Canada ce qui ne semble pas encore exister. Un tel modèle théorique peut notamment aider les universitaires à analyser les engagements futurs, de même qu'il peut assister les acteurs

---

[5] NATO, 2010, http://www.nato.int/cps/en/natohq/opinions_66727.htm (accessed January 16, 2016).

[6] UK, 2010, p. 9, http://www.publications.parliament.uk/pa/cm200910/cmselect/cmdfence/224/224.pdf (accessed January 16, 2016).

dans leur propre prise de décisions exécutives dans le cadre de ces mêmes engagements. Qui plus est, en adoptant une perspective de management stratégique en regard de *l'Approche Compréhensive*, nous proposons d'ouvrir de nouvelles perspectives dans le champ de la Sécurité Nationale et de la Défense, un domaine traditionnellement dominé par les sciences politiques et plus spécifiquement, par les relations internationales. Somme toute, nous avons trouvé que la *synergie* explique mieux les dynamiques complexes qui sont en jeu dans *l'Approche Compréhensive*. Ce faisant, les assises d'une théorie plus compréhensive sont proposées en <u>annexe A</u>, propice au développement ultérieur d'une théorie de la synergie.

Abstract

The comprehensive approach has been a new and emerging theme in international security. Although Canada and many NATO allies subscribed to the comprehensive approach as a philosophy for their global engagements, there does not appear to be a working framework, model or theory for this new and emerging approach. This presents itself as a dichotomy between rhetoric and reality, where executives are not providing an overarching architecture to go about delivering comprehensive results in effect. This is required in light of global interdependencies and conflict complexities. As such, we asked ourselves: What would be an applicable decision-making model of the comprehensive approach? Working with grounded theory (Glaser and Strauss 1967) and from a corpus of 178 documents on the subject, this research proposes a new executive-level decision-making model for the comprehensive approach. Noting the importance of synergy as a construct at the heart of the comprehensive approach, a more integrated, holistic and dynamic theoretical model is developed based on six dimensions: the situational context, the socioculture, the organisational structure, the strategic policy, the systemic process and the synergy dynamic. Our model could be employed as a tool in the executive suite to assist during reflexive thinking about global systemic practices, like in the case of Canada's current and future engagements or that of the United Nations. Indeed, it appears that in order to achieve higher degrees of collaboration and synergy, all six dimensions must be taken into consideration. More specifically, executives should deliberately create and sustain synergy by working through space-time conditions, by establishing a common understanding and comprehension, by coordinating and by cooperating in concertation—all in order to achieve greater collaboration and synergy. As such, this research concludes that our theoretical model of synergy can become an important reference for executive decisions that require a comprehensive approach in effect. Indeed, synergy fosters greater collaboration.

Résumé

L'Approche Compréhensive est un thème nouveau et émergeant en Sécurité Internationale. Quoique le Canada et plusieurs alliés de l'OTAN aient souscrit à *l'Approche Compréhensive* en tant que philosophie pour leurs engagements globaux, il ne semble pas exister de cadre de référence, de modèle ou de théorie fonctionnelle pour cette approche nouvelle et émergeante. Ceci se présente donc comme une dichotomie entre la rhétorique et la réalité, où les cadres exécutifs ne disposent pas d'une architecture pour effectivement livrer des résultats compréhensifs, lesquels sont requis à la lumière des interdépendances globales et de la complexité des conflits. Nous nous sommes donc demandés : Quelle serait un modèle de prise de décision applicable de *l'Approche Compréhensive*? Partant de la théorisation enracinée (Glaser & Strauss (1967)) et ayant travaillé avec un corpus de 178 documents sur le sujet, cette recherche propose un nouveau modèle de prise de décisions exécutif de *l'Approche Compréhensive*. Notant l'importance de la *Synergie* comme construit au cœur de *l'Approche Compréhensive*, un modèle théorique plus intégré, holistique et aussi dynamique est développé basé sur six dimensions : Le contexte situationnel, la socio-culture, la structure organisationnelle, la stratégie politique, le processus systémique et la dynamique de la synergie. Ce modèle pourrait être utilisé comme outil dans la suite exécutive pour assister lors de séances de réflexions comme dans le cas d'engagements actuels et futurs du Canada ou encore des Nations Unies. Il appert en effet que pour atteindre un plus haut degré de collaboration et de *Synergie*, que les six dimensions doivent être prises en considération. Plus spécifiquement, les cadres exécutifs devraient délibérément créer et soutenir la *Synergie* en travaillant avec les conditions de l'espace-temps, en établissant un climat propice à la compréhension commune, en coordonnant ainsi qu'en coopérant dans le cadre de concertations, et ce afin d'atteindre un plus haut degré de collaboration et de *Synergie*. C'est en ce sens que cette recherche conclut que notre modèle théorique de la *Synergie* peut devenir une référence importante pour les décisions exécutives qui requièrent effectivement une *Approche Compréhensive*. Il appert en somme que la *Synergie* favoriserait davantage de collaboration.

Keywords

Synergy, Comprehensive Approach, Canada, Afghanistan, Iraq

Biography

Eric is a senior university lecturer, an executive management consultant and military veteran who served for 25 years in the Canadian Forces. His research focuses on the strategic management nexus in national security and defence.

Image Credits

Interior photography courtesy of the Canadian Armed Forces – Combat Camera: http://www.combatcamera.forces.gc.ca/gallery/cc_photos/detail/?filename=IS2008-3154&assetId=18275

Back cover logo copyright of the Royal Canadian Legion.

Acknowledgments

The successful conduct and completion of a doctoral research project—in particular one of this scope on such a complex, contemporary, comprehensive public strategic management issue in the field of Canada's national security and defence—requires tremendous support. First and foremost, I wish to express my sincerest gratitude to my thesis director, Professor Lilly Lemay, for her unwavering and precious support, for her great responsiveness and for her open minded academic advice, which was essential for the realisation of this research. Such a project would not have been possible without her great leadership and mentorship.

I also wish to thank Professor Gerard Divay for presiding over my doctoral committee, and I wish to recognise the essential and critical challenge role played collectively by Professor Stéphane Roussel, Professor David Morin and Professor Rémi Landry. Thanks to their insights, this doctoral research project was able to go further. Finally, I dedicate this doctoral thesis to four beloved children, first to Audrey and Laurie, and also to Émilie and Tommy. I hope this doctoral research project will be a constructive legacy for them and their future, considering that this synergistic theoretical model can find many fruitful applications. Merci.

Introduction

In recent years, and in light of global instabilities, there has been a growing normative current in international relations regarding the necessity of greater collaboration in order to address the root causes of conflicts. The premise behind the idea is simple: By ensuring greater collaboration from the outset—and not only once conflicts or instabilities have emerged—solutions can be found, preventing and perhaps even pre-empting such issues from arising. This comprehensive approach, as it is called, is thus part of a strategic management paradigm where global rationality prevails and where, in theory, by working together as a team, global actors can collectively manage to find better solutions. What would be an applicable decision-making model of the comprehensive approach? Where, when, who and with whom, what, how, why and to what effect can such a comprehensive approach model be further employed? Through a grounded theory research design, this book will propose that synergy represents a more integrated theoretical model of Canada's comprehensive approach.

Overview

Canada's engagement in Afghanistan[7] had been a key foreign policy agenda issue for Canadians since the start of this new millennium. This followed directly from the tragic events of September 11, 2001. Indeed, not long thereafter, Canadian Special Forces were being engaged on the ground in Afghanistan (Horn and Balasevicius 2007, 13–14) as part of Canada's contribution to a coalition of willing nations, in a global war on terrorism, a campaign launched subsequently in December 2001 by the United States and the United Kingdom in northern Afghanistan in response to these unprecedented attacks. For Canadians, however, Canada's engagement

---

[7] *Canada's Engagement in Afghanistan,* http://www.afghanistan.gc.ca/canada-afghanistan/menu.aspx

1

in Afghanistan was mostly perceived as a military affair, perhaps even as a revolution in military affairs that saw Canada move closer to the US military, with Canada's defence spending higher than any level since World War II, as well as Canada's contribution reaching a high of about 3,000 troops in theatre. These important Canadian investments in blood and treasure never yielded expected results, coming short of the comprehensive achievements the approach promised.

Canada's engagement in Afghanistan saw the transformation of the Canadian Forces from a peacekeeping and peacemaking force, as it was perceived in the 1990s following the fall of the Berlin wall and the end of the Cold War, to a full fighting combat force alongside its allies in a complex counterinsurgency. This paradigm shift thus changed the Canadian Armed Forces, transforming its organisation, its equipment and its personnel concurrent with this key mission that was granted by three successive governments, based on the principled argument that this mission was strategic. Great synergies seemed to emerge from Canada's engagement in Afghanistan, in particular from many new and emerging constructs such as the three Ds of defence, diplomacy and development, as well as from the subsequent whole-of-government approach, the fundamental issue being that the comprehensive approach presented a much more significant challenge than at first expected that is both practically as well as intellectually.

Problem

Indeed, the comprehensive approach seems not to exist intellectually. Surely there must exist a framework, model or theory supporting the comprehensive approach, confirming this would seek to find one. However, systematic research on this topic has yielded little so far. This presents itself as a dichotomy between rhetoric and reality. Canada subscribed to the comprehensive approach through its policies on Afghanistan, but it never provided an overarching architecture to go about delivering comprehensive results in effect.

Questions

What would be an applicable decision-making model of the comprehensive approach? In order to further develop this overarching research question, we will seek to answer the underlying where, when, who, what, how and why questions through our original research design, answering each of the following sub-questions through six key dimensions.

✓ Where/when is the comprehensive approach situated today?
✓ Who are the comprehensive approach's societal stakeholders?
✓ What is the comprehensive approach's organisation structures?
✓ How is the comprehensive approach systematically designed?
✓ Why is the comprehensive approach a new strategic paradigm?
✓ Is the comprehensive approach creating positive synergies?

In developing comprehensive and comprehensible answers to these underlying questions, we propose to develop the comprehensive approach construct through concepts, categories and their correlations, as well as to provide a comprehensive answer to each question, in order to answer the overarching research question. As the final outcome of this doctoral research, we will answer whether the comprehensive approach can be better represented comprehensively.

> We can't solve problems using the same kind of
> thinking we used when we created them!
> —Albert Einstein

Objective

Our objective is to better understand the comprehensive approach as a new, emerging strategic management phenomenon, in order to propose a theoretical model that could assist executives in their decisions from a constructive, pragmatic view. Thus, the aim is to propose an academically acceptable, as well as professionally applicable, comprehensive theoretical model, seeking in essence to capture the key constructs and the key dimensions of such an integrated model. This will serve as a reference and will become a framework for organisations and operations in the field of national security and defence.[8] Henceforth, the aim of this doctoral research is to propose such a comprehensive theoretical model that could serve

---

[8] National Security and Defence, https://www.canada.ca/en/services/defence.html (accessed January 19, 2016). Senate Standing Committee, http://www.parl.gc.ca/sencommitteebusiness/CommitteeHome.aspx?comm_id=1076&Language=E

as strategic management framework to assist executives with pragmatic decisions. It was decided to exploit this theoretical void in order to propose what could be the basic constructs of a more integrated model and theory. Thus, finding a case of the comprehensive approach in practice is the cornerstone of this project, and as such the comprehensive approach has emerged as the key tenet of Canada's engagement in Afghanistan, without at least a parallel model, a theory and/or an integrated theoretical model.

Method

Perspective

Implementing a comprehensive approach is more about its management than politics. As such, this research proposes to study the comprehensive approach in a strategic management perspective. This is an innovative approach at looking inside the executive decision-making scheme for complex and multidimensional decisions, such as the political, economic, social, technological, legal and environmental dimensions, to name a few. In this research perspective, it is worth looking into Canada's engagement in Afghanistan, which in its comprehensive form only emerged from 2007 onward and ended in July 2011, in order to develop the intellectual constructs and the concepts, categories and correlations of such an integrated model, without being limited to a single, predominant perspective within the case-study and in the theory. Furthermore, this research will also consider other potentially applicable theories within a more integrated theoretical model of the comprehensive approach so as to offer future theoretical prospects (Annex A).

Background

The comprehensive approach emerged from the background that was Canada's engagement in Afghanistan, and so surveying this crucial case will be necessary. Henceforth, in order to study the theoretical subject of the comprehensive approach, the practical object of Canada's engagement in Afghanistan was thus crucial for setting the dimensions of analysis. We focus specifically on one country's engagement in Afghanistan (Canada's) and within a well-defined period of time from its original engagement (2001) to the approach emergence (2007) until its end in combat and comprehensive form (2011) and then in training form (2014). This research

4

will have as background a crucial case-study:[9] Afghanistan. Looking at this background holistically provides a better explanation for the practices and greatly assists in identifying the fundamental dimensions of management that are at play according to a grounded theory of the comprehensive approach. Afghanistan is the crucial background, and this unique case will de facto serve as reference to analyse the comprehensive approach.

Results

Contribution

The national security and defence of Canada in the 21st century is complex in nature and requires a comprehensive approach; Canada calls it a "whole of government," which theoretically is much less holistic than the comprehensive approach itself. Within the field of national security and defence, developing a comprehensive theoretical model represents an original contribution because, as mentioned, the field is dominated by policy and much less by management. Up to now, no other scholar has ventured to theoretically model this new, emerging approach, which is in essence the key contribution this doctoral research project proposes as its outcome. This has been achieved through the production and publication in journals of three academically peer-reviewed articles. The momentum for this research has been fuelled by many cognitive dissonances, as well as a sincere desire to serve beyond the call of duty to find better and smarter ways to operate within the field of national security and defence in Canada's interest.

Thesis

This doctoral thesis thus presents the central argument that synergy is a much smarter theoretical explanation for the decision-making scheme found within the comprehensive approach in Canada's engagement in Afghanistan. As such: synergy represents a more integrated, holistic and dynamic theoretical model for the comprehensive approach. By definition, synergy is "The interaction of two or more agents or forces so that their

---

[9]   "Case studies are the preferred method when how or why questions are being posed, the investigator has little control over events and focus is on contemporary phenomenon within a real-life context" (Yin 2009, 2).

combined effect is greater than the sum of their individual effects."[10] Henceforth, a dynamic notion of interactions is key, as well as the notion of greater and combined effects, which are enhanced.

Organisation

The book is divided into six chapters. The first two chapters serve to establish the basis of the thesis. The following three chapters serve to present results as three articles. The final sixth chapter serves as discussion on synergy. This doctoral research is essentially based on a systematic review of literature on the comprehensive approach in order to propose a more integrated decision model through a grounded theory design. Within a crucial case study as background, Canada's engagement in Afghanistan from 2001 to 2014, documentation content analysis allowed us to extract the codes, categories, and correlations to construct a new decision model and propose a supporting theory of synergy. Hence, this book is organised according to traditional academic standards but has essentially taken an unconventional academic approach.

Chapter 1 consists of the presentation of the fundamental issue: the fact that in spite of a clear focus within the literature on the topic of the comprehensive approach, there does not appear to be a working framework, model or theory to manage this so-called approach. Starting with an overview of the approach and following with its genesis, this first chapter then presents definitions of the comprehensive approach, as well as key constructs that have been its evolutionary precursors. After discussing Canada's approach, this chapter thus concludes that the so-called comprehensive approach is quite literally a Gordian knot.

Chapter 2 presents the research logic supporting this doctoral thesis. Starting with the key elements of a constructive and pragmatic epistemology, and following with our strategic management and our systemic ontology, it then presents our entire research methodology. By explaining the grounded theory method which was employed, this chapter describes the important selection of the corpus of literature on the topic. It further explains the content analysis process from which a theoretical model was constructed,

---

[10] *Oxford English Dictionary*, "Synergy," https://en.oxforddictionaries.com/definition/synergy

which was iterated three times at different points in the spiral, following the analysis of 88, of 105 and of 178 texts in total. This chapter is central for understanding our bottom-up and inductive approach, which through grounded theory has led us to the construction of a synergistic theoretical model. Chapters 3, 4 and 5 present the results of this analysis as original articles published or submitted for publication to peer-reviewed academic journals.

Chapter 3 consists of the first article published in Defence Studies and is entitled "Canada's Comprehensive Approach in Afghanistan: A Critical Review of Literature, 2001–2011." As such, it first presents the systematic and critical review of literature on the topic and goes on to identify three important contributions, as well as three serious limitations. First, there is the obvious security apparatus, and then there are the political strategy and the emerging normative, which all represent important contributions. Conversely, the efficiency assumption, the international relations and the intellectual complexity present serious limitations within the literature, particularly in the case of Canada's engagement in Afghanistan from 2001–2011. Noting the weakness of current frameworks in explaining the approach, the problem appears critically: In order to assess the success of the comprehensive approach, analyzing it more comprehensively is quintessential, but this appears impossible without a theoretical model.

Chapter 4 is entitled "Constructing Canada's Synergistic Model: Lessons from Afghanistan." Introducing Canada's engagement in Afghanistan and the comprehensive approach, it goes on to present our grounded theory methodology for the construction of this model. After passing through content analysis, it states the spiral iterations that have been done, resulting in the proposition of a theoretical model composed of six dimensions: the situational context, the socioculture, the organisational structure, the strategic policies, the systemic processes and the synergy dynamics. This article discusses lessons learned and concludes that synergy has been the fundamental underlying construct. Employing our model for Canada's future engagements, as well as for the UN's, seems very promising.

Chapter 5 then takes our synergistic model a step further into the field of management and in its application to the case of Iraq and the Levant. It synthesises our grounded theory methodology and is entitled "Synergy as Canada's Comprehensive Approach." It takes our synergistic model into collaborative public management and further explains that in fact, collaborative public strategic management is the field for this original contribution. By applying our synergistic model to the case of Iraq (2017), this article presents a series of policy recommendations for the current engagement in Iraq, concluding in essence that our synergistic theoretical model, or synergy, can be Canada's comprehensive approach.

Chapter 6 finally discusses synergy and presents our contributions in six areas of strategic management, as well as in international relations and national security and defence studies. From strategic performance, structured planning, systemic process to synergic collaboration as contributions to the field of strategic management, it also develops situational relations and societal warfare as its main contributions to international relations and strategic studies.

Our conclusion overall thus explains how the three articles are the outcome of an overarching doctoral research project that could become a post-doctoral or academic research program, and it concludes that synergy can become Canada's comprehensive approach.

In spite of limitations—more specifically the fact that these conclusions may be more applicable to a class of cases, namely unconventional warfare including counterterrorism, counterinsurgency, counter-proliferation and counter-narcotics, for example—this research nonetheless offers very interesting strategic management insights. Although probably more applicable to national security and defence studies at large, synergy appears to be a fruitful avenue to explain the decision-making scheme behind its complexity. This is particularly so in the face of those new multidimensional, complex and dynamic threats. Indeed, most contemporary challenges facing Canada's national security and defence in the 21st century are complex in nature largely thanks to globalisation and information technology. Thus, proposing synergy as a theoretical model makes great theoretical and practical sense for Canada, the UN and allied future engagements.

Annex A is also an important piece of this work. Starting with a review of the literature on synergy, from complexity to biomedical and on to management and military literature, this annex then turns to discuss synergy theory. By presenting the fundamentals of a theory, it goes on to discuss theoretical integration of numerous theories within our synergistic theoretical model. After presenting our final meta-analysis of covariance and the related data that attest to the validity and reliability of this research, it concludes by discussing synergy. This annex could be the precursor for further theoretical developments on the idea of synergy.

Comprehensive Approach

This first chapter will systematically review the literature pertaining to the comprehensive approach after having overviewed the approach and presented the approach's genesis. Since 2001, the comprehensive approach has been a key emerging construct within the field of national security and Defence. Indeed, on August 22, 2001, then United Nations Secretary-General Kofi Annan suggested in a report that the UN adopt a "comprehensive approach to ending Afghanistan conflict." This was before the tragic events of September 11, 2001. Since then, there has been a growing body of empirical literature within international relations, and strategic studies in particular, discussing the comprehensive approach. This chapter presents the systematic review of this empirical literature on the subject of this approach, starting with an overview and its genesis.

The comprehensive approach emerged following the realisation that a more integrated, strategic management was required to solve some of the fundamental root causes of conflicts that are very social and economic in nature. It was also found that the comprehensive approach emerged in light of these international security concerns, which also explain the main security and defence orientation of the literature. Also, NATO's counterinsurgency campaign in Afghanistan provided the background from which this comprehensive approach emerged. As such, a new normative and narrative was developed underscoring the requirement for this *comprehensive approach* and often underlining its assumption of efficiency. Henceforth, it is found that the *comprehensive approach* is not simply a wicked problem; it also suffers from great intellectual complexity that arises from a weakness of current frameworks in explaining the approach.

As a starting point, this chapter will first present the overview of the comprehensive approach at large and then discuss its genesis. Following from this chronological survey of the idea, definitions will be reviewed, and an operative definition will be retained for this research. Thereafter, Canada's approach will be discussed before concluding the chapter.

Approach Overview

Although the idea of a comprehensive approach is hardly a new one, the employment of the concept as a whole is rather new within the field of strategic management. In itself, the comprehensive approach is an attempt to circumscribe any given issue comprehensively, simply meaning "of broad scope or content; including all or much." As such, it could be said the approach is comprehensive in both scope and scale, generally attempting to describe phenomena in a larger and wider perspective. Within life sciences, the comprehensive approach has been used to comprehensively study different aspects of the human body, from chronic fatigue to more encompassing topics such as *The Essence of Rational Psychotherapy: A Comprehensive Approach to Treatment* (by Ellis 1970).

Within management, the comprehensive approach is associated with a rationalist epistemology, employing a more deductive logic. Indeed, the development of a rationalistic comprehensive theory can be traced back to August Comte, one of the fathers of positivism. Comte applied the methods of observation and of experimentation to the field of sociology, believing that persistent social problems could be solved by applying certain hierarchical rules. He also believed that with the aid of science, mankind would progress towards a higher state of emancipation. These foundational ideas were adopted by Max Weber and Talcott Parsons, the main proponents of rationalist comprehensive theory. As such, there is an entire current in management, in particular related to management science that sees rationalistic, comprehensive decision making as possible but moreover as an ideal-type, as Weber would put it. This current is the modern foundation for the re-emergence of the comprehensive approach in management and in particular within strategic management, as we will see later.

As the rationalistic comprehensive model takes a scientific and rationalist approach to problem solving, in its purest application, it would result in a full analysis of all possible factors affecting a given set of circumstances and of all possible alternatives to resolving the problem under study. The objectivity and complexity of the rationalistic comprehensive model thus represent its greatest strength and its greatest weakness. Theoretically, it results in the best solution because it has taken into account the widest variety of variables. In practice, the processes it engenders can be overly complex, redundant, time consuming and expensive (Hostovsky 2006, 382). This explains why the comprehensive approach is generally undercited as a decision-making model and is often substituted with more satisficing ones, as Herbert Simon (1991) would put it. Indeed, rationality tends to ignore the reality of modern politics on the assumption that politicians will make the best decision (i.e., at the planner's recommendation) from a set of alternatives analyzed in the plan. Baum (1996, 371) states emphatically, "This assumption is unrealistic, and yet theorists still continue to hold it."

Hence, decision making in management science is based on the main assumption that complex problems can be broken down into smaller parts that are more easily analyzed, that alternatives can be easily identified and assessed and that systematic thinking increases the likelihood of better decisions. Management science techniques are largely based on models of rationalistic decision making, which are derived from mathematics and economics. As such, the literature of public administration, decision making, policy formulation and planning emphasised formalised methods for making decisions, but public agencies are often limited in their ability to practice the rationalistically comprehensive method as presented.

Henceforth, this same logic has been applied to political science and more specifically to international relations. From the study of "Comparative Politics: A Comprehensive Approach" by Spiro (1962) to "Developing a Comprehensive Approach to Canadian Forces Operations" by Leslie et al. (2008), the rationalist and comprehensive paradigm still seems to be very important. This rationalist and comprehensive decision-making approach often uses sequential, linear and static problem solving, whereas today most complex issues have multiple, retroacting and dynamic interdependencies within the comprehensive approach.

Approach Genesis

Within the field of national security and defence studies, a first discussion of the comprehensive approach appeared in "Legal Aspects of Aerial Terrorism" by Emanuelli (1975). At the time, his conclusion was simply that "The basic obstacles of the comprehensive approach should be solved at the piecemeal level before attempting further integration." It took until 2001 for the idea of the comprehensive approach to reappear. United Nations Secretary-General Kofi Annan suggested in a report on August 22, 2001, that the UN adopt a "comprehensive approach to ending Afghanistan conflict."[11] This was before the tragic events of September 11, 2001, which subsequently saw the launch by the US of Operation Enduring Freedom in Afghanistan in October of that same year, with the help of allies (namely the UK and Canada).

It was UK Joint Discussion Note 4/05 that provided the first definition of the comprehensive approach in 2005, but it was not until the promulgation of the Comprehensive Political Guidance following NATO's 2006 Riga Summit that the idea really emerged in the Afghan context. The comprehensive approach was only first officially introduced by the NATO Alliance Council at the Riga Summit of 2006 (Smith-Windsor 2008, 1). Although Kofi Annan at the UN mentioned the need for a comprehensive approach to end Afghanistan conflict as early as 2001, it seems the idea only crystallised under NATO's engagement in Afghanistan (2006).

Thus, in the following years, from 2007 onward, the literature on the subject of the comprehensive approach expanded threefold. In Canada, the Canadian Forces' Land Operations Manual (2008) and the Counter-Insurgency Manual (2008) provided definitions and explanations on the comprehensive approach and comprehensive operations. The US presented its comprehensive approach definition within Field Manual (FM) 3-07 on

---

[11] UNSC, *Comprehensive Approach Needed to End Afghanistan Conflict*, speech, Secretary General Kofi Annan, August 22, 2001, http://www.un.org/apps/news/storyAr.asp?NewsID=1165&Cr=Afghanistan&Cr1

Stability Operations, also in the same year. Numerous conferences and seminars were also being held, such as in Finland (2008).[12] Numerous reports were being published, such as in Norway (2009), discussing of the comprehensive approach in major ways. By 2010, upon realising the necessity of the comprehensive approach, NATO then promulgated a Comprehensive Operational Planning Directive primarily intended towards headquarters staff.[13] In the same year, the UK held a Commons Committee hearing that produced a report that was rightly entitled "The Comprehensive Approach: The Point of War Is Not Just to Win but to Make a Better Peace."[14] This report stated that "engagement in future conflicts is likely to require the use of the comprehensive approach" (p. 3).

But in the Canadian context, the termination of the combat mission in Afghanistan in July 2011 also brought the end of Canada's comprehensive approach. In the case of the allies, namely the United States and the UK, it continued to live up until 2014, at which time the realisation that the so-called comprehensive approach was becoming impossible to realise sunk in. This was the case of many departing non-governmental organisations and international organisations, as well as long-standing allies like Canada, which ended its training mission in July 2014, having already terminated its comprehensive operations in July 2011.

Thus, from this brief chronological survey of the emergence of the comprehensive approach, it appears that the key highlight was NATO's promulgation of its CPG in 2006, followed by the COPD in 2010. In the Canadian context in particular, 2008 was an important year for Canada's comprehensive approach, following the early publication of the "Independent

[12] Finland, "Comprehensive Approach: Trends, Challenges and Possibilities for Cooperation in Crisis Prevention and Management," 2008, http://www.defmin.fi/files/1316/Comprehensive Approach - Trends Challenges and Possibilities for Cooperation in Crisis Prevention and Management.pdf.

[13] LTC Geza Simon and MAJ Muzaffer Duzenli, "The Comprehensive Operations Planning Directive (COPD)," *NRDC-ITA Magazine* no. 16 (2010): 16–19, http://www.nato.int/nrdc-it/magazine/2009/0914/0914g.pdf (accessed January 19, 2016).

[14] UK, "The Comprehensive Approach: The Point of War Is Not Just to Win but to Make a Better Peace," House of Commons, 2010, http://www.publications.parliament.uk/pa/cm200910/cmselect/cmdfence/224/224.pdf

Eric Dion, CD, MBA, PhD

Commission on the Future of Canada in Afghanistan," also known as the Manley Panel Report, which called for a comprehensive strategy as well as following two Canadian Forces' publications on land operations and on counterinsurgency, which both discussed the comprehensive approach and comprehensive operations. This was Canada's comprehensive approach golden years, which only lasted until the end of the combat mission in Canada's engagement in Afghanistan in July 2011. Henceforth, it appears clearly that the comprehensive approach emerged out of the background that was NATO's Afghanistan campaign as strategic planning for international security in a counterinsurgency. It also appears the comprehensive approach was an emerging, normative-assuming efficiency. All in all, when faced with the weakness of current frameworks, it remained intellectually complex.

Before delving in the particulars of Canada's approach, it appears essential to provide key definitions to better understand the basic constructs and evolutionary precursors behind the so-called comprehensive approach in order to develop a conceptual idea of the phenomenon.

Definitions

NATO (2013) defines comprehensive approach as one that "seeks to produce coordinated actions aimed at realizing desired effects in order to achieve an agreed end-state." See Slide 48 in the Footnote.[15]

Some NATO allies describe the same concept with slightly different terminology: The United Kingdom also uses *comprehensive approach,* however others such as the United States uses *whole-of-government approach, integrated operations* and *unified action* to describe the same concept or aspects of a comprehensive approach (CF Land Operations 2008, 5–14). The United Kingdom Joint Discussion Note 4/05, defines comprehensive approach as "Commonly understood principles and collaborative processes that enhance the likelihood of favourable and enduring outcomes within a particular situation" (UK-JDN 4/05 2005, 1–5).

---

[15] NATO, *NATO Operational Planning Process (OPP) and the Comprehensive Operations Planning Directive (COPD),* Presentation, NATO School Oberammergau, 2013, slide 48, https://semanticu.files.wordpress.com/2014/09/02-1100-1200-nato-operational-planning-process-copd.pdf (accessed January 26, 2016)

In the United States Army Field Manual 3-07 on Stability Operations defines the *comprehensive approach* as one "that integrates the cooperative efforts of the departments and of the agencies of the US Government, intergovernmental and nongovernmental organizations, multinational partners and private sector entities to achieve unity of effort toward a shared goal" (FM 3-07 2008, 1–4).

In Canada, the Canadian Force's Land Ops manual defines *comprehensive approach* as

> The application of commonly understood principles and collaborative processes that enhance the likelihood of favourable and enduring outcomes within a particular environment. Note: The *comprehensive approach* brings together all the elements of power and other agencies needed to create enduring solutions to a campaign. The *comprehensive approach* is an overarching *philosophy* for the conduct of a campaign. (CF Land Operations 2008, 5–14)

Moreover, the Canadian Forces' Counter-Insurgency (COIN) Operations Manual states,

> The multi-agency approach is termed the comprehensive approach. The comprehensive approach sees the military working in a unity of purpose and ideally in a unity of effort in order to create enduring solutions to the root causes of the insurgency and reach the desired operational end-state. In all cases, successful counter-insurgency requires this comprehensive approach facilitated through a unity of purpose. (CF COIN 2008, 1–15)

Henceforth, as far as we can tell within this research, the best definition of comprehensive approach to be found is "Commonly understood principles and collaborative processes that enhance the likelihood of favourable and enduring outcomes within a particular situation."[16] As such, where there is discussion of the comprehensive approach in this book, this will be the

---

[16] UK, *The Comprehensive Approach: The Point of War Is Not Just to Win but to Make a Better Peace*, House of Commons, 2010, http://www.publications.parliament.uk/pa/cm200910/cmselect/cmdfence/224/224.pdf

definition retained. It is also crucial to understand that the comprehensive approach did not emerge from a vacuum and that precursor ideas and constructs existed before 2006, leading to its emergence.

Within a complex field of study such as national security and defence, basic constructs exist as building blocks to allow for a common understanding of the operating and theoretical concepts. Such constructs often serve as systemic parts within a larger system of systems perspective—that is to say, that each construct itself is a system but is also treated as a node within a conceptual network. It thus appears important to define at the outset these major constructs, as well as to propose a typology in order to facilitate the understanding of the main constructs employed in this research. Many new, emerging constructs were employed throughout the Afghan campaign without theorisation: the defence, diplomacy and development (3D); the joint, integrated, multinational, public (JIMP); and the whole-of-government approach (WoG or WGA) appear to have been the evolutionary precursors to the holistic comprehensive approach construct. The British even cite Effects-Based Approach to Operations (EBAO) as fundamental to the *comprehensive approach*,[17] and Americans talk of integrated operations, unity of effort and unified action much in the same sense.

Within the Canadian context, the expression *whole-of-government* (WoG) is often used by itself, but it's also used in conjunction with similar-meaning expressions such as *integrated* and even *comprehensive*. Hence in the spirit of a comprehensive approach, this systematic review of literature included the Canadian literature on whole-of-government and the three Ds, which to a large extent have been the evolutionary precursors of the comprehensive approach at least in the Canadian context. To some degree, this has also affected its global emergence within NATO. Indeed, while 3D essentially represented the extension of three departments into Afghanistan, the JIMP concept represented an interesting attempt by some practitioners and scholars to synthesise the different domains of the contemporary operating environment (COE).[18] The WoG was a refocus from JIMP in order to limit

---

[17] "Effects-based approach to operations (EBAO) is fundamental because that is the framework in which British military began to think about comprehensive approach in a more structured coherent way" (UK 2010, 13).
[18] US, 2008, "Chapter 1—COE," http://www.globalsecurity.org/military/library/report/call/call_02-8_ch1.htm

the comprehensive approach to its most structurational features, which can be found in the whole of government itself, although the approach has often been less than holistic.[19] Hence, the comprehensive approach is the embodiment of this same approach but at a global level, including multinational, multistakeholder and international and non-governmental organisations (essentially in order) to propose a higher degree of collaboration for positive and enduring outcomes. Henceforth, the following table presents these key constructs from the smallest to biggest idea.

Table 1—Key Constructs

Acronym	Construct	General Definition
3Ds	Defence, Diplomacy and Development	3D is a framework promoting development, diplomacy and defence as security strategies. The 3D framework recognises that security challenges like terrorism, nuclear proliferation, global warming, SARS, avian flu or Ebola epidemics require a variety of tools in addressing complex threats. These tools can be categorised broadly under three headings of defence, diplomacy and development, in order—the 3Ds of security.
OGA	Other Government Agency	A federal government or state agency is a permanent or semi-permanent organisation in the machinery of government that is responsible for the oversight and administration of specific functions, such as an intelligence agency. There is a notable variety of agency types. Although usage differs, a government agency is normally distinct both from a department or ministry and other types of public body established by the government. Functions of an agency are normally executive in character.

---

[19] See LTC Patrick Kelly, 2007, "Hole in Whole of Government," The Canadian Forces College (CFC), Advanced Military Studies Program 10 (AMSP), http://www.cfc.forces.gc.ca/papers/amsc/amsc10/kelly.pdf

OGD[20]	Other Government Department	A ministry (or department) is a specialized organization responsible for a sector of government public administration, sometimes led by a minister and a senior public servant who can have responsibility for one or more departments, agencies, bureaus, commissions or other smaller executive, advisory, managerial or administrative organisations. In Canada, both the provincial and federal governments use the term *minister* to describe the head of a ministry or department. The specific tasks assigned to a minister is referred to as its portfolio.
WoG or WGA	Whole-of-Government Approach	Whole of government is an approach that integrates the collaborative efforts of the departments and agencies of a government to achieve unity of effort towards a shared goal. Also known as the interagency approach, the terms *unity of effort* and *unity of purpose* are sometimes used to describe cooperation amongst all actors, government and otherwise.[21]
NGO	Non-governmental Organisation	In its simplest definition, a NGO is an organization that is neither part of a government nor of a conventional business. It usually has for its mission a not-for-profit strategic objective.

---

[20] For OGD and OGA, see the alphabetical list of links to current Government of Canada Departments, Agencies, Crown Corporations, Special Operating Agencies, and others at https://www.canada.ca/en/government/dept.html.

[21] See United States Institute for Peace (USIP), http://glossary.usip.org/resource/whole-government-approach

IO	International Organisation	An intergovernmental organisation (IO) or an international governmental organisation (IGO) is an organisation composed primarily of sovereign states (referred to as member states) or of other intergovernmental organisations. Intergovernmental organisations are often called international organisations.
JIMP	Joint, Interagency, Multinational, Public	The demands of the current operational context are such that the Canadian Forces cannot conduct operations in isolation. Like never before, it is required to work closely and collaborate with people from OGDs and OGAs, NGOs and other civilian entities. To do this effectively, the CF must adopt a comprehensive approach to operations and collaborate and cooperate with a number of different actors (such as diplomats, development, corrections, police officers and local populations) who are all simultaneously working towards the same goals.[22] This is the essence of a Joint, Integrated, Multinational, Public (JIMP) construct.

CA	*Comprehensive Approach*	A comprehensive approach is commonly understood principles and collaborative processes that enhance the likelihood of favourable and enduring outcomes within a particular situation.[23] It integrates the cooperative efforts of departments and agencies of the WoG, IOs, NGOs, multinational partners and private sector entities in order to achieve unity of effort towards a shared goal.[24]

While following the presentation of these key constructs that have literally been the evolutionary precursors to the comprehensive approach, we also note the weakness of current frameworks and henceforth the confusion between these different constructs. This prompted the creation of a typology for these constructs in order to visually determine their respective fields of play within the global comprehensive approach. The following figure presents these key constructs within a visually referenced graphic, thus presenting the typology of the different approaches in order to better appraise their interdependencies as a whole system.

[22] Thomson et al., *Collaboration within the JIMP Environment,* Defence Research and Development Center (DRDC) Toronto, 2010, p. iii, http://cradpdf.drdc-rddc.gc.ca/PDFS/unc104/p534320_A1b.pdf.

[23] UK, *The Comprehensive Approach: The Point of War Is Not Just to Win but to Make a Better Peace,* House of Commons, 2010, http://www.publications.parliament.uk/pa/cm200910/cmselect/cmdfence/224/224.pdf.

[24] US, *Stability Operations,* Field Manual 3-07, 2008, pp. 1–4, www.fas.org/irp/doddir/army/fm3-24.pdf

Figure 1—Typology of Different Approaches

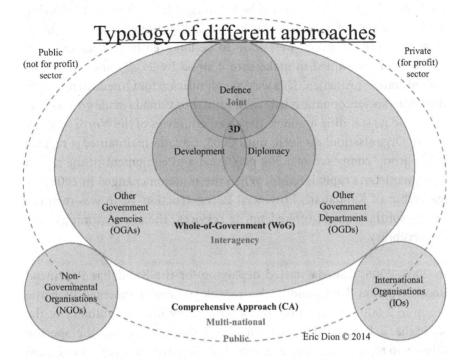

In essence, it appears from this typology of the different approaches employed within the comprehensive approach that a more integrated perspective can be offered, building on the different constructs employed. Indeed, what is interesting in regards to the comprehensive approach is that although it does not exist intellectually as a whole framework, model or theory, there are nonetheless these constructs that, when taken as a whole, better define the approach, as we have shown in our typology. However, this typology provides mostly an organisational structure perspective and does not account for other potential dimensions that should support comprehensive decision making. Henceforth, it appears quite important to review the empirical literature on the subject of the comprehensive approach in order to highlight some of these other fundamental dimensions found within Canada's approach, as it pertains for example to the situation, society, structure, strategy, systems and synergy.

Canada's Approach

From 2001 to 2014, Canada had been engaged in Afghanistan following the tragic events of September 11, 2001. Initially deploying Special Forces from the military, which were soon to be followed by regular forces in Kabul, Canada wanted to make sure it stood by its ally and friend, the United States of America. This was very significant for Canada in its North American socioeconomic relationship, and thus Canada made great efforts to uphold its standing amongst the allied countries of the North Atlantic Treaty Organisation. As such, until 2005, Canada maintained a regular battle group composed of 1,500 personnel and equipment in the region of Afghanistan's capital, Kabul. When the situation changed in 2005 and leadership of Kandahar's Provincial Reconstruction Team was required in the south, Canada offered up its services, thereby assuming more responsibility.

In 2005–2006, Canada started deploying for the Kandahar Provincial Reconstruction Team, and it also redeployed and augmented its battle group to 2,000 personnel on top of the 350 civilian and military of the Kandahar's Provincial Reconstruction Team, which had the specific mission to reconstruct Kandahar's critical infrastructure such as electrical dams, clinics, roads and more. Canada also took on the role of the Operational Liaison and Mentoring Team, advising local afghan military as well as deploying personnel in general support to the Regional Command South. Up until 2010, Canada's contribution to the southern province of Kandahar reached 3,000, at which point American forces started to affect an important surge of military personnel in order to retake key strongholds in Kandahar Province that were still under Taliban rule. The omnipresence of American, Commonwealth and Afghan forces troops in the south meant a strength of 35,000. By July 2011, the Canadian government decided to terminate Canada's engagement in Afghanistan[25] and finally established a military training mission in around Kabul and in the north of Afghanistan, a military training mission which ended in July 2014. The following histogram illustrates Canada's engagement in Afghanistan in terms of its number of military personnel per years and per area, superimposed on an Afghan map representing provinces and regions.

---

[25] *Canada's Engagement in Afghanistan,* http://www.international.gc.ca/afghanistan/index.aspx?lang=eng

Figure 2—Canada's Engagement in Afghanistan Histogram[26]

Eric Dion © 2011

For the Disposition of ISAF and Afghan Forces – November 2010, see Footnote, page 27.[27]

All along, Canada's engagement in Afghanistan evolved from a military to a defence, diplomacy and development (or 3D) mission, which in 2005 evolved into a whole of government and later transitioned to a comprehensive approach in 2007. This evolution was most notable in Canada's and NATO's engagement in Afghanistan. This followed from important changes in the geopolitical and strategic context—namely the fact that NATO's Afghanistan mission rapidly transitioned into a counterinsurgency in 2006–2007, leading to numerous policy and doctrine changes, such as the publication

---

26 Background Map courtesy of UN Dispatch: http://www.undispatch.com/how-the-american-military-sees-its-campaign-in-afghanistan_progressing/afghanistan_regional_commands_with_provinces/

27 Carl Forsberg, *Counterinsurgency in Kandahar: Evaluating the 2010 Hamkari Campaign*, 2010. http://www.understandingwar.org/sites/default/files/Afghanistan%20Report%207_15Dec.pdf .

of two Canadian Forces manuals[28] and US Field Manual 3-07 on stability. The publication in early 2008 of the Manley Report recommended more focused priorities, clear benchmarks, more frequent communications to Canadians regarding Canada's engagement in Afghanistan and integrated planning.[29] In essence, the Manley Panel, officially called the Independent Panel on Canada's Future Role in Afghanistan, stated, "Canada's civilian and military efforts in Kandahar, after just two years of close collaboration, are starting to achieve real operational synergy that would be difficult to replicate quickly with the forces of another country" (Manley 2008, 31).

As such, Canada was bringing real value in terms of its engagement in Afghanistan, in particular through the Kandahar Provincial Reconstruction Team, by helping local Afghans rebuild their clinics, schools and roads to further enable the economy. But the termination of the combat mission (2011) led to the closure of the comprehensive approach with the withdrawal of most of Canada's civilian-military assets and with focus on a training mission in northern Afghanistan until Canada's complete withdrawal in July 2014.

Within the Canadian context, the *comprehensive approach* is defined similarly to the UK:

> The application of commonly understood principles and collaborative processes that enhance the likelihood of favourable and of enduring outcomes within a particular environment. Note: The comprehensive approach brings together all the elements of power and other agencies needed to create enduring solutions to a campaign. The comprehensive approach is an overarching *philosophy* for the conduct of a campaign. It recognises that crisis situations and their surrounding environments are complicated and that an enduring solution cannot be reached by military forces alone. (CF Land Ops 2008, 5–14)

However, in spite of numerous papers that discuss the so-called comprehensive approach mostly from 2007 onward and mostly originating

---

[28] See *Canadian Forces Land Operations,* 2008, and *Canadian Forces Counter-Insurgency,* 2008.

[29] "Canada in Afghanistan—History," http://www.international.gc.ca/afghanistan/history-histoire.aspx?lang=eng

from Canada, Europe, the United States and NATO, no working framework, model or theory of the comprehensive approach could be found. In particular, this was the case when the author was deployed to Afghanistan. This situation presented itself as a fundamental cognitive dissonance where in spite of an important body of literature on the topic of the comprehensive approach and preceding constructs of 3D and whole-of-government, these concepts seemed to be further away from practical management and closer to philosophical policy statements, which was of no help to executives on the ground. Indeed, our own observation and participation attests to this reality.

The issue is that there never were commonly understood principles or collaborative processes that worked in harmony and that brought together all the elements of power, such as political, military, economic, social, infrastructure and information. On a daily basis, the operational planning staff within all levels of headquarters, from the tactical or local level to the operational or regional/provincial level and the strategic or national/international level, had to harmonise and synchronise operations and plans in order to achieve integrated effects. Oftentimes other departments and agencies—other than those relating to defence and security, that is—were just that, afterthoughts, and were not integral parts of the operational planning process.[30] In many instances, the level of integration was a direct corollary to the level of personal relationships in between people. Henceforth, the so-called comprehensive approach never fully developed the dimensions that would have seen it move beyond a mere philosophy and become a theoretical framework and practical model which would have helped executives with their strategic management in Afghanistan:

> The transformation of war requires integration of all elements of national power, civilian and military, at all levels of war. Whether termed *whole-of-government, comprehensive approach* or under some other appellation, civil and military activities must be integrated into a coherent, synergistic whole and this must be built into the campaign plan. (Canadian Forces Joint Publication 5.0 2008, 2–7)

---

[30] See *Operational Planning Process,* http://publications.gc.ca/collections/collection_2010/forces/D2-252-500-2008-eng.pdf

As the author himself deployed during the year 2010 as Chief of Joint Operational Plans (CJ35) for Task Force Kandahar within Regional Command South, it became quite apparent these so-called policy constructs were far away from real strategic and operational concerns. Indeed, the year 2010 was marked by an important surge in US troops of up to 35,000 in the Kandahar Province of southern Afghanistan, and Canada's civilian and military elements were at their maximum in terms of effective strength and their combined joint effects, at 3,000. During the best years of Canada's engagement in Afghanistan (2010–2011), which also saw an important surge of American troops in the region under Operation Hamkari[31] (meaning *together* in Pashtu), the main considerations were for the joint and multinational aspects of the military campaign, and much less for the integrated and public sides of JIMP.[32]

In practice, there was little systemic processes, no sociocultural considerations and no synergy dynamics that supported the execution of the so-called comprehensive approach. Mostly the organisational structure dimension (such as NATO and other international institutions like the UN) and the strategic policy dimension (such as the Afghan National Development Strategy) were used to attempt to achieve a higher degree of practical integration at the strategic-structural level, thereby leaving out other significant dimensions for achieving a comprehensive approach, like the sociocultural context, the systematic management cooperation between actors and the whole dynamics. Essentially, these holistic and comprehensive ideas were part of the strategic narrative, but they were not part of the daily execution of comprehensive operations that are closer to a strategic management perspective.

> The latest acronym used by the Canadian Army to describe this future environment is JIMP (Joint, Interagency, Multinational, and Public), and this term will soon permeate all aspects of Canadian military thinking, and consequently, approaches to operations. JIMP environment will pervade and serve as a prerequisite for not just

---

[31] See Operation Hamkari, 2010, http://www.understandingwar.org/sites/default/files/Afghanistan%20Report%207_15Dec.pdf

[32] See Joint-Integrated-Multinational-Public, http://www.cfc.forces.gc.ca/259/281/280/simms

success in Canada's international endeavours but in all operational considerations. Success in the current and the future operating environments, quite rightly require a truly integrated or a whole of government approach. (McIllroy 2008, 89)

Here again, it appears obvious that there is an intellectual complexity to the basic idea of the comprehensive approach. Indeed, the comprehensive approach recognises that crisis situations and surrounding environments are complicated and that an enduring solution cannot be reached by the military forces alone. It requires the use of a wide range of powers exercised through a variety of departments and agencies in order to solve the root causes and aggravate grievances that first led to the crisis, as indicated in CF Land Ops (2008, 5–14). Hence, the fundamental idea behind a comprehensive approach is that it supersedes the military, subjugating it to an overarching plan that "seeks to produce collaborative actions aimed at realising desired effects to achieve an agreed end-state," as per NATO's definition.

Based on the Comprehensive Approach Action Plan (CAAP) endorsed by the heads of state and government at NATO's 2008 Bucharest Summit, as well as in the Lisbon Summit decisions on the comprehensive approach, the North Atlantic Council (NAC)[33] agreed on March 4, 2011, to an updated list of tasks for the implementation of the Comprehensive Approach Action Plan.[34] Thus, putting the comprehensive approach into practice requires a wide spectrum of very different actors to work effectively together towards a shared goal. It was noted that the strengths of the various contributing organisations must be seamlessly tied together in order to make sure everyone is singing from the same sheet. This is even harder when non-state actors (such as the non-governmental organisation community) become part of the picture (Baumann 2010, 7). Indeed, there is no overarching

---

[33] The North Atlantic Council, http://www.nato.int/cps/en/natolive/topics_49763.htm

[34] NATO, "Implementation of the Comprehensive Approach Action Plan and the Lisbon Summit Decisions on the Comprehensive Approach," Private Office of the Secretary-General, 2011, pp. 1–6, https://jadl.act.nato.int/NATO/data/NATO/lm_data/lm_12820/999/objects/il_0_file_35471/20111130_NU_NATO-IS-NSG-PO(2011)0529-Action-Plan-Comprehensive-Approach.pdf (accessed February 25, 2016)

framework to guide the work of the NGO community in general, so it is important to consider a framework, model and theory where authority may be diffuse and remains collaborative.

Henceforth, the continuing challenge for Canada, the United States, and the other parts of the global community is to exploit the fact that contemporary security is, at its base, a holistic, political-diplomatic, socioeconomic, psychological-moral and military-police effort. The corollary is to move from a singular military approach to a multidimensional whole-of-government and whole-of-alliance paradigm that is much closer to the comprehensive approach lauded by Canada.

The Canadian whole-of-government approach and the NATO whole-of-alliance model to homeland defence and global security requirements do that, and they could be very useful as primary organisational principles to establish a comprehensive North American process for active intergovernmental and multilateral policy collaboration. That in turn requires a conceptual framework and an organisational structure to promulgate this unified civil-military planning and implementation of the multidimensional, multiorganisational and multilateral and multinational security concept (Manwaring 2006, 3). Fundamentally, then, the challenge is to find ownership for the approach and build a framework that would work as well for conflict prevention (perhaps even pre-emptively) as for conflict resolution.

Conclusion

In conclusion of this first chapter, it appears clearly from a systematic review of the literature on the subject of comprehensive approach that it is a victim of such intellectual complexity, perhaps arising from the lack of a consensual definition, and that it is practically not helpful on the ground at the executive level, needing further refinement. Such attempts have been made, namely through NATO's Comprehensive Operational Planning Directive (COPD) of 2010 and NATO's Comprehensive Approach Action Plan (CAAP) of 2011. The UN Integrated Mission Planning Process (IMPP) of 2006 and the US Integrated Civil-Military Campaign Plan (ICMCP) of 2010 were also attempts at institutionalising the comprehensive approach. However, in Canada there has been no such overarching institutionalisation attempt, and as such the *comprehensive approach* has simply remained a larger philosophy for future engagements. Henceforth, the so-called comprehensive approach can be said to be an empty shell, which in many ways was of no practical help for integrated executive management. So how can we theoretically model this comprehensive approach in a more synergistic management perspective to be useful?

In conclusion, this first chapter presented the systematic review of the empirical literature on the subject of the comprehensive approach. Here, the weakness of current frameworks of the comprehensive approach is most notable. Thus, the approach remains a philosophy which could leverage a more integrated, holistic and dynamic theoretical model. In the predominant military paradigm, the comprehensive approach simply appears as a new type of conflict that may be right, that which therefore also requires a new type of strategic thinking, especially when facing such threats as unrestricted warfare.[35] For example, the following figure represents the extent of the intellectual effort surrounding the comprehensive approach, presented by NATO militaries. See Slide 17 in the Footnote [36]

One can see that the comprehensive approach is composed of numerous constructs, such as diplomatic, information, military and economic (DIME), or political, economic, military, social, information and infrastructure (PEMSII) and military, political, economic and cultural (MPEC). Clearly, all these constructs lack higher level of integration, as if just by stating them along military weapon systems—such as Unmanned Aerial Vehicles (UAV), Unmanned Ground Systems (UGS) and Joint, Surveillance, Target, Acquisition, Reconnaissance and Suppression (JSTARS)—it would make them more operational ideas.

There is a strategic management requirement underscoring the comprehensive approach. As with the dominant defence outlook, international security predominates within the approach, here also precluding a more holistic perspective from emerging to lead the counterinsurgency. The approach further appears more and more as an emerging normative for international

---

[35] See Qao Liang and Wang Xiangsui, *Unrestricted Warfare*, 1999.
[36] NATO, *NATO Operational Planning Process (OPP) and the Comprehensive Operations Planning Directive (COPD)*, Presentation, NATO School Oberammergau, 2013, slide 17, https://semanticu.files.wordpress.com/2014/09/02-1100-1200-nato-operational-planning-process-copd.pdf (accessed January 26, 2016)

actors. An efficiency assumption further permeates the comprehensive approach, as though successful outcomes were more likely to occur following a systemic approach, although it's undemonstrated. Finally, there is an obvious intellectual complexity to the comprehensive approach, sometimes confusing and conflating numerous different frames of reference in an attempt to synchronise all. In essence, this appears as the real issue.

Moreover, the comprehensive approach is complicated by the preceding six trends noted from the review of the empirical literature on the subject. Indeed, some texts present the comprehensive approach as a strategic planning issue for international security within a counterinsurgency. It is also seen in some of those very same texts as an emerging normative that holds for valid an implicit efficiency assumption, and that henceforth consists of great intellectual complexity. As with the presentation of the overview and genesis of the approach, and of its definitions and key constructs, there appears to be an obvious confusion on the idea. Even Canada sometimes states the whole-of-government approach as its response to the comprehensive approach, which simply creates more issues. Henceforth, the comprehensive approach is not only a wicked problem—it is literally a Gordian knot. See Slide 21 in the Footnote.[37]

---

[37] NATO, *NATO Operational Planning Process (OPP) and the Comprehensive Operations Planning Directive (COPD),* Presentation, NATO School Oberammergau, 2013, slide 21, https://semanticu.files.wordpress. com/2014/09/02-1100-1200-nato-operational-planning-process-copd.pdf (accessed January 26, 2016)

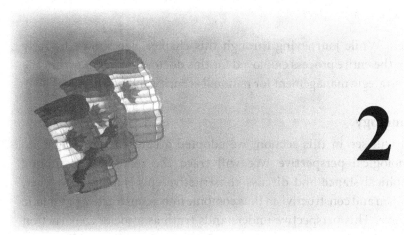

2

Research Logic

This second chapter first presents the key elements of the requisite epistemological and the ontological thinking that led to this research's methodology and research design. We will explain how we arrived at a constructive-pragmatic, epistemological perspective, and how we have employed a public strategic management approach as well as a systemic view. The logic behind this research flows from pragmatic philosophy to constructivist epistemology, in order to form an integrated constructive pragmatic perspective. This research logic is also based on a particular ontology—that is, strategic management but in a systems approach perspective, where interdependency is fundamental.

From these philosophical bases, this second chapter will then explain methodology in all its details, starting from the overarching grounded theory research design, which has led to key selections within the corpus of literature. Iterating between content analysis and theoretical analysis, this abductive research design further evolved into three iterations of the proposed theoretical model, incorporating content analysis with a meta-analysis. These mixed methods work in triangulating fashion, ensuring validity and reliability. Discussion will explicit the spiral development of this research and the unique opportunity for participation and observation the author was offered, providing more insights into the background of Canada's engagement in Afghanistan and Canada's comprehensive approach. While journeying through this chapter, you should be fully aware of the entire process employed for this doctoral research within the field of strategic management for national security and defence.[38]

Epistemology

As you will see in this section, we adopted a constructive pragmatic epistemological perspective. We will trace the road of this unique philosophical stance and discuss constructive epistemology. Together, pragmatism and constructivism thus combine into a constructive pragmatic perspective. This perspective understands truth as a social construction but also recognises its pragmatic worth. Pragmatism is a well-known and well-understood philosophy for strategic management in national security and defence, and constructivism for its part is best understood as a more fundamental epistemological perspective, in particular within academia. This provides for an original perspective on both the subject and the object of this research study. Indeed, it does not suffice to dispose of pragmatic decision making if it does not account for the stakeholder's overall perspective.

Epistemologically, there is a return to pragmatism within the political sciences, and in particular within the international relations, as Hildebrand (2005, 2008), and Shields (2008) explain it. This return to pragmatism is most notable within public administration as its own field of study. Moreover, there is also an important constructivist current, as Haas and Haas (2002) explain. Therefore, converging these two currents into a constructive pragmatic epistemology seemed very promising; our epistemology is on the cutting edge. In this next section, we will retrace the philosophical and epistemological roots that have combined to form the more constructive pragmatic perspective used throughout this research.

Pragmatic Philosophy

Pragmatism coming from James's *Pragmatic Maxim* (1878), as well as from Dewey in *How We Think* (1910) and *Logic: The Theory of Inquiry* (1938), have been foundational in the recent *Return to Pragmatism* by

---

[38] National Security and Defence, https://www.canada.ca/en/services/defence.html. Senate Standing Committee, http://www.parl.gc.ca/sencommitteebusiness/CommitteeHome.aspx?comm_id=1076&Language=E

Miettinen, Samra-Fredericks and Yanow (2009), as well as in a special issue of *Millennium—A Journal of International Studies* by Albert and Kopp-Malek (2002). Pragmatism is well-known in the national security and defence field as crucial for positive outcomes on the ground, and as such, the main criticisms formulated against pragmatism over the years have now become its strengths in light of the contemporary operating environment.[39] Indeed, practitioners understand the intrinsic value of a pragmatic philosophy for positive outcomes. What is less developed, however, are the intellectual and theoretical applications of pragmatism within national security and defence.

Pragmatism emerged as a philosophical movement in the latter part of the 19th century mainly through the works of Charles Pierce and John Dewey, as well as others who agreed in their rejection of positivist assumptions about the nature of knowledge and truth. They presented a sympathetic challenge to the notion that the application of a single method of inquiry—namely, the scientific method—would enable us to access the "real world" (Maxcy 2003, 52). Hence, pragmatism emerged as philosophy that remained grounded in practice and practical realities: "Here *Pragmatism* is treated as an approach which transcends all epistemological and ontological coordinate systems; and there is moreover a sometimes necessary attitude of cutting across these paradigms" (Albert and Kopp-Malek 2002, 455).

"Located between the 'paradigm wars' of an objective positivist epistemology and a subjective constructivist epistemology, pragmatism offers an immediate and useful middle position, both philosophically and methodologically" (Johnson and Onwuegbuzie 2004, 17). It is through social transactions that we come to understand the existence of multiple subjective realities, while at the same time seeking agreement via action. It is clear that pragmatism thus differs from the positivist notions of objectivity while endorsing collaborative action and acknowledging the participant's subjective realities (Vanderstraeter and Biesta; in Maxcy 2003, 59). This epistemological view thus appears to be fundamental in proposing a constructive pragmatic perspective to this research in that a pragmatic

---

[39] US, *Op Enduring Freedom (OEF): Tactics, Techniques and Procedures,* Handbook 02-8, 2008, "Chapter 1—COE," http://www.globalsecurity.org/military/library/report/call/call 02-8 toc.htm (accessed 25 Feb 2016)

philosophy appears to be commensurate with a constructive epistemology. In other words, as a middle epistemological position, pragmatism accepts many of the premises of both positivism and constructivism, such as deductive and inductive (also known as abductive) logic, objective and subjective viewpoints and qualitative and quantitative methods. Pragmatism provides a very integrative epistemological and philosophical perspective.

In pragmatism, there is no such thing as objective reality; everything is understood and interpreted through the eyes, ears and brains of analysts from specific social contexts (Davies 2007, 156). In a pragmatic philosophical perspective, truth is constructed from given paradigmatic views. As such, truth depends not on the accuracy with which an idea copies an antecedent reality or on its coherence with other truths, but on its capacity to guide the thinkers towards a successful or more satisfactory solution to any given problematic situation. As such, the notion that meaning is then attributed to the empirical world in order to respond to the practical problem of operating in it is amongst the cornerstone principles of pragmatist thought (Isacoff 2009, 614). Pragmatism is thus comprehensive.

In this perspective, one of the central ideas of pragmatist theories of knowledge is that epistemic claims are embedded within some practical context that in large part determines their relevant standards of justification and conditions of success. A truth claim is thus to be judged in light of its practical consequences. This practical turn of epistemology is especially relevant for the social sciences, whose main practical contribution, according to pragmatism, is to supply methods for identifying and solving problems (Bohman 2009, 499). This is a particularly useful philosophical perspective in light of complex issues facing public management in national security and defence. Pragmatism is characterised by the view that theories must be linked to experience or practice (Misak 2004, 1). Perhaps more important, the validity of any hypothesis is dependent upon both past and future in its success as reflection of experience and guide to practice (Kellogg 2007, 63).

> Pragmatism—the view that our theories must
> be linked to experience or practice.
> —Charles Sanders Pierce

Because it was there at the founding, and because it offers a comprehensive philosophy, classical pragmatism is the right vehicle for the field of public administration to assert itself conceptually and normatively. Classical pragmatism works for public administration because it fits this multidisciplinary field and can guide it through the inevitable "tides of reform" (Light 2006). "Classical Pragmatism has ideas big enough to inspire the public service, it has also well-developed theory of participatory democracy, and it is scientific enough to guide sophisticated policy analysis" (Shields 2008, 218). As such, pragmatism has been retained as philosophy underpinning this research, but it is insufficient in our view to form a holistic perspective on the issues at hand in managing national security and defence. A perspective that better accounts for the stakeholder is fundamentally required in order for a pragmatic theoretical model to be leveraged on the ground by management executives.

Constructive Epistemology

Unlike pragmatism, which proves more general philosophy than substantive logic,[40] constructive epistemology has been well-developed academically and theoretically by C. Wright Mills (1959) and Berger and Luckman (1966). More specifically, constructivism as a sociological approach has been a balancing force to the scientific and rationalistic, logical positivism that is rampant in security and defence circles. The constructivist paradigm assumes "A relativist ontology (there are multiple realities), a subjectivist epistemology (knower and respondent co-create understandings), and a naturalistic (in the natural world) set of methodological procedures" (Denzin and Lincoln 2003, 35). "Acting and thinking, practice and theory, are linked in a continuous process of critical reflection and transformation" (Schwandt 2003, 294–295). In a sense, we are all constructivists if we believe that the mind is active in the construction of knowledge. Knowing is active, which means the mind does something with impressions, forming abstractions or concepts at the very least. "Constructivism means that human beings do not find or discover knowledge so much as we construct or make it" (Schwandt 2003, 305).

---

[40] See James L. Golden, *The Rhetoric of Western Thought*, 2003, p. 527.

Eric Dion, CD, MBA, PhD

Henceforth, constructivism generally endorses an anti-objectivist, anti-foundationalist view of knowledge.[41] That is, knowledge of reality is not seen to be simply a matter of taking a look at the facts of the world in order to detect the degree of correspondence of those facts with our thoughts or beliefs (whether this be by direct perception or via representations). Rather, what we take to be a fact is assumed to be at least partly a function of our proactive outlook or framework of understanding (Stevens 1998, 286). Hence, we construct reality:

> Social constructionism, also called social constructivism particularly in political science, is often confused or conflated with constructivism, a related psychology theory associated primarily with Piaget, which assumes an objective reality that we apprehend through the construction of cognitive patterns in response to environmental influences. (Rohmann 2000, 363)

"Social constructionism locates the mind not within individuals, but in individuals-in-social-interaction" (Vygotsky 1978, 56). Thus, a constructivist epistemology recognises the very construction of truth claims and understands that the owner's perspective becomes key. In the process of institutionalisation, meaning is embedded in society. Knowledge and people's conception and belief of what reality is become embedded in the institutional fabric of society. Social reality, as Berger and Luckman (1966) point out, is therefore said to be socially constructed. This is fundamental.

Constructivist epistemology, combined to a more critical thinking, can uncover the key systemic processes that actually compose the key dimensions of a strategic management approach within national security and defence practices. Henceforth, the question is how inquiry can be not only both interpretive and explanatory, but also descriptive and normative at the same time. This distinctive standpoint characteristic of a critical social inquiry has also been called by Harbermas the "perspective of a critical-reflexive participant" (Bohman 2009, 503). "And so if there is any

---

[41] "Constructivism assumes that humans create knowledge in ever-changing contexts, rather than the more common view that nature reveals to us its own innate, foundational 'way that it is' that confers meaning to us" (McWilliams 2015, abstract), http://www.tandfonline.com/doi/pdf/10.1080/10720537.2014.980871

wisdom in philosophy at all, this wisdom will be active and it will teach us how to live and how to act" (Višňovský 2009, 1). "A focus on practice challenges us to bridge different levels of analysis and to do so in different ways as well" (Miettinen, Samra-Fredericks and Yanow 2009, 1309).

As such, critical thinking is crucial. This is a mode of thinking about any subject, content or problem in which the thinker improves the quality of his thinking by skilfully taking charge of the structures inherent in thinking and imposing intellectual standards upon them (Paul and Elder 2001; in Whetten 2002, 50). Unlike pragmatism, a constructive critical thinking posture is often missing from within the field of national security and defence studies, precisely because of the clear focus on practical outcomes that often do not question underlying assumptions. As such, a positively constructivist (or constructive epistemological) perspective is fundamental and allows a researcher to understand that reality is constructed from different points of view. Constructively incorporating these points of view is important for the decision-making process, and as such constructivism is important in proposing a new theoretical model because it accepts stakeholders' perspectives.

Constructive Pragmatism
In essence, what we propose as epistemological and philosophical underpinning for this research design is a constructive pragmatic perspective on our study. Indeed, with a clear purpose in mind to constructively and pragmatically guide us through the perspectives of stakeholders while maintaining critical reflexivity upon the object and subject, we nonetheless subscribe to a view of truth as constructed pragmatic reality based on overarching constructive pragmatic principles of knowledge:

> By guiding practice in accordance with four Ps [Practical, Pluralistic, Participatory, Provisional], classical pragmatism has potential to guide [Public Administration] toward its roots and toward fresh new useful approaches. (Shields 2008, 217)

Our epistemological point of view is simply that a balance between the different perspectives is quintessential and is the most likely (both practically and philosophically) to be a better outcome. This view is somewhat consistent with a win-win or with the best alternative to negotiated settlement, where neither of the parties to a negotiation wins completely or loses. In fact, the energy expanded and the synergy created between them is a better outcome overall.

In epistemic conclusion, it appears clearly to us that a constructive epistemology further shapes the ontological question by accepting complexity, by taking a process view or a systems approach to practical issues needing to be resolved and by opening up to a multitude of other approaches and a variety of disciplines, incorporating these metaphysical underpinnings within a more comprehensive methodology seeking to address *praxis* as well as *theos*. According to constructivists such as Clark (1994) in *Critical Theory and Constructivism*, there is no single valid methodology within science, but rather a diversity of useful methods. Thus, a constructive pragmatic epistemology coherently aligns with our ontology and our methodology. The following section thus discusses our ontological choices.

Ontology

This section will demonstrate how epistemology aligns well with our selected ontological position. We look at issues both from a strategic management and systems approach to better comprehend complex interactions, employing transdisciplinary and antidichotomic ontological principles in order to arrive to an ontologically comprehensive view that acknowledges the various dimensions that a comprehensive approach and model must accept at a meta-theoretical level (see Annex A). Indeed, in order to be theoretically comprehensive, our model should remain open and accept a multitude of ontological perspectives not only those arising from, for example, national security and defence. From an ontological point of view, our strategic management modelling of the comprehensive approach proposes to develop the constructs, concepts and categories of such a model, looking at things holistically and in a systemic approach. In this next section, we will explicit the ontology that bridges our epistemology and our methodology in a comprehensive, coherent research logic.

Ontology is the pre-methodological question that asks us how we perceive the social world. It is based on the basic premise that we all view those around us in unique ways. This fundamental fact has implications for our ability to achieve research neutrality, not only in the conclusions we draw, but also in the topics we choose to study, the way we go about the data collection task, and what we see, we hear and we interpret during the time of analysis and write-up. (Davies 2007, 240)

As such, promoting an open ontology rather than a closed ontology—that is, a *becoming* ontology over a *being* ontology—will allow constant revision or continuous improvement of the theoretical model. The basic idea is that the formula is never set but is rather a matter of circumstances, which opens the way to the usual criticism of constructivism and pragmatism as being relativistic. But if the real-life phenomenon at hand is relative, then it should be a well-grounded theory. Ontologically, it becomes possible to propose a practical academic theoretical model based on a strategic management perspective, so long as it also accepts a more systemic, holistic and dynamic view of the practical issues at hand.

Strategic Management

Instead of approaching the subject of comprehensive approach from a political science or from an international relations perspective, we approached it from a strategic management[42] perspective, focusing more on how to make things work pragmatically. Bozeman (1993) defines public strategic management research as being concretely concerned with prescription and prescriptive theory, indicating that some amount of interaction between the academics and practitioners is to be expected (Pitts and Fernandez 2009, 402). Public strategic management is a new field of study that is still developing norms and approaches to research, and key questions push at its identity (Pitts and Fernandez 2009, 399). Thus, from the field of national security and defence, the comprehensive approach is clearly one such area of growing interest, where there is indeed a public strategic management realisation that holistic approaches have now become quintessential.

One interesting feature of public strategic management is the strategic and executive-level perspective, the big picture or holistic view taken by

---

[42] Tom Christensen and Per Laegreid, "The Whole of Government Approach to Public Sector Reform; Profs of Administration," *Public Administration Review* 67, no. 6 (Nov/Dec 2007): 1059–1066

strategic management, in dealing with practical issues. An important assumption underlying this top-down perspective, however, is that the strategic managers can lead to success from the top, as if they somehow could be omni-scientists. As such, the comprehensive approach is part of a strategic and rationalistic perspective in management. From a more constructive and pragmatic perspective, it is acknowledged that some leadership must be exercised and that some management is required, but only to the degree where it leverages the other dimensions, which are also required from a more holistic point of view. Accepting that strategy is the answer, and that all can be strategically managed, are two ontologically false assumptions.

Henceforth, from an ontological point of view, our approach still fits within the public strategic management, but we do not concede that strategy as politics should dominate over other dimensions. From our ontological stance, we certainly acknowledge the importance of strategy, but as a subservient dimension equal in value to other categorical dimensions such as society. Ontologically, these other dimensions are well-developed from the field of strategic management—for example, the organisation structure, the strategic policies and the systemic functions. In a sociological perspective, the sociocultural and situational dimensions are also well-developed. Moreover, the synergy dynamics dimension appears to be fruitful dimension for further theorisation (see Annex A).

As such, we have considered the six main dimensions of management: where/when, who and with whom, what, why, how and with what effects. In this sense, a smarter comprehensive approach seems possible, but only if a systemic approach is accepted. Indeed, a more systemic perspective is required in order to better appraise the system's effects of the first, second and third order. In other words, taking a traditional stovepipe perspective is more likely to recreate fundamental issues. Hence, strategic management in itself proves to be insufficient to encompass an array of various ontologies, including bottom-up approaches and transdisciplinary views, mainly because of its predominant positivist and rationalistic view of strategy as dictating all other factors. Thus from our constructive pragmatic perspective, exclusively adopting a strategic management ontology appears unconstructive and unpractical. A more systemic approach is thus required.

Systemic Approach

Systems approach refers to the holistic and comprehensive analysis of complex and intensely challenging problems. Systems approach represents a growing body of transdisciplinary[43] knowledge about the structure, behaviour and dynamics of change within a specific category of complex systems known as complex adaptive systems (i.e., open evolutionary systems in which the components are strongly interrelated, self-organising and dynamic).

> Rain forests, businesses, societies, our immune systems, the World Wide Web, and the rapidly globalizing world economy can be thought of as Complex Adaptive Systems. Each of these systems evolves in relationship to the larger environment within which it operates. To survive, the system as a whole must adapt to change. As a result, we are witnessing the integration of knowledge across disciplines and the emergence of new concepts, tools, and a vocabulary of complex systems thinking. Across the frontiers of science, this new more complete, whole of systems approach is replacing the old reductionist paradigm, where scientists traditionally tried to understand and to describe the dynamics of systems by studying and describing their component parts. (Sanders 2003. 2)

Systems approach also appeared as a promising avenue to transcend the inherent positivistic stance of the strategic management ontology. Thus, the systems approach is well-documented in academic literature but more so in business administration than in public administration, as with strategic management, and it can prove very fruitful for a comprehensive modelling. A key distinction between the systems approach and strategic management is the former's acknowledgment of informal factors, as well as its implicit acceptance of yet more complexity. We have become all too familiar with the network talk, but we would argue that we have ontologically still not fully grasped the implications of the network walk, or if you may, of the networking, particularly in light of what it means for complexity research

---

[43] Transdisciplinary connotes a research strategy that crosses many disciplinary boundaries to create a holistic approach. Piaget introduced this usage of the term in 1970 and again in 1987 (Piaget 1970)

faced with global interdependencies represented by terrorism, insurgencies, narco-traffic and more.

Ontologically, in light of contemporary complexities, we understand a transdisciplinary approach has thus become necessary to comprehensively understand an important field of study, such as the national security and defence of Canada since 2001. From our own experience and expertise as strategist, we appreciate that short-sighted disciplinary views are in fact the root causes of some of our most crucial shortcomings. In light of global interdependence and information technology, a multiperspectival theorising as presented by Bohman (2002) appears important in supporting an emerging comprehensive approach such the one as adopted by Canada, NATO, the United States and UK, as well as a consortium of Scandinavian countries (Finland, Denmark, Norway) and the Netherlands. In essence, if a comprehensive approach is the answer to some of our more fundamental security concerns, then a more opened ontology is thus required, which can incorporate different positions. This perspective provides a system-of-systems view where issues are seen more holistically.

Overall Ontology

Ontologically, each academic and professional discipline has its own challenges and weaknesses, as well as their own advantages and strengths. Taken individually, any discipline is not likely to offer any more comprehensiveness than the limits of its own theoretical body of organising knowledge, which in the case of some disciplines (like physics or history) have now become so extensive it is humanly impossible for one person to appreciate the whole. This has led to further subdivisions of meso and micro perspectives that lost sight of the macro perspective. Conversely, the transdisciplinary field of strategic management and systems approach attempts to reintegrate the big picture.

Thus, a constructive pragmatic and transdisciplinary perspective is, in our view, a smarter and balanced approach to construct a practical comprehensive theory to better understand issues. Furthermore, the constant opposition of the positivist and interpretivist epistemologies, with their subsequent intellectual dichotomisations, have led to yet more complexity than is practical. Ontologically, not only is a strategic management perspective essential to better understand the decision-making scheme behind the comprehensive approach, but a systemic view is also crucial to better appreciate its effects. Henceforth, a more constructive epistemology seeks to construct, from a more pragmatic philosophical standpoint, a constructive and perhaps even a more systemic perspective in strategic management. As such, it then becomes obvious that a unique methodology is required to support this research logic.

Research Methodology

This book asks the central question: What would be an applicable decision-making model of the comprehensive approach? The idea is to offer executives a theoretical model that could support their strategic thinking in the case of Canada's future engagements, such as in Iraq and the Levant, the Middle-East, Eastern Europe and perhaps even here at home during crises. Indeed, executive officers should focus on the strategic and important issues facing the organisation as a whole, including where it is headed and what it should become. According to Mintzberg (1994), "Strategy is a plan, a pattern, a position, a perspective, even a ploy," which reflects well upon our own emerging dimensions of strategic management.

Moreover, "Strategy is linked to a strategic thinker's view of how the organisation should operate and function" (Hambrick and Frederickson 2001, 20; in Steptoe-Warren 2011, 243). In this strategic management perspective, Canada's engagement in Afghanistan will provide the background from which grounded theory methodology will be employed. This background is crucial because it is the only instance so far in which the so-called comprehensive approach has been deliberately cited as a key construct of the mission: "A crucial case is one in which a theory that passes empirical testing is strongly supported and one that fails is strongly impugned" (George and Bennett 2005, 9). This book thus aims to provide a theoretical model to support civil-military strategic management, and it further asks what are the major dimensions of this comprehensive approach, and how we can theoretically model them. The following methodology will assist us in providing answers.

Grounded Theory

To answer these underlying questions, this doctoral research employed the principles of grounded theory as outlined in *The Discovery of Grounded Theory* by Glaser and Strauss (1967). This theory-generation methodology is best suited for cases where there are no apparent or underlying models or theories. Henceforth, this book will propose a grounded theoretical model through a grounded theory research design, which is understood as

> A rigorous method of conducting research in which researchers construct conceptual frameworks or theories through building inductive theoretical analyses from data and subsequently checking their theoretical interpretations. Thus, researchers' analytic categories are directly "grounded" in the data. The method favors: 1) analysis over description, 2) fresh categories over preconceived ideas and extant theories, and 3) systematically focused sequential data collection over large initial samples. This method involves the researcher in the data analysis while collecting data. Data analysis and collection inform and shape each other in an iterative process. Sharp distinctions between data collection and analysis phases of traditional research are intentionally blurred within grounded theory. (Charmaz 2014, 343)

This grounded theory has been advantageously used by Guillemette and Luckerhoff (2009). We thus started by searching for the subject of the comprehensive approach within the professional literature, looking to find the dimensions of the underlying theoretical model.

> Grounded Theory methods consist of systematic, yet flexible guidelines for collecting and analysing qualitative data to construct theories from the data itself. Thus researchers construct a theory 'grounded' in their data. Grounded Theory begins with inductive data and analysis, uses comparative methods, and keeps you interacting and involved with data and emerging analysis. (Charmaz 2014, 1)

In our search for a theory of the comprehensive approach, we searched for documents which in the first instance contained the expression *comprehensive approach*. Documents were read and analysed qualitatively by interpretatively coding and categorising them, and quantitatively by searching for the occurrence of keywords within the texts themselves.

Within this book, a model is thus understood as the visual, approximate or mathematical representation of a phenomenon. A theory is understood as a set of abstract and general propositions of this same phenomenon. Indeed, according to Denscombe (1998, 240), "A theory is a proposition about the relationship between things," which grounded theory seeks to produce by iterating between data collection, data analysis and (in our case) a meta-analysis. Moreover, a theoretical model is understood as "A description or representation used to understand the way in which a particular system or process works."[44]

Henceforth and for the purpose of this research, we propose to develop a theoretical model. Content analysis thus materialised hermeneutically through our interpretation of the texts. "Hermeneutics is the research activity of interpreting whatever in the target situation is seen, heard or sensed. The 'hermeneutic circle' consists of the original data and the interpretative transformation of it by the researcher" (Davies 2007, 237). This research followed the principles of grounded theory outlined by Glaser and Strauss (1967), and there was no predetermined number of texts to read. Rather, theoretical saturation of the categories according to our interpretative analysis and subsequent quantitative analysis was the goal.

> Glaser and Strauss (1967) originally did not clearly name the data analysis process as open coding or theoretical coding, but emphasised the constant comparative method for generating theory. They proposed that a researcher starts by coding each incident (incident refers to each identifiable unit of meaning in a line; often a sentence, a clause, a few sentences, or very occasionally a paragraph); compares the code with the previous incidents in the same and different groups; creates categories and properties in the constant comparative process; and integrates categories and their properties by reduction. (Tan 2009, 102)

As such, we proceeded with the corpus.

Corpus Selection

For this research, initial coding started by qualitatively interpreting the fundamental texts on the topic of comprehensive approach. Many sources came from Canada, and some came from Scandinavian countries and

---

[44] See Oxford English Dictionary Online, https://en.oxforddictionaries.com/definition/theoretical_model

Europe (including the United Kingdom). Other texts originated from the United States and the North Atlantic Treaty Organisation. These initial texts were selected on the basis of an initial Internet search for the term *comprehensive approach* in the first instance. Most were official political and strategic documents discussing the comprehensive approach originating from these different countries. Following initial readings on the topic, which included many writings on comprehensive approach as applied by Canada in Afghanistan through such reports as the Manley Report (2008) and doctrinal documents such as CF Land Ops and CF COIN (2008), as well the US Manual on Stability Operations (2008), all of which are publicly accessible, no actual integrated model or theory could be found, creating a fundamental cognitive dissonance.

As the data and material started to accumulate regarding comprehensive approach, this further meant that our categorising scheme had to be established in order to process incoming documents.

> Unlike selective sampling where the researcher decides ahead of time who and where to collect data, in Grounded Theory sampling is an ongoing process of data analysis and collection. It is theoretical because an emerging theory cannot be predetermined but tentatively develops and is determined during this process. (Tan 2009, 97)

As such, employing the major dimensions of strategic management, which emerged from our first iteration of 88 texts: the situational context, the socioculture, the organisational structure, the strategic policies, the systemic processes and the synergy dynamics; we thus started to conceptualise about the comprehensive approach in a more holistic and integrated manner, incorporating more texts and data as the coding scheme further evolved. Moreover, in the spirit of a comprehensive approach, we expended this review of documentation to include as well the Canadian literature on whole-of-government and the three Ds of defence, diplomacy and development, which to a large extent have been the evolutionary precursors of the comprehensive approach, at least in the Canadian context.

The overall global context of this selection was also of critical importance to our understanding. Indeed, it became obvious through our review of the literature on the topic that studying comprehensive approach meant also studying the background of Afghanistan. The approach emerged from that crucial case and from its main precursors of defence, diplomacy and development (3D) and whole-of-government (WoG). Canada was now subscribing to the comprehensive strategy in countering the threat of terrorism, as it became apparent from the 2005 International Policy Statement.[45] This was followed shortly thereafter by NATO's 2006 Riga Summit, leading to the countries adopting the Comprehensive Political Guidance (CPG). As for the UN, it had long discussed the requirement of a comprehensive strategy to fight terrorism, but the idea only gained maturity through NATO's engagement within Afghanistan. As such, precursor concepts (3D, WoG, Civil-Military Cooperation and Network-Enabled Operations, to name a few) were now pointing towards greater interdependencies and more civil-military collaboration, which later became embodied within the comprehensive approach, but that in fact was before the letter.

During the summer of 2006, Canadians started to experience greater difficulty in the southern provinces of Kandahar and part of Helmand for which they were tasked, leading to more casualties, more debate at home and abroad and more data. It was decided to circumscribe the study of the comprehensive approach with Canada and Afghanistan as secondary keywords. This somewhat limited the quantity of data, but nonetheless during the year of 2007, Canada's national security and defence, as well as foreign affairs, were full of political discussions regarding Canada's engagement in Afghanistan. By default, this provided the required focus for this research in that it created a practical object to a still-evolving, fluid subject. At that time (2007), the precursor concepts for the comprehensive approach were being conflated: the three Ds were often associated with the whole-of-government and with an integrated approach. Hence, looking for the comprehensive approach was still not a clean-cut research venture.

---

[45] "Counteracting this threat [of terrorism] requires a comprehensive strategy that includes, but is broader than, coercive instruments. Canada, in collaboration with other likeminded states, will take advantage of every available tool: intelligence, law enforcement, financial instruments and military force. We will ensure that our approach is consistent with the democratic values we hold dear, and maintains the utmost respect for civil liberties" (Canada—IPS 2005, 12), http://www.isn.ethz.ch/Digital-Library/Publications/Detail/?lang=en&id=156830

The comprehensive approach was still an emergent idea at the time. In parallel to Canada's engagement in Afghanistan, NATO's own engagement in Afghanistan was also morphing from a counterterrorism operation into a larger counterinsurgency campaign, which meant that the overall strategic, political and military background was also radically changing in 2006–2007.

From a data collection standpoint, this meant a threefold increase in documents and various media to the point where this research's topic had to be refined. By 2007, the comprehensive approach only started to emerge regarding Afghanistan. A posteriori quantitative analysis of the retained documents highlights that the comprehensive approach emerged in 2007.

Figure 3—Number of Texts Retained per Year

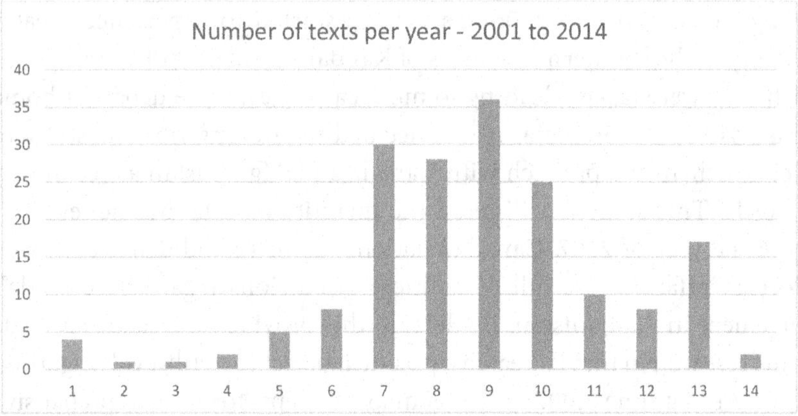

By 2007, keywords started to emerge as the basic concepts for researching the comprehensive approach in a strategic management perspective, leading to a snowballing where one document on the topic led to another with the same keywords, and so on. Keywords were employed mainly using Google and Google Scholar from the Internet, because the documents contained in other systems were restricted due to their government classification. Snowballing with basic keywords (*Afghanistan, Canada* and *comprehensive approach*) led to sufficient unclassified documentation to warrant a full doctoral research on this topic. In an electronic folder held by the author, over 615 individual texts and media were collected between the years 2006–2014, employing the basic non-mutually exclusive keywords as indicated. This included numerous books, reports, articles, theses and media reports, as well as other sources of multimedia. Between 2001–2014, it thus appears Canada was at the forefront of the comprehensive approach, in particular between 2007 (when the comprehensive approach itself emerged) and 2011 (when Canada's combat and so-called comprehensive approach mission was terminated and transitioned into a military training mission until 2014). The following table represents the number of texts retained by country or organisation of origin, as well as in percentages.

Table 2—Origin of Selected Texts

Origin	Count	Percent
Canada	104	58%
Europe and UK	26	15%
United States (US)	18	10%
NATO Alliance	15	8%
United Nations (UN)	10	6%
Afghanistan	5	3%
Total Count	**178**	100%

Content Analysis

According to grounded theory methodology, data collection was done in parallel with analysis, where documents were first read, hermeneutically interpreted, codified and categorised and subsequently meta-analysed using a word-counting software. Reading in the first instance was done without the actual coding scheme fully developed, so in some instances a second reading was made necessary: This had the undesired effect of creating some doubles within our dataset, which had to be removed at later stages. During that same timeframe, the context and the background for the topic also evolved, from the three Ds to the WoG as explained earlier, as well as from different sets in Afghanistan: from Kabul to Kandahar in 2006, to a southern surge in 2009–2010, to a training mission from

July 2011 to 2014. As the iterations of documentation analysis evolved, our original coding was established within the first 88 texts analysed. Subsequent iterations of the model were produced with 105 and 178 texts, when it was thought a significant level of theoretical saturation could be achieved. However, without any quantitative meta-analysis of the correlations between the categories, there was no way of knowing whether indeed the model as a whole was sufficiently well-integrated. In parallel, the codification behind this grounded theory research design had also evolved, becoming more focused and integrated, and now it included further keywords, which were also being employed with Primitive Word Counter.

As a word counting software, Word Counter version 1.09 has a very interesting functionality in that it allows to discriminate actual words employed, and not simply count them. That is to say that a full list of all words employed within a chosen text are shown in absolute numbers as well as in percentages, allowing further discrimination. This software is known as a search engine optimiser, but it can very well be used in checking for keywords. This was precisely the usage this research made, employing concepts within categories to quantitatively capture the occurrences of each in any given text document. The captured data was then recorded traditionally in an Excel spreadsheet, and percentages were calculated in order to give a relative weight to each of the known dimensions of management. Using Word Counter, comma-separated value (CSV) files were created for most texts analysed and imported in an excel sheet that allowed to calculate the occurrence of codes into categories and thus ensure reliability.

Our grounded theory research design worked from the ground up, building the theoretical model as the analysis evolved in parallel with data collection, and so the categories were not well known for sure. Within the management literature, the basic categories of structure, strategy and systems were well-recognised, and each had well-established corpus of literature. Within the sociology literature, the society category occupied a cognitive space, whereas the situational category is better known within the military for situational awareness purposes and for better appraisal of the overall context. The dynamic category appeared as an interesting category within a system-of-system perspective. Starting from these simple categories, codes were clustered according to their main dimension. This process was obviously very similar to grounded theorisation, where categories are constructed from codes and concepts and thereafter analysed for their relevance into each of these categories. The following table presents the keywords that were researched under each of the six dimensions.

Table 3—List of Keywords Researched

Strategic Management Dimensions	Root Keywords Researched
Situational-Context	Situ(*); context(*); histor(*)
Sociocultural	Soci(*); cult(*); people(*) **Excluded:** association and agriculture
Organisational Structure	Struc(*); organisa(*); agen(*) **Included:** (recon and decon)struction
Strategic Policy	Strat(*); politic(*); plan(*) **Excluded:** (demon and illu)strate
Systemic Functions	Sys(*); function(*); process(*)
Synergy Dynamics	Syn(*); dynam(*); coll(*)

Model Iterations

As codes started to appear alongside the texts, using ample Post-It notes and exploiting the margins to their maximum for this interpretative coding scheme, many similar codes started to emerge from one text on the topic to the next text, and so on.

> Seen by many as illustrating the stark difference between qualitative research and experimental research (in which data is collected to test a pre-stated theory), grounded theory emerges from the data. The process requires the researcher, during the data-gathering phase of a project, to examine the material as it builds up and to place it into categories—to classify it. Once this process has been started, the researcher returns to the field to gather more data and see whether the additional material fits into the established categories or whether the classificatory system needs to be adapted to accommodate fresh data. (Davies 2007, 237)

Eric Dion, CD, MBA, PhD

Once codes and categories started to saturate, after having read 88 texts, a first iteration of the model was proposed. After 105 texts, a further iteration of the model was produced. The final analysis and the final iteration of the model was produced following 178 texts. The following figures represent the number of texts read per year and the iterations of the model:

Figure 4—Iterations of the Model

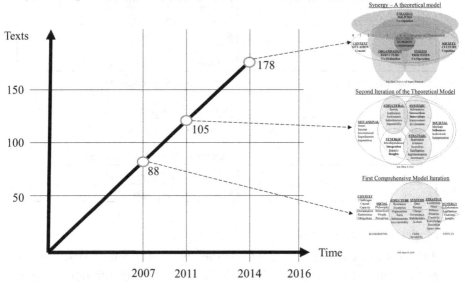

Eric Dion © 2016

54

54

Figure 5—First Iteration of the Model at 88 Texts

First Comprehensive Model Iteration

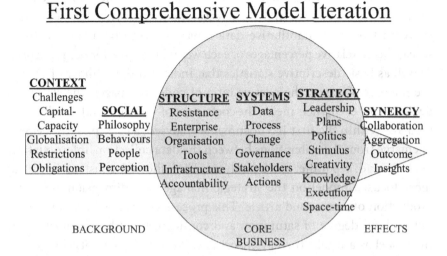

Eric Dion © 2009

Figure 6—Second Iteration of the Model at 105 Texts

Second Iteration of the Theoretical Model

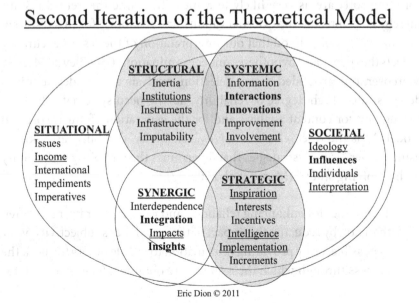

Eric Dion © 2011

Each of these iterations was done with theoretical saturation in mind, with the model being constructed of the original 88 texts, being refined with 105 texts and saturated with 178 texts read. As each text on the comprehensive approach was first read and then researched employing the keywords in Word Counter, quantitative data thus started to populate an Excel spreadsheet. Relative percentages of each were earmarked for our reference, as well as basic descriptive statistics that indicated the number of codes, the number of pages, the relative ratio of codes per pages, the standard deviation for each, their mean, the coefficient of variation and finally their median. Within the first 105 documents analysed, a clear pattern seemed to emerge from these iterations between the data collection, interpretative analysis and a parallel meta-analysis. This allowed construction of a more focused model on the strategic management dimensions and the production of our second article. This process was carried over and over until a high degree of saturation and confidence had been achieved for the model as a whole, thereby ensuring validity and reliability for the six dimensions. By that time, 178 texts had been read, memos had been noted in a Word document along with our analysis, and data had been compiled in an Excel spreadsheet.

As such, a researcher reading the same 178 texts and employing the same coding and categorisation scheme from grounded theory, as well as word counting software, is very likely to achieve the same theoretical results, thereby guaranteeing the external validity and reliability for this research. Validity is "the likelihood that our interpretation of the results accurately reflects the theory and hypotheses under examination" (Hoadley 2004, 204). Moreover, our grounded theory selection, analysis and model iterations demonstrate a high degree of reliability, having been systematically used throughout for content analysis and for the generation of our theoretical model. "It is the researcher's creativity, sensitivity, flexibility and skill in using the verification strategies that determines the reliability and validity of the evolving study" (Morse et al. 2002, 17).

> Techniques for enhancing reliability and validity operate, more often than not, by reducing the impact of the researcher's subjectivity as far as possible, or by providing information to enable others to check the process through which the results were obtained. (Gagnon 2010, 15)

Indeed, we have leveraged both of these techniques.

Finally, in regards to our overall research methodology, we also argue in the same vein that

> Strategies for ensuring rigor must be built in the qualitative research process per se. These strategies include investigator responsiveness, methodological coherence, theoretical sampling, sampling adequacy, an active analytic stance, and saturation. These strategies, when used appropriately, force the researcher to correct both the direction of analysis and development of the study as necessary, thus ensuring reliability and validity of the completed research project. (Morse et al. 2002, 17)

Conclusion

In essence, it appears clearly from a systematic review of literature that the *comprehensive approach did* not exist as framework, model or theory. Even the literature on the topic states,

> The comprehensive approach is an overarching *philosophy* for the conduct of a campaign. It recognises that crisis situations and their surrounding environments are complicated and that an enduring solution cannot be reached by military forces alone. (CF Land Ops 2008, 5–14)

As such, the constructive pragmatic epistemological perspective that we have presented allows us to take into consideration other perspectives than simply the military's mainly positivistic and rationalistic stance. Indeed, a more open epistemology is required as a working philosophy. Ontologically as well, a more open position on issues at stake is required, adopting a strategic management and systemic approach in order to find more practical, integrated, holistic and dynamic solutions. This is the benefit of open paradigms.

Methodologically faced with the weakness of current frameworks, it was proposed to develop a theoretical model, thereby employing grounded theory for its generation. Starting our content analysis with the principal writings on the *comprehensive approach*, it was realised that theoretical saturation was the goal in developing such a theoretical model. After iterating between the content analysis, its interpretation and its quantitative meta-analysis, and employing a word-counting software, our original model was iterated at 88, 105 and 178 texts. In doing so, six dimensions emerged for further analysis, and the model spiral developed.

Complementing this research methodology composed of triangulation between a systematic review of literature, its content analysis and a meta-analysis, a unique opportunity for participation and observation was offered to the author whom deployed in Afghanistan in 2010 at the height of the campaign as Chief of Joint Operational Plans (CJ35) for Task Force Kandahar (TFK). This deployment helped to confirm there was no working framework, model or theory for the comprehensive approach.

In the following chapters, the result of this iterative theoretical model development is presented as three articles that have been published or submitted for publication in peer-reviewed journals. Following these three articles, a general discussion on synergy ensues.

3

Canada's Comprehensive Approach in Afghanistan

Abstract

We present the first article published in *Defence Studies*[46] for this doctoral research, entitled "Canada's Comprehensive Approach in Afghanistan: A critical review of literature, 2001–2011." This article follows our systematic review of the literature on the topic of Canada's comprehensive approach in Afghanistan from 2001 to 2011. It traces the genealogy of the approach and identifies three major contributions as well, as three serious limitations. A subsequent qualitative analysis of the content of this literature, as well as a quantitative meta-analysis, provides a deeper than ever understanding of the complexity of Canada's so-called comprehensive approach, and as such it presents the theoretical underpinnings of a pragmatic executive decision-making model for Canada's future engagements to be developed through further iterations of grounded theory.

---

[46] Eric Dion, "Canada's Comprehensive Approach in Afghanistan: A Critical Review of Literature, 2001–2011," *Defence Studies* 14, no. 2 (2014): 192–215, http://www.tandfonline.com/doi/abs/10.1080/14702436.2014.891854 (accessed February 3, 2016).

Introduction

In this article, through a systematic review of literature, we seek to confirm the hypothesis to the effect that the comprehensive approach does not exist as an intellectual construct. If this hypothesis is valid, no framework, no model and no theory of the comprehensive approach will be found from this systematic review of this extensive body of literature on this topic. Conversely, if such a comprehensive approach intellectual construct or framework is found, it would render a null hypothesis. Henceforth, we have strived to find such intellectual construct throughout this review of literature. However, no working framework, model or even theory of the *comprehensive approach* could be found.[47]

As a research project, while reviewing this extensive body of literature, it thus became interesting to determine with a good degree of confidence what could be the key dimensions of such model. Indeed, extrapolating what could be the comprehensive approach's crucial dimensions from this systematic review of the literature can yield the basic intellectual constructs for such a framework. This is of particular interest for Canada in light of lessons still to be learned in the face of global instability and insurgencies for which the comprehensive approach has emerged in response.[48] Better understanding this holistic approach thus seems to be a quintessential intellectual venture, and through this systematic review of the literature on the comprehensive approach, we propose to verify our hypothesis, and once verified, present what could be its basic intellectual constructs.

As such, we first present three major contributions of the mostly political and professional body of literature on the topic of Canada's comprehensive

---

[47] "At present, there are no clear measures of effectiveness to accurately assess the performance of the Canadian CA in Afghanistan. The absence of performance indicators, trend analysis, and objectives, impairs iterative and objective assessment of organizational efficiency. Without functional measures of effectiveness, no authoritative judgements can be made regarding the suitability of the CA as expeditionary conflict tool" (Ritchie 2010, 119), http://www.cfc.forces.gc.ca/papers/csc/csc36/mds/Ritchie.pdf.

[48] "Strategic decision-makers assigned missions to NATO forces that are impossible to complete with military means alone. Thus the *Comprehensive Approach* exists to draw on civilian capabilities to support these overarching political-military strategies" (Rotmann 2010, 4), http://www.ndc.nato.int/download/downloads.php?icode=231

approach in Afghanistan from 2001 to 2011, followed by three serious limitations also apparent from this review of literature. Thereafter, we present the theoretical underpinnings of what could be a pragmatic executive decision making model for Canada's future engagements, which has emerged from the dual qualitative content analysis and quantitative meta-analysis of the codes, concepts, categories and their correlations. This article thus sets the stage for further grounded theory research in complex decision making.

Research Logic

A different research logic is required in circumstances where no model or theory seems to exist as a starting point. Instead of opting for a traditional top-down approach, where a theoretical premise is stated and then verified, a more grounded and bottom-up theory construction approach is required—one that will allow the emergence of key dimensions from the ground.[49] Academically speaking, an inductive logic was used for this research in lieu of traditional deductive logic.[50] In this case, the ground is composed of the extensive body of literature on this key topic, complemented by my own participation and observation of this mission in the year 2010, where I served as Chief of Joint Operational Plans within Regional Command South for Task Force Kandahar (CJ35-TFK) as a lieutenant-colonel.

More specifically, this review of literature of the comprehensive approach, which has emerged through its Afghanistan mission as new policy and practice, has provided great insights. Composed of 88 articles, reports and books, this extensive body of mostly political and professional literature on the approach and its mission has provided a fertile ground for analysis. Employing the principles of grounded theory,[51] key concepts and categories

---

[49] "The promise of a formal top-down campaign introducing the *Comprehensive Approach* is very limited. Instead, new ways of pragmatic collaboration below the strategic level need to be encouraged. Most examples are drawn from Afghanistan, the alliance's most demanding mission that permeates both its other operations and largely shapes its institutional evolution" (Rotmann 2010, 1), http://www.ndc.nato.int/download/downloads.php?icode=231

[50] For more on inductive logic, see the Stanford Encyclopedia, http://plato.stanford.edu/entries/logic-inductive

[51] Dennis L. Rennie, "Grounded Theory Methodology as Methodical Hermeneutics: Reconciling Realism and Relativism," *Theory and Psychology*

Eric Dion, CD, MBA, PhD

emerged from over 14,515 citations extracted from within the body of this systematic review of literature. Following this review of literature of the comprehensive approach, out of which emerged the approach's genesis as well as three major contributions and three serious limitations, we proceeded to further analyse its contents qualitatively, and we proceeded to meta-analyse the data we extracted.

We proceeded qualitatively to analyse its content, following a pragmatic philosophy as well as a constructivist epistemology: We accepted what was written by the authors to mean it, and we also accepted that it was their own views. Thus the main points being made in each text were taken as such, and we extracted all key quotations into a code and related them to a concept and category. This qualitative content analysis was conducted simultaneously while the review of the literature was ongoing, according to the principles of grounded theory, clustering codes into concepts and categories. Subsequently, we proceeded to meta-analyse our own content analysis for a degree of significance.

This was also accomplished simultaneously by counting the number of occurrences of keywords within each text and by quantitatively meta-analysing each concept and category to determine their degree of significance as well as their overall correlation to one another in a whole model.[52] This pragmatic and constructive methodology yielded a good degree of validity and reliability to the three major contributions and three serious limitations that we present herein.

Approach Genesis

We need what we call a Comprehensive Approach. And that is the first lesson of this mission. The days when the military could defeat the enemy, then hand the baton off to the civilians and go home, are

---

10 (August 2000): 481–502. http://tap.sagepub.com/content/10/4/481.short (accessed February 25, 2016)

[52] "The logic of looking at the body of evidence, rather than trying to understand studies in isolation, is always compelling. Meta-analysis refers to the statistical synthesis of results from a series of studies. While the statistical procedures used in a meta-analysis can be applied to any set of data, the synthesis will be meaningful only if the studies have been collected systematically" (Borenstein 2009), http://www.meta-analysis.com/pages/why_do.html

past us. And Afghanistan is not unique. There are 16 major armed conflicts underway today. All of them are within, rather than between states. In many cases, it is the basic pillars of society that need to be rebuilt. This means that the military and civilians need to work much more closely than they have in the past. That might seem obvious and easy to do. It isn't. And there is a bit of a strange paradox in how this has evolved. At the national level, NATO Governments have generally moved towards a "Whole of Government" approach to Afghanistan. Diplomats, defense ministries and development experts sit together, plan together and operate together, including in Provincial Reconstruction Teams all over Afghanistan. But at the international level, this lesson has simply not yet been learnt.... To my mind, none of this is abstract theory. The less effective we are at adopting a Comprehensive Approach, the longer it will take for this mission to succeed. Last year, NATO lost more than one soldier a day, on average, in Afghanistan. That math is clear. And behind the math are lost lives. And it must not be ignored. We cannot allow old-think to hold us back. The cost is far too high. (Anders Rasmussen 2010)

Over the last dozen years, an extensive body of literature has emerged in regards to various aspects of the international mission in Afghanistan. As such, an important part of this literature has revolved around security concerns and policy issues, thus often focusing more on symptoms and approaching comprehensiveness from a professional, political and international perspective, and as a metaphor. Conversely, a more disjointed and less mainstream part of this extensive body of literature on the Afghanistan mission has been more concerned with its fundamental root causes, comprehensively approaching the topic from a systemic, sociological and almost metaphysical perspective. Both views have sought to converge however, in order to present an integrated comprehensive approach.

It was Kofi Annan who first urged a comprehensive approach to end the Afghanistan conflict,[53] and that was before it started in most Western minds—that is, before September 11, 2001. The case for a comprehensive collective security was then put forward by the United Nations in a 2004

---

[53] See Afghanistan News Center, http://www.afghanistannewscenter.com/news/2001/august/aug23h2001.html

report entitled "A More Secure World: Our Shared Responsibility." It was the report of the High-level Panel on Threats, Challenges and Change, and it specifically articulated a comprehensive strategy in order to meet the challenges of preventing further terrorist acts.[54]

In the United Kingdom (UK) a 2005 Joint Discussion Note (JDN)[55] defined the comprehensive approach as "Commonly understood principles and collaborative processes that enhance the likelihood of favourable and enduring outcomes within a particular situation" (UK-JDN 4/05). In the United States (US), a 2007 Army Field Manual (FM) on Stability Operations[56] defined a comprehensive approach as one "That integrates the cooperative efforts of the departments, and agencies of the US Government, intergovernmental and nongovernmental organizations, multinational partners, private sector entities, to achieve unity of effort toward a shared goal."[57] As for the NATO Alliance, the comprehensive approach was first officially introduced by the NATO Alliance Council (NAC) at the Riga Summit of 2006 (Smith-Windsor 2008, 1).

In the Canadian context, the 2004 National Security Policy has been heralded as "The first comprehensive functional articulation of what a defence of Canada means," which merged into the Canada First Defence Strategy in 2007 (Cappe Speech at CDAI Symposia 2008, 16). The 2008 Canadian

---

[54] UN, *High-level Panel on Threats, Challenges and Change*, 2004, http://www. un.org/secureworld/report2.pdf

[55] UK, *The Comprehensive Approach*, Joint Discussion Note (JDN) 4/05 Ministry of Defence, 2005, http://www.mod.uk/NR/rdonlyres/BEE7F0A4-C1DA-45F8-9FDC-7FBD25750EE3/0/dcdc21_jdn4_05.pdf

[56] US, *Stability Operations*, Field Manual 3-07, 2008, pp. 1–4: www.fas.org/irp/doddir/army/fm3-24.pdf

[57] "3D—Defence, Diplomacy and Development—reflects the reality that today's complex operations require a more comprehensive, holistic, and integrated approach that 'match our military might with a mature diplomatic and development effort worthy of the task ahead.' This focus is similar to the whole of government approach described in FM 3-07, Stability Operations, which describes the integration of "the collaborative efforts of the departments and agencies of the United States Government to achieve unity of effort toward a shared goal". However, some areas of the U.S. government view the 3D approach as merely a descriptor for what each department's role and responsibilities are in a conflict and based on how the 3D activities will be funded" (Finney 2010, 1).

Army Counter-insurgency Manual simply copied the UK's original idea.[58] As such, this review of literature encompassed the evolutionary concepts of the three *D*s and WoG as precursors to the comprehensive approach, sometimes also referred to as the integrated approach.

Thus through this literature review, it has become obvious the alleged comprehensive approach has not achieved a degree of intellectual maturity with the end of Canada's engagement in Afghanistan in July 2011. Indeed, the approach evolved[59] from the three *D*s of defence, diplomacy and development, which first emerged in 2003, and the subsequent *whole-of-government* as of 2005, along with other emerging intellectual constructs such as the Civil-Military Cooperation (CIMIC) and the Joint, Interagency, Multinational and Public (JIMP) concepts. Three major contributions can be noted from this review of literature: a security apparatus, a political strategy and an emerging normative. Conversely, three serious limitations have also been noted: an efficiency assumption, international relations and an intellectual complexity.

Security Apparatus

"If the only tool you have is a hammer, you tend to see every problem as a nail," Abraham Maslow once famously remarked. The first significant dimension to emerge from this literature review is the clear predominance of the security apparatus. More than 25 percent of the literature reviewed had a primary emphasis on security, defence and military concerns, which are generally associated with governmental structures and agencies, as well as government-contracted private security companies. What's more, a structuration[60] view is also very much reflected in numerous

---

[58] Canadian Forces, *Counter-Insurgency Ops*, 2008, 1–5, http://info.publicintelligence.net/CanadaCOIN.pdf
[59] "From participation in the search for Osama bin Laden, to taking command of the Kabul-based International Security Assistance Force, to operating in Kandahar, to assuming responsibility for the Provincial Reconstruction Team as well as security for much of Kandahar province, Canada's responsibilities evolved rather than being part of a unified strategic vision and implementation plan" (Fitz-Gerald and McNamara 2012), http://www.ipolitics.ca/2012/03/07/canada-needs-a-more-comprehensive-approach-to-national-security
[60] Structuration, http://www.istheory.yorku.ca/structurationtheory.htm, http://www.theory.org.uk/giddens2.htm

documents that discuss widespread destruction, reconstruction teams and requirements for infrastructure and industry, and that (according to structuration theory) discuss reinstitutionalisation, namely through security. Furthermore, organisational concerns for Afghan national independence, as well as the state of the Afghan institutions, are often cited as key considerations justifying this engagement and approach. Most instances place overwhelming emphasis on organisational and structural aspects of security, and none can be said to be objectively or subjectively comprehensive in its structural approach.

Many authors cite directly the central role played by security organisations in the comprehensive approach and Canada's engagement in Afghanistan. As such, it appears that a military prism[61] permeates the literature as a hammer. Security is an overwhelming consideration, casting a shadow upon all other organisations. Diplomacy and development are outmatched by defence in comprehensive approaches. Although best practices suggest that such partnerships work best amongst partnerships of equals,[62] defence seems to have outmatched diplomacy and development in most current, comprehensive global interventions (Cornish and Glad 2008, 8). A recent call by the Conference of Defense Associations (CDA) for the Canadian government to commission a "comprehensive National Security Strategy"[63] further underpins this crucial point, where comprehensiveness is subsumed to the security apparatus's policies and practices.

This predominance of the security apparatus is clearly apparent in official reports emanating from the government of Canada. For Canada, the success of this whole-of-government strategy depends on a balanced contribution from across the departments. Yet so far, there has been a sense that the military contribution has been disproportionately large. According to Manley (2008, 28), there is an urgent need for Canada to complete "practical and significant development projects of immediate

---

[61] *PRISM* is also a journal of the US National Defense University: http://www.ndu.edu/press/prism.html

[62] Patrick and Brown, *Greater Than the Sum of Its Parts?* International Peace Academy, 2007, pp. 128–129

[63] Paul Chapin and George Petrolekas, "Canada Needs a National Security Strategy," 2012, http://www.ipolitics.ca/2012/02/21/cda-institute-canada-needs-a-national-security-strategy (accessed February 25, 2016)

value to the Afghans," while at the same time contributing more to the capacity and legitimacy of the Afghan government institutions. Yet even to date, Canada's civilian programs have not achieved the scale or depth of engagement necessary to make a significant impact (Manley 2008, 28). In spite of signature projects,[64] the same held true by the end of the combat mission in July 2011.

It is also obvious from the review of literature that security is the most pressing concern for most, if not all, of the stake-holders involved (NATO, the UN and OSCE),[65] but also for non-governmental organisations such as OXFAM and CARE.[66] What's more, the overwhelming ratio of the security apparatus, in comparison to any other organisation involved, skews the perspective. Claims of egalitarian 3Ds, or whole-of-government, have clearly become rhetoric over reality.[67] Indeed, most of what works across agencies and national boundaries, such as the PRT concept,[68] predates the comprehensive approach and operates on the tactical level. In terms of operational and strategic effect, NATO's efforts and those of member states in key theatres are as fragmented as they were before the comprehensive approach was ever put on paper (Rotmann 2010, 4). Hence in order to counter such structural disintegration, it appears that a political strategy was required.

---

[64] "Canada's Three Signature Projects, "http://www.afghanistan.gc.ca/canada-afghanistan/projects-projets/index.aspx

[65] NATO, "Comprehensive Approach," http://www.nato.int/cps/en/natolive/topics_51633.htm?selectedLocale=en and UN Peacekeeping: http://www.un.org/en/peacekeeping/operations/peace.shtml and OSCE: http://www.osce.org/sg/75766

[66] CARE, *NGO Insecurity in Afghanistan*, 2005, http://www.care.org/newsroom/specialreports/afghanistan

[67] "Despite its reputation as a catchphrase of little consequence, NATO's *Comprehensive Approach* is a necessary response to practical coordination challenges and capability gaps that affects all of the Alliance's operations. While the need for 'comprehensiveness' is therefore well founded, the record of its implementation in key missions, such as the International Security Assistance Force (ISAF) in Afghanistan, is not encouraging" (Rotmann 2010, 1).

[68] "While PRTs are related to humanitarian efforts, unlike NGO and UN relief organizations, they seek to achieve the political ends of their sponsoring governments by extending the reach of the host government and providing strategies to improve security and governance in conflicted regions" (Woodrow Wilson School—PRTs 2008, 5).

Eric Dion, CD, MBA, PhD

Political Strategy

The second key dimension to emerge from this literature review is the political strategy. Almost 25 percent of the literature reviewed had a secondary focus on the political strategy discussing the Afghan intervention in light of national interests and international influence, as well as from a planning and implementation perspective within a global time and space, to achieve an impact.[69] It is obvious from this review of the literature that strategizing at the national, international, political and even organisational level has been a significant part of the discussion. From convincing the Canadian audience of the mission's success and worthiness[70] to quarterly reports to Parliament on Canada's engagement in Afghanistan,[71] to garnering international support for the mission, to raising Canada's voice[72] and demonstrating our national resolve and our firm engagement, the political strategy dimension is obvious but sometimes much more subtle.[73]

[69] "In other words, to strengthen the impact of an integrated approach, Canada must become more adept at directly linking its development efforts to its security operations while launching capacity building initiatives in the same geographic location" (Jorgensen 2008, 36), http://www.cfc.forces.gc.ca/papers/nssc/nssc10/jorgensen.pdf

[70] "Over the course of the Canadian involvement in Afghanistan, there were two relatively divisive parliamentary votes (May 2006, March 2008) occasioned by concern over the essential character of the mission and its duration, along with the highly politicized public and parliamentary debates over the government's Afghan detainee transfer policy" (Coombs 2012, 5), http://www.cdainstitute.ca/images/CDAInstitute_WOG_Dec2012.pdf

[71] Canada, "Quarterly Reports to Parliament on Canada's Engagement in Afghanistan," http://www.afghanistan.gc.ca/canada-afghanistan/documents/qr-rt.aspx?lang=eng

[72] "The objective of this diplomatic effort should be to raise Canada's voice, commensurate with the Canadian contribution in Afghanistan, to establish a comprehensive political-military ISAF strategy; to press for improvements in NATO/ISAF force structure, command organization and operational effectiveness; and to advocate the deployment of more forces to Afghanistan by other NATO partners" (The Manley Report 2008, 27), http://dsp-psd.pwgsc.gc.ca/collection_2008/dfait-maeci/FR5-20-1-2008E.pdf

[73] "The idea that UN peacekeeping is—or should be—a central pillar of Canada's international security policy has major political and potentially strategic implications. First, it has led to a perceptible change in political rhetoric regarding the mission in Afghanistan. The Conservative government has put greater emphasis on 'rebuilding,' 'stabilization,' human security, and non-military dimensions of the mission, as well as Canada's international

A key thread that runs through such concerns are an imperative to develop a global strategy for fighting terrorism that addresses root causes and strengthens responsible states and the rule of law and fundamental human rights. "What is required is a comprehensive strategy that incorporates but is broader than coercive measures" (UN Report 2004, 48). Thus, through the evolution of the Afghan mission, the prevailing view is that military force on its own is an insufficient—and in some regards an inappropriate—instrument to achieve our aims and therefore needs to be integrated with efforts that are mainly civilian in nature (Baumann—RUSI 2008, 70). Today, military legitimacy and successful operations are not defined by military power alone. Because conflict today is driven by material, ethnic, religious and ideological demands, and because it requires "winning the hearts and minds" of the local populations, the "ability to bear all instruments of national and coalition power and influence upon a problem in a timely, coordinated fashion (i.e., diplomatic, economic, military, and informational) is increasingly essential to achieving effective results" (Leslie et al. 2008). However, the only answer to the degradation of security has been (at least up until 2009) to send more troops to face the growing insurgency. Here, the tendency of any institution to ask for more resources, especially when things are going wrong, can be recognised. In fact, the question of a change in the political strategy had not been discussed before the end of 2008, even though deterioration of security began as early as 2002–2003 (Dorronsoro 2009, 3).

In effect, two trends that discuss political strategy can be noted within the literature: one inward looking, concerned with national political strategy for example in Canada, and another more outward focused on the Afghan political strategy. Indeed, in 2007 the government struck an independent panel under former Liberal Deputy Prime Minister John Manley to make recommendations on the future course of this mission.[74] Among the consequences were improved recognition of the breadth and the complexity of the Afghanistan challenge and a substantial evolution in both the strategic whole-of-government coordination framework in

---

responsibilities, with fewer references to 'retaliation' and 'war.' The objective is to frame the mission as a nation-building intervention" (Massie 2009, 638), http://ijx.sagepub.com/content/64/3/625.full.pdf+html

[74] The Manley Report, 2008, http://dsp-psd.pwgsc.gc.ca/collection_2008/dfait-maeci/FR5-20-1-2008E.pdf

Ottawa and the corresponding mission structure and civilian resourcing in Afghanistan (Coombs—CDAI 2010, 6). Conversely, aid has become overtly politicised and used as a tool to stabilise fragile states in the name of anti-terrorism. Thus, comprehensive approaches to stabilisation where political, military and development are complimentary instruments have changed the nature of aid. Development and humanitarian assistance is no longer based on criteria of need and aid effectiveness, but is used as a strategy to appease communities and win hearts and minds (Cornish and Glad 2008, 3).

As a blended approach, NATO's new strategic concept of 2007 promoted coordination and integration in the political and military dimensions, harnessing two core instruments of security. Although donor governments in the developed world cannot agree on the policy prescriptions to address failed states, how to prioritise failed states or even a single definition for failed state, there is a consensus that policy responses should use the whole-of-government approach. The 2005 IPS placed Canada firmly within this global consensus (Baker 2007, 15–16). Hence it is obvious that the political strategy dimension is significant within the literature reviewed, and it also influenced a more narrative dimension that appears to be a new emerging normative.

Emerging Normative

Indeed, the third significant dimension, which represents 15 percent of the literature reviewed on the comprehensive approach and Canada's engagement in Afghanistan, is an emerging normative. In particular, this dimension discusses social and cultural factors through ideological, individual or informal lenses, involving a larger stakeholder perspective and intersubjective understanding. Working together as equal partners, the various arms of donor governments and others (like aid agencies) are intended to act not only to resolve a conflict but also to transform societies, lifting failed and failing states into a new era of responsible governments that serve their people's best interests (Cornish and Glad 2008, 9). Experience in Afghanistan, and Kosovo demonstrated that today's challenges require a more comprehensive approach by the international community involving a wide spectrum of civil and military instruments (Riga 2006, para. 10). In light of significant, complex conflicts with important implications for stability and international security, Canada recognised the growing need for a coordinated whole-of-government approach to respond to countries in or at risk of crisis, such as Sudan, Afghanistan and Haiti (START 2006, 1).[75]

Attempting to address the root causes of the insurgency phenomenon and not simply target its most visible symptoms—perhaps an integrated 3D approach, combining elements of diplomacy, defence and development— is the best strategy for supporting states that suffer from a broad range of interconnected problems (Baker 2007, 1). Ultimately, however, the alleviation of poverty must become a primary strategy for achieving security in Afghanistan. Yet Afghanistan still receives far less funding from the international donor community overall than most other post-conflict nations (Smith 2007, 5). More fundamentally, support for the creation of Joint, Interagency, Multinational and Public (JIMP) capability stems from a growing consensus that outward focused, integrated and multidisciplinary approaches to those security threats and challenges must become the norm to address the complex problems and challenges posed by an increasingly multidimensional security environment. That environment is increasingly dynamic, uncertain and challenging (Gizewski and Rostek 2007, 58). As such, the hearts and minds theory suggests that insurgency-threatened countries ought to attack the two basic political problems behind insurgency: bad administration and a lack of administration (Grandia 2009, 14).

Even US Senators McCain and Lieberman argued in 2009 that the way forward in Afghanistan required "a comprehensive civil-military counterinsurgency approach."[76] COIN literature, from David Galula to David Kilcullen, recognises that good governance and sustainable development are the prize, relegating capture and kill missions to secondary status (Welle 2010, 54). A preponderance of evidence suggests that *whole-of-government* strategy, based on the converging elements of "political will, effective military enforcement capacity, and the sufficient economic resources," can help a failed state complete the transition to a peaceful and

---

[75] Stabilization and Reconstruction Task Force—START, http://www.international.gc.ca/START-GTSR/about-a_propos.aspx

[76] John McCain and Joe Lieberman, "Our Must-Win War," *The Washington Post* (March 19, 2009), http://articles.washingtonpost.com/2009-03-19/opinions/36770352_1_afghanistan-war-plan-terrorists

prosperous society (Jorgensen 2010, 41). However, there is a compelling lack of evidence to suggest that such a comprehensive approach may work and may even be successful as a working approach to resolve those complex insurgencies and crises. It is increasingly recognised that approaches to resolving conflict will no longer reside exclusively within the military domain, but rather will increasingly require more integrated approaches (Brown and Adams 2010, 9).

Stabilisation, as well as contested state building, requires a carefully synchronised application of different forms of power, from organised violence to effective governance, relief and development assistance (Rotmann 2010, 2). For coordination challenges, pragmatic and creative officials in the field have found ad-hoc and informal ways of working together long before the Riga Summit or the comprehensive approach (Rotmann 2010, 2). Canada's whole-of-government efforts in Kandahar involved a host of players in Canada and abroad, including Canadian field partners, members of the international community and Afghan authorities at all levels. The effort also reflected a wide variety of perspectives and philosophies, along with a multitude of objectives, plans, programs and activities, all of which impacted how Canada tackled the tasks it confronted in Afghanistan (Coombs 2012, 13). So in spite of the clarity of the emerging normative from the comprehensive approach throughout the literature, there does not appear to be a working framework for such coordination— and yet there is a further efficiency assumption underlying the approach.

Efficiency Assumption

The fourth significant dimension that emerged from this review of literature is an efficiency assumption that concerns 13 percent of the literature reviewed. Indeed, one of the goals of the JIMP framework (and of the associated whole-of-government approach) is to remove overlap and duplication amongst government agencies. In theory, these approaches should make the Canadian government agencies more efficient by increasing the chances for achieving interoperability and collaboration among key players (Leslie et al. 2008). Within the Canadian government, Ottawa has espoused the importance of whole-of-government approaches in its strategies and activities in Afghanistan, Haiti and the Sudan (Patrick and Brown 2007). Current government efforts using a whole-of-government or comprehensive approach are intended to optimise service delivery. Such initiatives are further intended to improve coordination among domestic and international operations (Brown and Adams 2010, 53). Thus, comprehensive approaches have been widely adopted by the troop contributing countries in Afghanistan, and there is a broad agreement that a combination of military, political and development efforts is the only way to obtain a peaceful and stable Afghanistan (Cornish and Glad 2008, 10). However, much in the same vein as the emerging normative dimension of the *comprehensive approach*, there have yet to be clear and objective demonstrations of the efficiency assumption within the approach without any model. Therein lies fundamental assumptions with regards to how such systemic efficiencies could be achieved through information exchange, personal interrelations, education and interoperability.

The criteria for success of Canada's strategy in Afghanistan and the metrics associated therewith continue to be a matter of debate. However, the criteria for failure are very clear: failing to apply a *whole-of-government* strategy. Where a comprehensive and integrated WoG approach is applied, Canada's efforts are generally met with success. Where Canada's WoG strategy is being applied in Afghanistan, and in Kandahar specifically, there are numerous signs that progress is being achieved. Significant improvements have been registered in the areas of governance, security and socioeconomic development. In Kandahar, where security operations have been synchronised with capacity building, community development councils (CDCs) have been established, which in turn have produced development plans that were ultimately implemented. Where the security forces accompanied food and medical shipments, food and medical aid was delivered to Afghans outside of Kabul (Jorgensen 2008, 26). It is increasingly clear that only a WoG strategy can achieve the necessary coherence and focus needed to achieve measurable and sustainable progress. Three separate efforts are neither sustainable nor effective; only an integrated, adequately resourced WoG strategy is viable. For Canada, the Manley report served to highlight the effectiveness of *whole-of-government* strategy (Jorgensen 2008, 43).

More broadly, a similar methodology needs to be developed to study how well quick impact projects (QIPs) are being coordinated with respect to the whole-of-effort approach. The initial evidence of the coordination between elements of the Kandahar PRT and other civilian actors operating within the area suggests this has been limited. The additional (and much more problematic) variable in assessing the whole-of-effort approach is the lack of a superordinate authority. Unlike the WoG approach, in which all government departments are subordinate to the will of the Canadian cabinet (which insists on unity of effort), is it feasible for this methodology to create dimensions for actors such as NGOs over whom there is no executive authority (Baker 2007, 14)? Indeed, there is an expectation that most non-UN external actors will participate in the overall comprehensive approach, and that there will be various processes, mechanisms and structures to facilitate the coordination, harmonisation and alignment processes necessary to achieve this system-wide coherence (De Coning 2009, 12). Although the comprehensive approach has tremendous potential as a stabilisation tool in counterinsurgency (COIN), there is no direct correlation between the use of comprehensive approach and the probability of success (Ritchie 2010, 63). Hence, poor results overall in Afghanistan tend to demonstrate the efficiency assumption is false—probably because comprehensive results are intimately tied to international relations.

International Relations

The fifth dimension that emerged from this review of literature is that the *comprehensive approach* is an international relations issue, and one that is indeed in search of super-coordination, as reflected in almost 11 percent of the literature. This is often traced to lessons of history, geostrategic situations and incidents that have created immediate moral or international imperatives because of general instability, insecurity or insurgency with larger implications, such as in the case of so-called failed or failing states. Indeed, for Canada, the Afghan challenge also came in the broader context of a US-Canadian crisis regarding Washington's invasion of Iraq; Canada opposed this move and declined to send troops. However, sending a second deployment of 2,000 Canadian soldiers to Kabul in 2003 in the multilateral setting of NATO and the International Security Assistance Force (ISAF) allowed Ottawa to avoid Washington's opprobrium for staying out of Iraq by making this significant contribution to the "US global war on terror." Beyond its bilateral relations with Washington, Canada has thus sought to maintain a significant role within NATO that, together with various UN resolutions, has provided a legitimizing multilateral umbrella for Canadian military participation in Afghanistan (Smith 2007, 11).

In fact, the role that Canada plays in the international arena is founded on the Canadian values of diplomacy, human security, international stability and viable international relations (Brown and Adams 2010, 31). Only until recently, with a more clearly defined international campaign leadership in late 2009 and the influx of tens of thousands of additional American troops, have these national undertakings been fully integrated into broader international counterinsurgency and nation-building campaigns, which have now begun to coalesce. It was in this context that, of necessity, a relatively robust Canadian whole-of-government campaign was finally able to evolve within Kandahar Province (Coombs—CDAI 2012, 4). But putting the *comprehensive approach* into practice requires a wide spectrum of very different actors to work effectively together towards a shared objective. It was noted that the strengths of the various contributing organisations must be seamlessly tied together to make sure everyone is singing from the same sheet. This is even harder when non-state actors such as the NGO community become part of the picture (Baumann 2010, 7). Indeed: "The issue of the coordination of all activities between military and civil actors in a crisis is important. It impacts substantially on the ability of the international community to adequately respond to complex emergencies. As such, it must be hoped that civil-military relations will be increasingly carefully monitored, as has been the case over recent years (Jenny 2001, 32)". But such intellectual complexity is intractable.

Intellectual Complexity

The sixth dimension to emerge from this review of the literature at 10 percent is an intellectual complexity within the comprehensive approach, compounded by its lack of a clear construct: No single element of national power on its own is sufficient to deal with all the complexities of failed and failing states (Capstick 2006, 1). It is further recognised that governments and their security-related institutions must develop appropriate organisational mechanisms that will achieve an effective unity of effort, with the intent to ensure that the application of the various civil-military instruments of power directly contribute to a viable and mutually agreed political end-state. Generating a more complete unity of effort will require conceptual and organisational contributions at the international, as well as the national, level (Manwaring 2006, 1). Hence the combination of political, military and development measures to foster peace, security, economic resurgence and good governance took on several names: integrated, comprehensive,

3Ds (defence, diplomacy and development) or the whole-of-government approach (Cornish and Glad 2008, 10). Given the number of possible agencies implicated within the interagency context and the fact that the concept of the Joint, Interagency, Multinational, Public (JIMP) framework is still also quite new, determining exactly which organisations fall into the interagency category is somewhat difficult. Using the whole-of-government approach as opposed to a comprehensive approach helps minimise some of the efforts of categorisation. WoG refers only to the activities of those other government departments (OGDs) and other government agencies (OGAs) of a particular country (i.e., Canada), whereas *comprehensive* includes all actors, from IOs and NGOs to private companies and corporations (Thomson et al. 2009, 3). Thus, another critical feature of the relationship amongst JIMP players and local publics is its sheer complexity (Brown and Adams 2010, 30).

For a truly comprehensive approach to emerge, each part of government needs to transform not just the military (Rotmann 2010, 4). So as the JIMP construct and framework are refined, it will be important to ensure collaboration with key people shaping this construct. One of the current challenges is the complexity of the JIMP context and the need to capture the overall perspectives of economics, anthropology, sociology, psychology and many other related fields. In this very sense, the efforts to refine and understand the JIMP construct must themselves be comprehensive. They need to take the best knowledge and experience from a range of domains, and they should attempt to integrate this knowledge and experience in a way that captures the unique perspectives in play (Brown and Adams 2010, 78). Task Force Kandahar and its whole-of-government collaborators were able to fight the insurgency in a number of ways: Canadian military efforts were oriented towards removing destabilizing influences, as well as establishing and maintaining population and community-centric security. These in turn created the conditions for an integrated interagency approach that generated and promoted local governance and development mostly from the bottom up. As part of this whole-of-government effort, wherever possible, the approach taken was to establish and reinforce partnerships that put Afghan officials and security forces in the forefront and the population's interests first. As conditions evolved towards responsible and functioning governance, burgeoning local economies, effective rural and urban interface, and capable Afghan National Security Forces, the aim was for districts to transition to complete Afghan control (Coombs 2012, 12–13).

Nonetheless, synchronisation still remains the critical flaw, exposing coalition vulnerabilities for incremental targeting by insurgents. Internal inefficiencies continue to plague the comprehensive approach's efficiency, impairing the unified pursuit of shared national goals (Ritchie 2010, 121). This conclusion is reinforced by many. As much as we like to look back and say, "We Canadians made a contribution, there never was a comprehensive plan."[77] Hence, it is obvious the comprehensive approach suffers from great intellectual complexity, one that has not been solved at the practical ground level, much less at the theoretical framework level. Perhaps is it the essence of a comprehensive approach metaphor or its metaphysical construction? Or if a comprehensive approach is the answer, perhaps the real problem then may be the lack of it? There is of course another very simple potential explanation for all of this: The comprehensive approach is not actually required to meet our objectives because our "objectives are actually far more modest than we are politically willing to admit" (Owen 2011). Such intellectual complexity thus presents a serious limitation to the comprehensive approach, especially without a model.[78]

Content Analysis

Henceforth, the idea of a comprehensive approach is not about comprehensiveness in scale or in scope. Rather, it is about its aggregated effect which in theory can be larger than the sum of its parts. Consequently, in order to achieve such synchronising effect, a pragmatic model is required that can be as metaphysically comprehensive as it can be metaphorically comprehensible. Thus, following our review of this extensive body of literature, we proceeded to analyse its content, firstly through a hermeneutic qualitative analysis and then through a quantitative meta-analysis, with a view to present what could be the theoretical underpinnings of such an executive model.

By employing the principles of grounded theory, we thus noted the important citations from the texts (i.e., articles, reports and books), according to

---

[77] Susan Sachs, "Newsmakers 2011: In Their Own Words," *The Globe and Mail* (December 24, 2011), A11.
[78] "No one nation can solve all the problems. There is no single means of addressing the problems. Military solutions on their own manifestly do not work. How are the varied problems of different theatres to be addressed when there is no single model?" (Rose; in Crawshaw 2007, 1).

the key points made by their authors, consistent with a constructivist epistemology. We subsequently coded these citations into concepts and categories, which we presented above as major contributions and serious limitations of the body of literature on the topic of Canada's comprehensive approach in Afghanistan for 2001–2011. This hermeneutic content analysis reveals in essence that the so-called comprehensive approach seems not to exist intellectually as an integrated construct, and that it probably does not exist practically, presenting a rhetoric-reality gap. For policymakers and practitioners, this is not new, but for pragmatic theorists, this is of concern. Without an intellectual construct or a framework, there is only muddle,[79] such as in Afghanistan. This poses a challenging double-hermeneutic problem,[80] which needs to be solved for Canada's future similar engagements.[81] Indeed, "Nothing is more practical than a good

---

[79] "The comprehensive approach arguably emerged from the identification of needs on the ground and the recognition of shortfalls in the response and was never meant to act as a set template fixing roles once and for all. Yet while definitional debates may appear secondary in light of pressing operational concerns, they are noteworthy in that they might reveal a degree of uncertainty behind the overall project of stabilisation" (Baumann 2010, 3).

[80] "Because the JIMP construct has yet to be fully and clearly defined, there are imminent dangers in moving ahead until there is more clarity around what the concept represents from the perspectives of all relevant parties. The theoretical underpinnings of the construct will need to be fully elaborated before it can serve as an adequate base for future research and development efforts (p. 68).... Although certainly framed from primarily a CF perspective, at least implicitly, the current conceptualization of JIMP seems to run somewhat counter to the true inclusive spirit of JIMP. The 'M' in JIMP is presumably not just about working in multinational military coalitions and alliances, but in theory, should also include the CF's ability to work with both military and non-military players of all diverse cultures. As the conceptual clarification of the JIMP concept proceeds, it might also be important to consider a more inclusive term to replace 'JIMP.' The JIMP construct (and particularly the joint and multinational components) seems most relevant when applied exclusively to the military context. The term 'comprehensive approach' may be better suited for conceptualizing the nature of the diverse collaboration necessary" (Brown and Adams 2010, 70).

[81] "Canadians should value what they have learned from their Afghanistan experience and make a determined effort to ensure that that learning is not lost before they next find themselves engaged in an international peace operation. If Canadians aspire to play an international leadership role, the expertise required in future will not be in traditional peacekeeping but in complex

theory," as Kurt Lewin noted (1952). As such, what this content analysis of the literature reveals from our grounded theory research logic is that the basic constructs of such framework of a comprehensive approach are reflected through its literature, which may provide the basic intellectual constructs for a framework.

Meta-Analysis

Furthermore, through the meta-analysis of the occurrences of keywords throughout the literature reviewed and subsequent quantitative analysis, we were able to identify the relative weight and the statistical significance of each of the three major contributions and three serious limitations that we extracted employing the principles of grounded theory.

Table 4—Percentage Related to Threads

SA= 25.1%	PS= 24.8%	EN= 15.1%	EA= 13.3%	IR= 10.6%	IC= 9.7%	SUM= 98.6%
26 texts	26 texts	16 texts	14 texts	11 texts	10 texts	105 texts

Each of these six dimensions proved to be statistically significant according to $T = 5$, $N = 105$ and $B = 0$, where Cohen's effect size was 0.95 with a desired statistical power of 0.05 for significance. This represents the total number of separate texts selected in our review for statistical saturation, comprised specifically of 24 articles, 59 reports, and 22 books, for a total population of $N = 105$. This statistically significant body of literature also provided great theoretical saturation, which is a crucial point for future modelling of the comprehensive approach as it presents itself.

Over 25 percent of the literature epitomises a security apparatus, almost 25 percent focuses on political strategy, 15 percent discusses the comprehensive approach as an emerging normative, and 13 percent of the literature is concerned with an efficiency assumption. Those factors create 78 percent of the review, and these constitute the bread and butter of the literature on the approach and mission. These are not new to any astute reader and observer of the comprehensive approach. However, another 20 percent of the literature can be attributed almost equally at 10

---

operations combining the skills of both military and civilians" (Coombs 2012, 15).

Eric Dion, CD, MBA, PhD

percent to international relations and to intellectual complexity. As much as the predominance of the security apparatus and the political strategy are obvious, the emerging normative and the efficiency assumption are more implicit but relatively easy to demonstrate. The international relations dimension to the comprehensive approach is also generally recognised, but what is less recognised is intellectual complexity, which as demonstrated probably emerges from the weakness of current frameworks in explaining the approach. But thanks to grounded theory, retracing the key dimensions of the comprehensive approach is possible, extracting citations into codes, concepts, categories and calculating correlations:

Figure 7—Comprehensive Overview

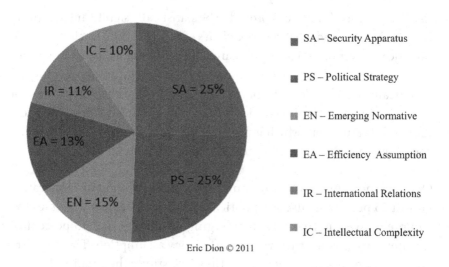

Eric Dion © 2011

Conclusion

Interestingly, the June 2013 issue of the *International Journal*[82] highlights all of the dimensions this independent review of literature has presented

---

[82] *International Journal* 68, 2 (June 2013): 269–377, http://ijx.sagepub.com/content/current.

80

long before it was ever published. For example, Massie states that "his article provides a comprehensive assessment of Canada's engagement in Afghanistan," however, without ever referencing a working comprehensive theory, model or framework; neo-classical realism is rather an epistemological perspective and much less a pragmatic tool. The other authors also highlight to various degrees the dimensions we presented herein: When Zyla discusses the norm of external responsibility; when Fitzsimons talks of Canada's engagement in light of international considerations for NATO and ISAF; when Burtch discusses the OMLT mentorship as "possible exit strategy"; when Tchantouridzé discusses the failure to win the hearts and minds of locals; when Veilleux-Lepage discusses public support for Canada's mission; and finally when Leprince talks of efficiency to Canada's recently adopted whole-of-government approach through the KPRT lens. These articles collectively underscore our own frame of analysis, giving great credence to this article's independent literature review, content and meta-analysis, thus validating its theoretical underpinnings.

However, by failing to implicitly link Canada's security operations with tangible examples of Canadian reconstruction and development, the Canadian strategy failed to exploit the potential synergistic effect of these major activities. In particular, up until the end, there appeared to have been a sharp disconnect between the work of the CF and that of CIDA. Despite all indications that security and development are inseparable elements of nation-building, CIDA has failed to focus its efforts and resources on supporting programs aimed specifically at Kandahar to help Afghans make a connection between Canada's security operations and Canadian reconstruction support. DFAIT has similarly shown a marked failure to engage with the necessary resources and focus "across the entire diplomatic spectrum" (Smith 2007, 6). Conversely, the dominance of the security apparatus was probably not conducive to more collaborative dynamics overall. In the end, Canada has been wholly unable to fully harmonise the 3Ds of defence, development and diplomatic—elements of a more strategic, longer-term assistance to achieve a sustainable end-state. Failing to harmonise strategies at the conceptual level first has increased the potential for miscommunications on the ground in Afghanistan, and it has created a significant potential to come into conflict in their efforts to rebuild

Afghanistan (Jorgensen 2008, 31). Genuine efforts are required to harmonise departmental efforts, empowering collaborative action in the spheres of security, governance, reconstruction and development (Ritchie 2010, 105).

But the comprehensive approach is not an end in itself—it is a means to an end. The aim is not to build new structures and hierarchies, but to achieve better outcomes and to resolve a crisis in a sustainable way.[83] However, in order to do so, a holistic framework is required—one which, if rigorously constructed from grounded theory, can provide a comprehensive, pragmatic model. Hence the fundamental issue, as determined from this systematic review of the literature on the comprehensive approach and Canada's engagement in Afghanistan from 2001 to 2011, is that a comprehensive approach does not seem to exist intellectually as whole construct, posing a serious double-hermeneutic problem. Indeed, without a model or theory supporting this approach, there can be no clear political or managerial directions, and neither can there be feedback in order to adjust actions.[84] In order to assess whether the application of the comprehensive approach has been successful, analysing the approach comprehensively is quintessential, but it's impossible without a framework.[85] Henceforth,

---

[83] Finland, Comprehensive Approach Research Team Report, 2008, p. 9m http://www.defmin.fi/files/1316/Comprehensive_Approach_-_Trends_Challenges_and_Possibilities_for_Cooperation_in_Crisis_Prevention_and_Management.pdf

[84] "Without benchmarks there can be neither success nor failure; only muddle" (State of Readiness 2012, 51).

[85] "The continuing challenge for Canada, the US, and the other parts of the hemispheric and global communities, then, is to exploit the fact that contemporary security—at whatever level—is, at base, a holistic political-diplomatic, socio-economic, psychological-moral, and military-police effort. The corollary is to move from a singular military approach to a multidimensional whole-of-government and whole of alliance/coalition paradigm. The Canadian whole-of-government approach and the NATO whole-of-alliance model to homeland defense and global security requirements do that, and could be very useful as primary organizational principles to establish a comprehensive North American process for active intergovernmental and multilateral policy cooperation. That, in turn, requires a conceptual framework and organizational structure to promulgate unified civil-military planning and implement the multidimensional, multi-organizational, and multilateral/multinational security concept" (Manwaring 2006, 3).

it objectively appears that the comprehensive approach is almost entirely subjective and that it fundamentally lacks a more theoretically grounded and practical intellectual construct. Thus through subsequent grounded theory methodological research designs, we propose to develop such an executive model.

References

Annan, Kofi. 2001. Comprehensive Approach Needed to End Afghanistan Conflict. Speech as United Nations Secretary General. August 22, 2001. http://www.afghanistannewscenter.com/news/2001/august/aug23h2001.html and http://reliefweb.int/report/afghanistan/annan-suggests-un-adopt-comprehensive-approach-ending-afghanistan-conflict (accessed January 16, 2016).

Baker, Jon. 2007. "Quick Impact Projects: Towards a 'Whole of Government' Approach." *Norman Paterson School of International Affairs Review* 8: 1–22. http://diplomatonline.com/mag/pdf/PatersonReviewVolume8_2007.pdf#page=9 (accessed February 21, 2016).

Baumann, A. B. 2008. "Clash of Organisational Cultures? The Challenge of Integrating Civilian and Military Efforts in Stabilisation Operations." *Royal United Services Institute* 153, no. 6: 70–73. https://rusi.org/publication/rusi-journal/clash-organisational-cultures-challenge-integrating-civilian-and-military (accessed February 21, 2016).

Brown, Andrea L., Barbara D. Adams. 2010. "Exploring the JIMP (Joint, Interagency, Multinational, Public) Concept: Literature Review." Defence Research and Development Center (DRDC) Toronto, CR 2010-021, February. http://cradpdf.drdc-rddc.gc.ca/PDFS/unc100/p533781_A1b.pdf (accessed February 21, 2016).

Canada. 2006. "Mobilizing Canada's Capacity for International Crisis Response." Department of Foreign Affairs and International Trade (DFAIT)—Stabilisation and Reconstruction Task Force (START), Brochure. http://www.international.gc.ca/START-GTSR/

about-a_propos.aspx and http://www.unitar.org/ny/sites/unitar.
org.ny/files/START%20Canada_UNITAR_Oct%202008.pdf
(accessed February 21, 2016).

Canada. 2008. "Independent Commission on the Future of Canada in
Afghanistan (The Manley Report)." http://dsp-psd.pwgsc.gc.ca/
collection_2008/dfait-maeci/FR5-20-1-2008E.pdf (accessed
February 21, 2016).

Capstick, Mike. 2008. "The Civil-Military Effort in Afghanistan: A
Strategic Perspective." *Journal of Military and Strategic Studies*
3: 35–52. http://jmss.org/jmss/index.php/jmss/article/view/35/33
(accessed February 21, 2016).

Coombs, Howard. 2012. "Canadian Whole of Government Operations;
Kandahar—Sept 2010 to July 2011." Conference of Defence
Association Institute (CDAI), Vimy Paper, December. http://
www.cdainstitute.ca/images/CDAInstitute_WOG_Dec2012.pdf
(accessed February 21, 2016).

Cornish, S., M. Glad. 2009. "Civil-military Relations: No Room
for humanitarianism in Comprehensive Approaches."
CARE International, the Norwegian Atlantic Committee.
http://reliefweb.int/sites/reliefweb.int/files/resources/
C312D751A2DA554F852575B300577460-care-civil-military-
jan09.pdf (accessed February 21, 2016).

De Coning, Cedric. 2008. "The United Nations and the
Comprehensive Approach." The Danish Institute for
International Studies (DIIS), Report No. 14. http://
subweb.diis.dk/graphics/Publications/Reports%20
2008/Report-2008-14_The_United_Nations_and_the_
Comprehensive_Approach.pdf (accessed February 21, 2016).

Dorronsoro, Gilles. 2009. "Running Out of Time: Arguments
for a New Strategy in Afghanistan." Center for
International Policy Studies (CIPS), Ottawa U, July.
http://mercury.ethz.ch/serviceengine/Files/ISN/103579/

ipublicationdocument_singledocument/c0ff9f35-0e1b-4f25-bc4a-104b35e23fe8/en/CIPS_WP_Dorronsoro_July2009.pdf (accessed February 21, 2016).

Fitz-Gerald, Ann, Don McNamara. 2010. "Comprehensive Security Requires Comprehensive Structures—How Comprehensive Can We Get?" Canadian Defence and Foreign Affairs Institute (CDFAI) and Canadian International Council (CIC), March. https://d3n8a8pro7vhmx.cloudfront. net/cdfai/pages/95/attachments/original/1413683635/ Comprehensive_Security_Requires_Comprehensive_Structures. pdf?1413683635 (accessed February 21, 2016).

Gizewski, Peter, Michael Rostek. 2009. "Toward Joint, Interagency, Multi-national, Public (JIMP)-Capable Land Force." *Canadian Army Journal* 10, no. 1. http://www.army.forces.gc.ca/caj/documents/ vol_10/iss_1/CAJ_vol10.1_09_e.pdf

Grandia, Mirjam. 2009. "The 3D Approach and Counterinsurgency. A Mix of Defence, Diplomacy and Development: The Case of Uruzgan." Master's thesis, University of Leiden, the Netherlands. http://www. cimic-coe.org/wp-content/uploads/2014/06/3DandCOINThesis. pdf (accessed February 21, 2016).

Jenny, J. 2001. "Civil-military Cooperation in Complex Emergencies: Finding Ways to Make It Work." *European Security Journal* 10, no. 2: 23–33. http://www.tandfonline.com/doi/abs/10.1080/09662830108407492 (accessed February 21, 2016).

Jorgensen, M. P. 2008. "A Strategy for Effective Peace-Building: Canada's Whole-of-Government Approach in Afghanistan." Canadian Forces College (CFC) Toronto, National Security Studies Program, Course No. 10 (NSSP 10), May 2008. http://www.cfc.forces. gc.ca/259/281/280/jorgensen (accessed February 21, 2016).

Leslie, Andrew, Peter Gizewski, Michael Rostek. 2009. "Developing a Comprehensive Approach to Canadian Forces Operations."

Canadian Military Journal 9, no. 1. http://www.journal.dnd.ca/vo9/no1/doc/04-leslie-eng.pdf (accessed February 21, 2016).

Manley, John. 2010. "Canada's New Role in Afghanistan: Leading Rather Than Following Public Opinion." Institute for Research on Public Policy (IRPP)—Policy Options, December. http://policyoptions.irpp.org/fr/magazine/the-year-in-review-2/canadas-new-role-in-afghanistan-leading-rather-than-following-public-opinion/ (accessed February 21, 2016).

Manwaring, Max G. 2006. "Defense, Development, and Diplomacy (3D): Canadian and US Military Perspectives." Colloquium brief, Strategic Studies Institute (SSI), US Army War College, Kingston, June. www.strategicstudiesinstitute.army.mil/pdffiles/pub732.pdf (accessed February 21, 2016).

Massie, Justin. 2009. "Making Sense of Canada's "Irrational" International Security Policy: A Tale of 3 Strategic Cultures." *International Journal* 64, no. 3: 625–645/ http://ijx.sagepub.com/content/64/3/625.full.pdf+html (accessed February 21, 2016).

NATO. 2006. *Comprehensive Political Guidance.* 29 November. http://www.nato.int/cps/en/natolive/official_texts_56425.htm (accessed February 21, 2016).

Owen, Taylor. 2011. "More on the Integrity of the Comprehensive Approach." OpenCanada.org, Canadian International Council (CIC) blog, July 1: http://opencanada.org/features/more-on-the-integrity-of-the-comprehension-approach/ (accessed February 21, 2016).

Patrick, Stewart, Kaysie Brown. 2007. "Greater Than the Sum of Its Parts? Assessing "Whole of Government" Approaches to Fragile States." Center for Global Development (CGD). http://www.cgdev.org/doc/weakstates/Fragile_States.pdf (accessed February 21, 2016).

Rasmussen, Anders Fogh. 2010. "Afghanistan and the Future of Peace Operations." Speech at the University of Chicago, 8 April. http://

www.nato.int/cps/en/natolive/opinions_62510.htm (accessed February 21, 2016).

Ritchie, Robert T. 2006. "Stabilization in the Afghanistan Counter-Insurgency (COIN): Assessing the Comprehensive Approach in Kandahar Province." Canadian Forces College (CFC)—Joint Command and Staff Programme, Course 36 (JCSP 36), February 26. http://www.cfc.forces.gc.ca/papers/csc/csc36/mds/Ritchie.pdf (accessed February 21, 2016).

Rostek, Michael, Peter Gizewski. 2011. *Security Operations in the 21ˢᵗ Century: Canadian Perspectives on the Comprehensive Approach.* McGill-Queen's University Press http://mqup.mcgill.ca/book.php?bookid=2727 (accessed February 21, 2016).

Rotmann, Phillip. 2010, "Built on Shaky Grounds: NATO Comprehensive Approach." NATO Defence College, Rome, Research Division Paper, No. 63, December. http://www.ndc.nato.int/download/downloads.php?icode=231 (accessed February 21, 2016).

Smith, Gordon. 2007. "Canada in Afghanistan: Is It Working?" Canadian Defence and Foreign Affairs Institute (CDFAI). https://depot.erudit.org/bitstream/001776dd/1/Canada-Afg_is_it_working_2007-03-01_.pdf (accessed February 21, 2016).

Smith-Windsor, Brooke. 2008. "Hasten Slowly; NATO's Effects Based and Comprehensive Approach to Operations." NATO Defence College, Rome, Research Division Paper, No. 38, July. http://www.ndc.nato.int/download/downloads.php?icode=10 (accessed January 2, 2016).

Thomson, Michael H., Barbara D. Adams, Courtney D. Hall, Craig Flear. 2010. "Collaboration within the JIMP (Joint, Interagency, Multinational, Public) Environment." Defence Research and Development Center, Toronto, CR 2010-136, August. http://cradpdf.drdc-rddc.gc.ca/PDFS/unc104/p534320_A1b.pdf (accessed January 2, 2016).

Travers, Patrick, Taylor Owen. 2008. "Between Metaphor and Strategy: Canada's Integrated Approach to Peacebuilding in Afghanistan." *International Journal* 63, no. 3 (Summer): 685–702. http://www.academia.edu/575431/Between_Metaphor_and_Strategy_Canadas_Integrated_Approach_to_Peacebuilding_in_Afghanistan (accessed February 3, 2016).

United Nations. 2004. "A More Secure World: Our Shared Responsibility." Report of the High-level Panel on Threats, Challenges and Changes, UN 59th General Assembly, December 2. http://www.un.org/en/peacebuilding/pdf/historical/hlp_more_secure_world.pdf (accessed February 20, 2016).

Welle, J. W. 2010. "Civil-Military Integration in Afghanistan; Creating Unity of Command." *Joint Forces Quarterly*, no. 56. http://www.dtic.mil/dtic/tr/fulltext/u2/a515092.pdf (accessed February 2, 2016).

4

Constructing Canada's Synergistic Model

Abstract

A systematic and critical review of literature of Canada's engagement in Afghanistan and of the so-called comprehensive approach—that is, "commonly understood principles and collaborative processes that enhance the likelihood of favourable and enduring outcomes within a particular situation" (UK 2006)—has demonstrated that this approach has not been theorised or modelled since Afghanistan. This article thus proposes to theoretically model the comprehensive approach in order to provide executive managers with a more synergistic construct. It is based on six dimensions: The situational context, socio-culture, organisational structure, strategic policies, systemic processes and synergy dynamics. This theoretical model allows us to tackle some of the fundamental lessons learned, namely from Canada's engagement in Afghanistan, with a view to applying them generally to the UN's future engagements. In particular, it is found that synergy is the central theme underlying the comprehensive approach, also called the integrated approach. Thus, constructing a theoretical model from this dynamic synergy dimension is key in order to provide greater effects.

Introduction

This article considers a previous critical review of literature on the *comprehensive approach* and *Canada's engagement in Afghanistan*, in order

Eric Dion, CD, MBA, PhD

to propose a more theoretically grounded executive management model. By employing grounded theory, having retained a corpus of 178 texts on the topic and having analysed their content, iterations of an executive management model were done, and a theoretical model is proposed that could generally be applied in similar engagements, and generally during unconventional warfare, asymmetric conflicts, insurgencies and their related crises.

As such, this article considers *Canada's engagement in Afghanistan* as the background within which the study of the *comprehensive approach* as a phenomenon can take place. Working from grounded theory with the aim of developing an executive management model, we retained 178 texts and we analysed their content in order to hermeneutically interpret codes and categories, as well as meta-analyse the 178 texts for correlations.

Following a previous critical review of literature, three important contributions were found, namely the security apparatus, the political strategy and the emerging normative. There were also three serious limitations identified, namely the efficiency assumption, the international relations aspect and intellectual complexity. These strengths and weaknesses are taken into account in this theoretical model in order to build on the former and offset the latter.

The literature reviewed also helped construct the six fundamental dimensions for our executive management model, which are the situational context, socioculture, organisational structure, strategic policies, systemic processes and synergy dynamics. Following the lessons learned, this article further proposes that synergy is a fruitful and promising avenue for the further theorisation of the so-called comprehensive approach.

Canada's Engagement

Canada's engagement in Afghanistan started in October 2001 when a small contingent of Canadian Special Operations Forces operators was initially deployed in direct support to the United States in the aftermath of the September 11, 2001, terrorist attacks (Horn and Balasevicius 2007, 13–14). By February 2002, Canada's first battle group was deploying to Afghanistan while Canada launched its own Operation Athena in early August 2003.[86] Not long after, the first mentions of the three Ds of defence, diplomacy and development started to appear within Canada's engagement in Afghanistan to identify the early contribution of the three respective departments involved. Thus "It was the Canadian government that originally developed the 3D concept, later adopted by many other governments" (Friis and Jarmyr 2008, 4), and more specifically by NATO allies.

When Canada assumed leadership of the Kandahar Provincial Reconstruction Team in 2005, discussion of the whole-of-government approach started to appear.[87] By their presence and coordination efforts, Provincial Reconstruction Teams have certainly brought aid and reconstruction into regions that were neglected. They also signal that a simplistic Manichean military approach has been abandoned for a more comprehensive understanding of the conditions that will facilitate a durable solution to the violence in Afghanistan and beyond (Smith 2007, 19). At the time, the Kandahar Provincial Reconstruction Team was composed of approximately 350 military, police, foreign affairs, correctional services and development personnel with the mission of assisting Afghans with the provision of security, governance and development.[88] The practice was less than the whole of government, however, still alluding to a few key departments from Canada—namely National Defence, Foreign Affairs, Public Safety and Canada's International Development Agency. Although the concept had evolved from the three Ds of defence, diplomacy and development to the whole-of-government, Canada's engagement in Afghanistan still remained largely marked by the original structuralist and stovepipe idea.

In the Canadian context, it took until 2008, after Canada's engagement in Afghanistan had moved to the southern province of Kandahar in 2005–2006—and more specifically, following the release of the report of the Independent Panel on Canada's Future Role in Afghanistan, also known

---

[86] Canada—Operation Athena, http://www.forces.gc.ca/en/operations-abroad-past/op-athena.page

[87] Canada (2005), "International Policy Statement."

[88] USAID (2006), "Provincial Reconstruction Teams (PRTs) in Afghanistan: An Interagency Assessment."

as the Manley Report, in January 2008[89]—for the comprehensive approach to emerge. It seemed that previous intellectual efforts at the idea had not reached maturity in Canada, while the United Nations in particular had been promoting an integrated mission planning process for some time, since 2006.[90] NATO had also discussed the *comprehensive approach* at its 2006 Riga Summit, leading to the publication of its "Comprehensive Political Guidance."[91] But Manley's main recommendation was simply that "The objective of this diplomatic effort should be to raise Canada's voice, commensurate with the Canadian contribution in Afghanistan, to establish a comprehensive political-military strategy." From a Canadian perspective, the idea thus started to grow around the requirement for a comprehensive approach, from 2008 onwards. However, the end of the combat mission in 2011 also signalled the end of Canada's comprehensive approach in Afghanistan, providing a circumvented and crucial background to study the purported comprehensive approach.

Comprehensive Approach

Within the Canadian government, Ottawa has espoused the importance of whole-of-government approaches in its strategies and activities in Afghanistan, Haïti and the Sudan (Patrick and Brown 2007). Indeed, the whole-of-government approach required the Canadian Armed Forces to work closely with other government departments and other government agencies to achieve operational goals. But preparing members to work with a multiplicity of players in a non-traditional role (i.e., enabling development and diplomacy) demanded a new way of thinking (Mulroney 2007). It can thus be said that the three *D*s of defence, diplomacy and development, as well as the whole-of-government approach, have been the evolutionary precursors to the comprehensive approach. However, the key structural idea according to Lévi-Strauss's structuralist theory (1958), is that a deterministic perspective, that pre-empts a more integrated model from emerging, had been the most central theoretical theme underlying the so-called comprehensive approach.

---

[89] Canada (2008), "Independent Commission on the Future of Canada in Afghanistan" (Manley Report).

[90] UNITED NATIONS – UN (2006), *Integrated Missions Planning Process* (IMPP).

[91] NATO (2006), Comprehensive Political Guidance, Endorsed by NATO Heads of State and Government.

Comprehensiveness basically means to address the range of threats and challenges by the full menu of instruments in order to contribute to overall stability and security. On the implementation level though, there is no single common understanding on the essentials of a comprehensive approach. There is broad agreement that in the international realm, it implies the pursuit of an approach aimed at integrating political, security, development, rule of law, human rights, and humanitarian dimensions of international missions and operations. (EU 2008)

As such, it appears that the very idea of structural integration was central to the comprehensive approach that an overarching form of organisation had since become a requirement. Indeed, today the 3Ds concept has become a general catch-phrase for the comprehensive approach because it so concisely captures the main axis of the interrelationship (Friis and Jarmyr 2008, 4). In Canada, the whole-of-government approach has become the pendant of the comprehensive approach, probably for the lack of an overarching integrated and comprehensive framework. The *whole-of-government approach* has become a familiar mantra among Canadian military officers and government bureaucrats when they describe the unique way that this country embarks on overseas missions. The idea is straightforward: "Government departments and agencies, aligned with the military, working together as a team for the desired outcome" (Pugliese 2014). This approach is particularly understood as a requirement during counterinsurgency operations, where international forces try to convince the local population against the insurgencies.[92] But limiting the comprehensive approach only to the governmental aspects through 3D or whole-of-government approach leaves out other non-structural dimensions required of comprehensiveness. Such a structural 3D or *whole-of-government approach* does not help address some of the more fundamental, root causes of insurgencies required for conflict resolution, such as the economy and sociocultural aspects of the insurgencies.

By definition, the comprehensive approach literally entails "Commonly understood principles and collaborative processes that enhance the likelihood of favourable and enduring outcomes" (UK 2006, 9). This

---

[92] Johnson, Thomas H., M. Chris Mason, (2008), "All Counterinsurgency Is Local."

definition offers a much more sociocultural, systemic and even dynamic perspective in that it relates to ideas of common understanding as well as collaboration, while ensuring positive and lasting outcomes. The comprehensive approach presents the distinctively unique, holistic perspective required in order to face complex conflicts and insurgencies, such as is the current Allied engagement in Iraq and Syria.[93] As the UK government aptly noted following its own comprehensive approach, "The point of war is not just to win but to make a better peace."[94] Henceforth, a multidimensional and more holistic perspective on the comprehensive approach is required, deconstructing our traditional paradigm of organisations working in isolation and trying to (re)connect horizontally through new structures.[95] "The comprehensive approach holds significant promise for governments in search of more holistic approaches to security challenges such as Afghanistan" (Gammer 2012, 11). Thus fundamentally, an integrated and comprehensive approach is required. And indeed, "The comprehensive approach not only makes sense—it is necessary."[96]

Methodology

Following a preceding critical review of the literature on the comprehensive approach,[97] three important contributions and three serious limitations were noted. Indeed, an efficiency assumption, international relations and intellectual complexity were noted as serious limitations, whereas the security apparatus, political strategy and emerging normative were noted as important contributions to the literature on this crucial topic. As a follow-on, this article thus asks the central question: How can we model the comprehensive approach in a more synergistic management perspective? The idea is to offer executives a theoretical model that could support their strategic thinking in the case of Canada's future engagements, such as in

---

[93] US Combined Joint Task Force—Op Inherent Resolve (CJTF–OIR), Central Command (CENTCOM).
[94] UK (2010), "The Comprehensive Approach: The Point of War Is Not Just to Win but to Make a Better Peace."
[95] Pugliese (2014), "'Whole of Government' Is Old Wine in a New Bottle."
[96] NATO (2010), http://www.nato.int/cps/en/natohq/opinions_66727.htm (accessed January 16, 2016)
[97] Dion (2014), "Canada's Comprehensive Approach in Afghanistan: A Critical Review of Literature."

Iraq and the Levant, the Middle-East, Eastern Europe and perhaps even here at home, in the Arctic and during domestic or regional crisis.

"Strategy is linked to a strategic thinker's view of how the organisation should operate and function" (Hambrick and Frederickson 2001, 20; in Steptoe-Warren 2011, 243). In this strategic management perspective, Canada's engagement in Afghanistan provided the case study from which grounded theory methodology was employed. This case study is thus crucial because it is the only instance so far in which the so-called comprehensive approach has been deliberately cited as a key construct of the mission: "A crucial case is one in which a theory that passes empirical testing is strongly supported and one that fails is strongly impugned" (George and Bennett 2005, 9). This article thus aims to provide a theoretical model to support executive management, and it further asks what the major dimensions of this Canadian comprehensive approach are, and how can we theoretically model them?

Systemic Perspective

In order to construct a valid and reliable theoretical model for the comprehensive approach, a systemic perspective was fundamental to consider the implications of a holistic view.

> Systems approach refers to the holistic and comprehensive analysis of complex and intensely challenging problems. The systems approach represents a growing body of transdisciplinary knowledge about the structure, behavior, and dynamics of change within a specific category of complex systems known as Complex Adaptive Systems, i.e.: open evolutionary systems in which the components are strongly interrelated, self-organizing, and also dynamic (Sanders 2003, 2).

Systems approach appeared as a promising avenue to transcend the inherently positivistic stance of the strategic management ontology. Thus, the systemic approach, well-documented in academic literature but more so in business administration than in public administration, can prove very fruitful for a comprehensive theoretical modelling. From our own experience and expertise as a strategist, we appreciate that short-sighted disciplinary views are in fact the root causes of some of our most crucial shortcomings. In essence, if a comprehensive approach is the answer to some of our more fundamental security concerns, then a more opened ontology is thus required, which can incorporate different positions. This perspective provides for a system-of-systems view, where issues are seen more holistically within a larger strategic management perspective. The recent Design and Systems Thinking Symposium[98] held by The Centre for National Security Studies (CNSS) at the Royal Military College St-Jean, is one example of systems thinking.

Grounded Theory

To answer its underlying questions, this research has employed the principles of grounded theory as outlined within *The Discovery of Grounded Theory* by Glaser and Strauss (1967). This theory-generation methodology is best suited for cases where there are no apparent or underlying models or theories. From this methodology, we thus started by searching for the subject of the comprehensive approach within the professional literature, looking to find the dimensions of the underlying theoretical model in a system-of-systems perspective:

> Grounded Theory methods consist of systematic, yet flexible guidelines for collecting and analysing qualitative data to construct theories from the data themselves. Thus researchers construct a theory "grounded" in their data. Grounded Theory begins with inductive data and analysis, uses comparative methods, and keeps you interacting with the data and emerging analysis. (Charmaz 2014, 1)

Within this article, a model is understood as the visual, approximate representation of a phenomenon, and a theory is understood as a set of abstract and general propositions of this same phenomenon. Indeed, according to Denscombe (1998, 240), "A theory is a proposition about the relationship between things," which grounded theory seeks to produce. In our search for a theory of the so-called comprehensive approach, we searched for documents that in the first instance contained the expression *comprehensive approach*. Documents were read and analysed, both qualitatively by hermeneutically coding and categorising them, and quantitatively by searching for the occurrence of keywords within the

---

[98] Centre for National Security Studies (CNSS): https://www.cfc.forces.gc.ca/237/394-eng.html

texts themselves. This research followed the principles of grounded theory as outlined by Glaser and Strauss, and so there was no predetermined number of texts to read. Rather, theoretical saturation of the categories (dimensions) according to our interpretative analysis and subsequent quantitative analysis was the goal for our content analysis. This saturation was achieved after having analysed and meta-analysed 178 texts.

Corpus Selection

For this research, initial coding started by qualitatively interpreting the fundamental texts on the topic of the comprehensive approach, with many from Canada and some from Scandinavian countries, Europe, the United States, and North Atlantic Treaty Organisation. These initial texts were selected on the basis of an initial Internet search for the term *comprehensive approach* in the first instance. Most were the official political and strategic documents discussing the comprehensive approach originating from these different countries. Following initial readings on the topic, which included many writings on the comprehensive approach as applied by Canada in Afghanistan, through such reports as the Manley Report and doctrinal documents such as the Canadian Forces *Land Operations Manual* and Canadian Forces *Counter-Insurgency Manual* (2008),[99] as well the United States *Manual on Stability Operations* (2008),[100] no actual integrated model or theory could be found, creating a fundamental cognitive dissonance.[101] As the data and material started to accumulate regarding the comprehensive approach, this meant that a categorising scheme had to be established in order to process all the incoming documents.

> Unlike selective sampling where the researcher decides ahead of time who and where to collect data, in Grounded Theory, sampling is an ongoing process of data analysis and collection. It is theoretical because an emerging theory cannot be predetermined but tentatively developed and determined during this process. (Tan 2009, 97)

---

[99] Canada (2008), Canadian Forces, *Counter-Insurgency Operations* and (2008) CF *Land Operations*.
[100] United States (2008), *Stability Operations Field Manual 3-07.*
[101] Van De Ven (1989), "Nothing Is Quite so Practical as a Good Theory."

As such, we started to conceptualise about the comprehensive approach in a more holistic manner, incorporating more texts and data as the coding scheme evolved and developed to achieve saturation. Henceforth, the context, the socioculture, the organisational structure, the strategic policies, the systemic processes and the synergy dynamics all appeared as important dimensions for executive management through our content analysis of the first 88 texts found in the case of Canada's engagement in Afghanistan from 2001 to 2014.

During the summer of 2006, Canadians started to experience much greater difficulty in the southern provinces of Kandahar and part of Helmand for which they were tasked, leading to more casualties, more debate at home and abroad and more data. It was decided to circumscribe the study of the comprehensive approach to Canada-Afghanistan as secondary keywords. This somewhat limited the quantity of data, but nonetheless during the year of 2007, Canada's national security and defence, as well as foreign affairs, were full of political discussions regarding Canada's engagement in Afghanistan. By default, it provided the required focus for this research in that it gave a practical object to a rather still-evolving, quite fluid subject. In parallel to Canada's engagement in Afghanistan, NATO's own engagement in Afghanistan was also morphing from a counterterrorism operation into a larger counterinsurgency campaign, which meant that the overall strategic context was also radically changing in 2006–2007. From a data-collection standpoint, this meant a threefold increase in documents and various media from the Internet to the point where this research's topic had to be further refined. By 2007, the comprehensive approach only started to emerge regarding Afghanistan. A posteriori quantitative analysis of the retained documents highlights the number of texts retained per year between 2001 and 2014. A slight bias was introduced in 2013 by selecting a special issue of the *International Journal* on this topic.[102]

---

[102] *International Journal* (2013), vol. 68, no. 2 (June): 269–377, http://ijx.sagepub.com/content/68/2.toc

Figure 3—Number of Texts Retained per Year

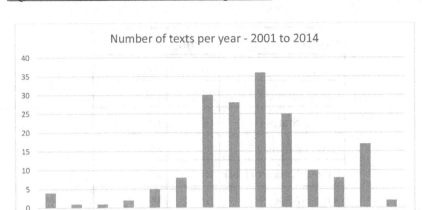

By 2007, keywords had started to emerge as the basic concepts for researching the comprehensive approach in a strategic management perspective,[103] leading to a snowballing where one document on the topic led to another with the same keywords, and so on. Keywords were employed mainly using Google and Google Scholar from the Internet because the documents contained in other systems were restricted due to their government classification. Snowballing with the basic keywords *comprehensive approach* and *Afghanistan-Canada* led to sufficient unclassified documentation to warrant full doctoral research on this topic. In an electronic folder held by the author, 615 individual texts and media were collected in between the years 2006–2014, employing the basic non-mutually exclusive keywords as indicated. This included numerous books, reports, articles, thesis and media reports, as well as sources such as multimedia transcripts. In between 2001–2014, it thus appears Canada was at the forefront of the comprehensive approach, in particular between 2007 (when the comprehensive approach itself emerged) and 2011 (when Canada's combat and comprehensive approach mission was terminated and transitioned into a military training mission until 2014). The following table represents the number of texts retained in the end by their country of origin and in relative percentages.

---

[103] Rintakosi, K. and M. Autti, eds. (2008), *Seminar Publication on the Comprehensive Approach.*

Table 2—Origin of Selected Texts

Origin	Count	Percent
Canada	104	58%
Europe and UK	26	15%
United States (US)	18	10%
NATO Alliance	15	8%
United Nations (UN)	10	6%
Afghanistan	5	3%
Total Count	**178**	**100%**

Content Analysis

According to grounded theory methodology, data collection was done in parallel with analysis, where documents were read, hermeneutically interpreted, codified and categorised and then subsequently meta-analysed using word-counting software. Reading in the first instance was done without the actual coding scheme fully developed, so in some instances a second reading was made necessary. This had the undesired effect of creating some doubles within our dataset that had to be removed at the later stages. During that same timeframe, the context and the background for the topic also evolved from the 3Ds to the whole-of-government, as explained earlier, as well as from different sets in Afghanistan: from Kabul to Kandahar in 2006, to a southern surge in 2009–2010,[104] to a training mission from July 2011 to 2014.[105] As the iterations of documentation analysis evolved, our original coding was established within the first 88 texts analysed as explained. Subsequent iterations of the model were produced at 105 and 178 texts when it was thought a significant level of theoretical saturation could be achieved. However, without any quantitative meta-analysis of the correlations between the categories, there was no way of knowing whether indeed the model as a whole was sufficiently well-integrated. In parallel, the

---

[104] Coombs (2012), *Canadian Whole of Government Operations.*
[105] Dorronsoro (2009), *Running Out of Time: Arguments for a New Strategy in Afghanistan.*

codification behind this grounded theory research design had also evolved, becoming more focused and integrated, and now included further keyword searches that were thus being employed with Primitive Word Counter version 1.09, for a further quantitative analysis.

As word-counting software, Word Counter has a very interesting functionality in that it allows one to discriminate the actual words employed, and not simply count them. That is to say that a full list of all the words employed within a chosen text is shown in absolute numbers as well as in percentages, allowing for further research discrimination. The following table represents the list of root keywords researched in our corpus of texts.

Table 3—List of Keywords Researched

Strategic Management Dimensions	Root Keywords Researched
Situational-Context	Situ(*); context(*); histor(*)
Sociocultural	Soci(*); cult(*); people(*) **Excluded:** association and agriculture
Organisational Structure	Struc(*); organisa(*); agen(*) **Included:** (recon and decon)struction
Strategic Policy	Strat(*); politic(*); plan(*) **Excluded:** (demon and illu)strate
Systemic Functions	Sys(*); function(*); process(*)
Synergy Dynamics	Syn(*); dynam(*); coll(*)

Word Counter is known as a search engine optimiser but can be used in checking for keywords. This was precisely the usage this research made of the software, employing concepts within categories to quantitatively capture the occurrences of each in any given text document. The captured data was then recorded traditionally within an Excel spreadsheet, and percentages were calculated in order to give a relative weight to each of the known dimensions of management. Using Word Counter, comma-separated value files were created for most texts analysed and imported in an Excel sheet, which allowed us to calculate the occurrence of codes into categories and thus ensure reliability.

Model Iterations

Our grounded theory research design literally worked from the ground up, and so building the theoretical model as the analysis evolved in parallel with data collection; the categories were not well-known for sure. Within the management literature, the basic categories of structure, strategy and systems were well-recognised and each had a well-established corpus of literature. Within the sociology literature, the society category occupied a cognitive space while the situational category is better known within the military for situational awareness purposes, which is to better appraise the overall context. Starting from these emerging categories, codes were clustered according to their main dimension. This process was obviously very similar to grounded theorisation where categories are constructed from codes and concepts and thereafter analysed for their relevance into each of these categories, where correlations can be calculated.

As codes started to appear alongside the texts, using ample Post-It notes and exploiting the margins to their maximum for this interpretative coding scheme, many similar codes started to emerge from one text on the topic to the next.

> Seen by many as illustrating the stark difference between qualitative research and experimental research (in which data is collected to test a pre-stated theory), grounded theory emerges from the data. The process requires the researcher, during the data-gathering phase of a project, to examine the material as it builds up and to place it into categories—to classify it. Once this process has been started, the researcher returns to the field to gather more data and see whether the additional material fits into the established categories or whether the classificatory system needs to be adapted to accommodate fresh data. (Davies 2007, 237)

Once codes and categories started to saturate, after having read 88 texts, a first iteration of the model was proposed. After 105 texts, a further iteration of the model was produced, as well as an article written and also published on the critical review of this literature. The final analysis and the final iteration of the model were produced following 178 texts. Each of these iterations was done with theoretical saturation in mind, with the model being constructed of the original 88 texts, being refined with 105 texts and saturated with 178 texts read. As each text on the comprehensive approach was first read and then researched employing the keywords in Word Counter, quantitative data thus also started to populate an Excel spreadsheet. Relative percentages of each were earmarked for reference, as well as basic descriptive statistics that indicated the number of codes, the number of pages, the relative ratio of codes per pages, the standard deviation for each, their mean, the coefficient of variation and their median.

Within the first 105 documents analysed, a clear pattern seemed to emerge from these iterations between the data collection, interpretative analysis and parallel meta-analysis. This allowed construction of a more focused model on the executive management dimensions, and this process was carried over and over until a high degree of saturation and confidence had been achieved for the model as a whole, thereby ensuring validity and reliability for the six dimensions. By that time, 178 texts had been read, memos had been noted in an ongoing Word document along with our analysis and data had been compiled in an Excel spreadsheet for ease of access.

As such, it can be said that our grounded theory selection, analysis and model iterations demonstrate a high degree of reliability at having been systematically used throughout for the content analysis and for the generation of our synergistic theoretical model for Canada.

> Techniques for enhancing reliability and validity operate, more often than not, by reducing the impact of the researcher's subjectivity as far as possible, or by providing information to enable others to check the process through which the results were obtained. (Gagnon 2010, 15) It is the researcher's creativity, sensitivity, flexibility and skill in using the verification strategies that determines the reliability and validity of the evolving study. (Morse et al. 2002, 17)

Theoretical Results

In order to study the comprehensive approach as it emerged from the Canadian context, between 2001 and 2014, it was necessary to consider its precursors of 3Ds and the whole-of-government approach. It was also fundamental to consider the Afghan mission background from which these concepts were born. Because the aim of this article is to provide a theoretical model to support executive management, a grounded study of the Afghanistan case was conducted in order to create the major dimensions for such a model. Indeed, as explained, the context, the socioculture, the organisation structure, the strategy and the system were already well-recognised dimensions that helped explain the comprehensive approach. Only the synergy dynamics dimension was new and emerged from our grounded analysis:

> A typological theory provides one way of modeling complex contingent generalizations. They frequently draw together in a framework the research of many social scientists, cumulating their individual efforts into a much larger body of knowledge. (George and Bennett 2005, 7)

This is precisely the effect the six dimensions have as a whole, and the following figure illustrates these six dimensions as circles with their overlapping areas, indicating the interactions and the holistic interdependence of the entire theoretical model.

Figure 8—Synergy: A Theoretical Model

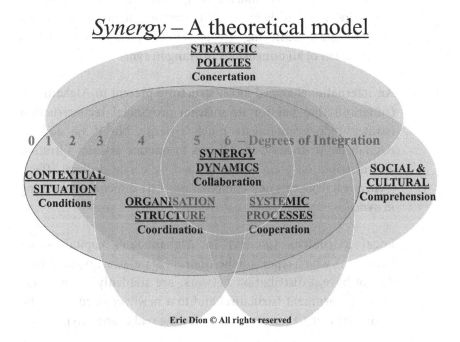

Synergy – A theoretical model

STRATEGIC
POLICIES
Concertation

0 1 2 3   4   5   6 – Degrees of Integration

SYNERGY
DYNAMICS
Collaboration

CONTEXTUAL
SITUATION
Conditions

ORGANISATION
STRUCTURE
Coordination

SYSTEMIC
PROCESSES
Cooperation

SOCIAL &
CULTURAL
Comprehension

This key figure presents our grounded theoretical model of the comprehensive approach, where each dimension is represented as a virtuous circle with overlapping areas to other dimensions. Each circle could further represent the percentages extracted for each executive management dimension, with the strategy being a top-down consideration. Synergy is in the middle, representing the central theme of the comprehensive approach. The percentages presented in Table 4, represent the usage of the respective dimension within the comprehensive approach extracted from our content analysis and meta-analysis of the 178 texts retained. In essence, these percentages represent the relative importance given to it by all the authors. Together, these six dimensions form a more holistic model of Canada's comprehensive approach and help explain the decision-making—for example, with regards to Kandahar's Provincial Reconstruction Team's role implementing the Afghan National Development Strategy within Dand district by playing a role in securing the governance for the Pashtuns within Afghanistan. Different cases can be explained employing such a theoretical model:

- Pashtuns (society) in Afghanistan (situation) living off agriculture (system) do not create much synergy, but if we build a highway (structure) allowing them to sell their produce to market (strategy), then we start achieving greater effects (synergy) from this combination of all dimensions working in sync.

- An international armed force (structure) present in Afghanistan (situation) that has for its mission provincial reconstruction (strategy) does not create much synergy, but if we add an Afghan team (society) that learns to operate a water filtration and distribution plant (system), then we create positive effects (synergies) from this new combination of six dimensions working in sync.

- Local journalists (society) in Afghanistan's capital Kabul (situation), which report on the affairs of State (strategy) but which do not have a distribution network, are suddenly given access to the government (structure) and to a newly constructed radio station (system), then they start affecting real change (synergy).

As such, it appears that six executive management dimensions consistently explain cases. Following our hermeneutic interpretation of the 178 retained texts, as well as our meta-analysis of keywords, we also calculated the correlations of each dimension to the others to verify the degree of integration of the model. Our analysis of covariance demonstrates that all six dimensions are important for the model as a whole because they are statistically significant. Given a different background, the relative weight of these dimensions could be reflected by circumstances and change slightly, albeit all six dimensions would still be key. Moreover, all six dimensions are also positively correlated, each one to the other five. This demonstrates a good degree of integration within Canada's synergistic theoretical model. The following table thus presents these positive correlations ranging from low to very high:

Table 5—Meta-Analysis of Covariance

Correlation	Situ	Soci	Struc	Strat	Sys	Syn
Situ	1,00	0,64	0,75	0,69	0,78	0,56
Soci	0,64	1,00	0,60	0,48	0,54	0,39
Struc	0,75	0,60	1,00	0,86	0,82	0,88
Strat	0,69	0,48	0,86	1,00	0,84	0,91
Sys	0,78	0,54	0,82	0,84	1,00	0,81
Syn	0,56	0,39	0,88	0,91	0,81	1,00

Hence, the sociocultural dimension is the least positively correlated dimension within the model. Strategy appears as the most highly correlated of the other five dimensions, pointing towards its overall effect. Synergy appears as the most innovative of all six. In order to explicit these six dimensions, the theoretical analysis of each is given below.

Situational Context

This dimension refers to the where and when questions with the aim of situating executive management actions in space and in time. Often understood as the background of where and when actions take place, and thus often held as implicit knowledge, the situational context is nonetheless important for setting other dimensions in our theoretical model. The background is relative to each situation and is the first consideration for executives. It often serves as the first few paragraphs for orders and directives for military and civilians alike, and it is supported by academic disciplines such as history, geography and archaeology. As one of the least positively correlated dimensions to the others and coming in at 10.3 percent, the situational context dimension nonetheless appears important for explaining the context.

This situational context helps explain the international relations aspect of the case overall, which following from a review of the literature has proven to be a serious limitation in that Canada's engagement in Afghanistan was indeed often presented in relations to the United States. For example, in studying the comprehensive approach, the historical relations between Afghanistan and America provide part of the background to understanding Canada's role, allowing Ottawa to avoid Washington's opprobrium for staying out of Iraq in 2003. However, Canada's international relations with the United States were not the only consideration, and a whole host of factors also needs to be accounted for within the other decision dimensions.

Socioculture

This dimension refers to the who and with whom questions with the aim of socialising the executive management with regards to people. Often understood as the civil society with who and for whom actions take place, it is generally also held implicitly, which unlike the context creates important knowledge gaps filled by looking at people more considerately. As such, the sociocultural dimension is often not mentioned explicitly and is conflated with the overall background within which actions take place. This underscores the importance of the sociocultural dimension, which in conflict zones like Afghanistan needs a separate treatment from the other dimensions, establishing itself as a standing dimension. Indeed, the sociocultural dimension is an important consideration showing up at 15.5 percent. However, it is the less positively correlated dimension, indicating its integration is required.

The sociocultural dimension helps explain the emerging normative aspect of the approach that, following from a review of the literature, has proven to be an important contribution in that the comprehensive approach appeared as a new norm for international interventions. For example, there is growing recognition that society is a key intervention consideration, and that intervening powers should be more concerned with the values of the local people. Under the latest counterinsurgency doctrine (2008),[106] this was indeed a crucial dimension, and winning the hearts and minds was always an important Canadian doctrine overall.

Organisational Structure

This third dimension, in a logical order of analysis from the context and society to organisations, refers to the what question with the aim of representing the structural aspects. Treated as key consideration for executive management, organisational structures represent the bureaucracy, the administration and technocracy. They are one of the major dimensions in that many questions and issues revolve around it. It was established in most, if not almost all, of the retained 178 texts, and it represents with the

---

[106] Canada (2008), Canadian Forces—*Counter-Insurgency Operations.*

strategic policy dimension—the quintessence of executive management. Showing up significantly at 20.3 percent with highly positive correlations to other dimensions, it is thus an important dimension in our theoretical model.

The organisational structure dimension helps explain the structural and organisational domination of the security apparatus, which following from a review of the literature has proven to be an important contribution along with the security apparatus's omnipresence. Indeed, within Canada's use of the comprehensive approach through its engagement in Afghanistan, security was the single most important consideration for any intervention. For example, Canadian Task Force Kandahar's role in Dand District of Kandahar Province, working closely with the governor and his team, was to stabilise the entire district, thus allowing Kandahar's Provincial Reconstruction Team to engage in quick-impact projects. The reverse methodology would have been near impossible for international organisations.

Strategic Policies

This dimension refers to the why question with the aim of explaining executive management strategic and political actions. Generally understood by all executive management, it is also the most intellectually complex dimension, with numerous definitions, interpretations and actions, ranging from the tactical to the operational and strategic levels. As the most critical of other dimensions, as many seem to think, it does not explain the holistic effect of executive management actions, and this strategic policies dimension is very much focused on integrating executive actions with the daily political considerations. Representing the most employed dimension of the six at 26.9 percent and being highly correlated to structure, system and synergy, its importance overshadows the other five dimensions.

Strategy is so important within the 178 retained texts that it appears predominantly. "If all considerations are strategic then real strategy consideration become nothing more."[107] The strategic policies dimension helps explain political and strategic aspects of the mission, which following from a review of the literature has proven to be an important contribution.

---

[107] Lemay, Pre Lilly (2016), Conversation with the author on Strategy.

For example, the Strategic Advisory Team, Afghanistan, was instrumental in advising the Afghanistan cabinet of ministers on their roles within the Afghan Compact made in London. The Afghan Compact[108] was a strategic policy aimed at stabilising Afghanistan as a country and was a forefather to Afghanistan's National Development Strategy that followed. Strategy henceforth is thus a crucial dimension.

Systemic Processes

This dimension refers to the how question with the aim of understanding processes and the mechanics of executive management actions. Often understood as the implementation phase and somewhat as the strategy policy dimension, this dimension emphasises how to get things done through the processes. In general, it is found to be very explicit within orders and directives in the military and civilian life alike, precisely because of the level of detail that executive actions require to achieve full project implementation. As a significant dimension at 13.7 percent, it is possible to consider an expanded view of the systemic processes dimension compared to strategy and structures.

The systemic functions dimension helps explain the efficiency assumption to the approach, which following from a review of the literature has proven to be another serious limitation in that in spite of integration attempts, it appears that efficiency was not the outcome of a comprehensive approach or of Canada's engagement in Afghanistan in spite of rhetoric. For example, one of Canada's three signature projects was to rebuild the Dahla Dam and its irrigation system.[109] "When Canada's diplomats, development specialists and soldiers left Kandahar in 2011, our involvement with the dam ended and the government declared the $50-million project a success. It wasn't."[110] Indeed, efficiency has proven unattainable and a serious limitation in the Afghanistan context, where effectiveness was not even guaranteed.

---

[108] The Afghanistan Compact (2006), http://www.nato.int/isaf/docu/epub/pdf/afghanistan_compact.pdf

[109] *Canada's Engagement in Afghanistan*, http://www.international.gc.ca/afghanistan/

[110] Pugliese (2016), "More Problems for the Dahla Dam—One of Canada's Afghan Signature Projects."

Synergy Dynamics

This dimension refers to the "So what?" question with the aim of looking at effects holistically. It presents a system-of-systems perspective, where a systemic approach is fundamental to better appreciate the effects and the consequences of executive management actions daily. More than the other dimensions, the synergy dynamics presents issues in a dynamic and constantly iterating circle of virtue. Of course, dynamics can also be negatively reinforcing (vicious circles), such as the drug trade, black market and insurgencies, but we have to trust the vast majority of human endeavours will be virtuous, thus creating and fostering the emerging synergy. As a new dimension for executive management, we have found it to be significant at 12.7 percent with highly positive correlations to strategy, structure and systems. The synergy dynamics dimension explains intellectual complexity.

> To survive, the system as a whole must adapt to change. As a result, we are witnessing the integration of knowledge across disciplines and the emergence of new concepts, tools, and a vocabulary of complex systems thinking. Across the frontiers of science, this new more complete, whole of systems approach is replacing the old reductionist paradigm, where scientists traditionally tried to understand and to describe the dynamics of systems by studying and describing their component parts. (Sanders 2003, 2)

The synergy dynamics dimension helps explain the sum that is larger than its parts, which following from a review of the literature has proven to be the final important contribution. For example, as one officer explained, "In Afghanistan and in Iraq, you don't do security independent of governance, and you don't do governance independent of development. They all have to happen simultaneously or near simultaneously." A key village approach was thus employed to great effect by the Canadians and demonstrated positive synergies, as the Maliks (leaders) were "buying into their own processes ... To me, that's success."[111] As such, the synergy dynamic appears as the most innovative and interesting dimension, with the aim to propose a synergistic executive model that can cut through complexity.

---

[111] Brown (2010), "Troops Seek to Replicate Gains Made in Afghan Village."

General Discussion

We looked into numerous examples within Canada's engagement in Afghanistan and found that these also underscore the dynamics of the comprehensive approach. Moreover, each example highlights different dimensions within our model, from the situational context to the socioculture, to the organisational structure and strategic policies, to the systemic processes and the synergy dynamics. They demonstrate in essence that there exist these six management dimensions to consider in order to propose a much more comprehensive approach. However, it also appears that the whole idea of comprehensiveness might not be the best supporting theory to explain the decisions made. Indeed, the synergy dynamics have emerged as a central theme within our theoretical model, underscoring such terminology as synchronisation of effects (i.e., military for *synergy*).

As such, it was found that a grounded theory could be proposed, building on the different dimensions highlighted within our examples. Indeed, it is notable that all six dimensions of our executive management model have been employed throughout instances of examples, albeit in a yet-to-be-integrated fashion, the case of the key village approach employed in Kandahar being the most integrated of all. Together however, these six dimensions form a more comprehensive approach model, and in fact they help explain the emergence of synergy as a valid and reliable theory to support the comprehensive approach. In theory, better integrating government actions will help achieve strategic and policy objectives, as well as provide greater clarity and transparency into decision making. Thus, the comprehensive approach should be understood in the context of increasingly complex and interdependent international conflict management system. The scope of the crises faced by the international community is often of such a scale that no single agency, government or international organisation can manage them alone (Friis and Jarmyr 2008, 2). Moreover, what appears to be required is much greater integration within a model.

The idea of achieving greater effects than the sum of the parts is not a new one, but it bodes well with the innovative and central idea of our theoretical model for achieving synergy. In order to achieve such synergy, all six dimensions must be present, albeit their relative percentages will vary according to the situation, the society, the structures, the strategy, the systems and the synergy. This will be reflected differently from one example to the other. Nonetheless, each dimension is significant and important to construct a more holistic model. Proposing the dimensions leading to synergy is the real contribution of this research, whereas other research on synergy simply stated the idea of the greater sum from the parts. Moreover, because this research was built employing the key principles of grounded theory, our synergistic theoretical model best reflects the practice as it emerges from the ground, presenting in an integrated fashion these six dimensions that help explain key examples. This article does not yet explain how the synchronisation of these six dimensions actually helps foster greater synergy, which will be the work of further grounded research. Nonetheless, this research has constructed for Canada a new synergistic theoretical model, and as such applying lessons learned from Afghanistan to emerging cases is fundamental.

Lessons Learned

Learning from the previous analysis, it appears there are many lessons that could be implemented within the newer case of Canada's engagement in Iraq and the Levant. Although these concepts have been clearly articulated, little has been done in the intervening years to institutionalise the lessons identified, in order to actually make them lessons learned.

> As the Canadian government looks forward towards involvement with other fractured and war-torn environments, like Iraq and Syria, ... it needs to heed the lessons identified by our contribution in southern Afghanistan and increase the effectiveness of its whole of government efforts overall. (Coombs 2015, 30)

As such, one of the most fundamental lessons learned from this holistic analysis is that the 3Ds, the whole-of-government approach or even the comprehensive approach as conceptually described in the literature reviewed are not necessarily the answer. These are structuralist approaches with three departments, whole-of-government and more. Such a structuralist approach appears deterministic, pre-empting a more integrated model. Indeed, what appears to be required is a higher degree of instrumental integration to foster synergy and its dynamics. "A key consideration is to recognise the implicit requirement for coordination between the various power instruments. Consequently, an explicit synchronisation mechanism must be derived and implemented in order to achieve cross-cutting synergy" (Ritchie 2010, 65). Such integration would see humanitarian assistance, governance and development synergised under a single, overarching campaign plan, beyond the military's own plan. Hence, the military piece of the puzzle was relatively well-synchronised; not so for the rest while achieving synergy is quintessential.

Conclusion

> Looking back to Canada's engagement in Afghanistan, rather than a strategy document focused on fixed signature projects, a more comprehensive framework and approach to the whole-of-government mission that provided clarity on the roles and responsibilities of each department particularly with respect to activities in support of governance and development, would have improved our effectiveness, as it would have guided our consistent progress. (Unterganschnigg 2011, 8)

"Synchronization still remains the critical flaw, exposing coalition vulnerabilities for incremental targeting by insurgents. Internal inefficiencies continue to plague the comprehensive approach" (Ritchie 2010, 121). Indeed, "This is a moment when the world's leading powers need to work toward greater collaboration, set clearer priorities, and focus on the long-term issues (many economic and social in nature) associated with stabilizing the regions at risk from which these spreading problems are emerging," according to Rothkopf (2015). As such, this article sought to provide a new executive management theoretical model to support Canada's future engagements, such as in Iraq and the Levant. It was found that synergy is an important and innovative dimension for integrated and holistic executive management because it does appear to be greater than the sum of its parts, and it provides the central explanation for our holistic theoretical model.

Moreover, our theoretical model presents the six dimensions that help foster synergy, which is the real and innovative contribution of this research for executive management. Indeed, the situational context, the socioculture, the organisational structure, the strategic policies and the systemic processes are already relatively well-developed dimensions within strategic management literature: Not so for the synergy dynamics dimension.

Synergy dynamics best helps explain integrated and synchronised effects within the comprehensive approach, and it furthermore provides a theoretical model to support future engagements. The innovation is here in the holistic model that supports synergy.

For example, leveraging our theoretical model would be for executive management to recognise the low percentage of attention given to the sociocultural dimension in this case and thus refocus some of their executive efforts on this dimension to benefit "the people." Moreover, giving more attention to the synergy dynamics dimension would purposefully refocus some attention to the necessary collaboration between all stakeholders involved within a given situation, working with organisational structures to systematically implement the strategic policies—all in order to synchronise and harmonise greater effects. Synergy thus proves to be a central integrating dimension, interdependent with the others, and as such, purposely giving more executive management's attention to it appears crucial.

This article has allowed us to construct a synergistic model for Canada's engagements. One potential limitation of our synergistic theoretical model is that it has not explained how such a model would actually work in other issue management cases, such as in the Middle East and perhaps even at home for crisis management. However, in the current contemporary operating environment, and probably in the near future operating environment,[112] insurgency-like conflicts are omnipresent, requiring a comprehensive approach and a synergistic executive management theoretical model. It will require further research for the model to be confirmed as an executive management tool. As such, that research will seek to present the levers of action for this theoretical model, leveraging the lessons learned from examples presented in this grounded study of the case. Meanwhile, it is noteworthy that synergy has been the fundamental underlying construct, and employing our model for Canada's future engagements (such as Iraq) seems promising.

---

[112] United Kingdom (2015), *Future Operating Environment—FOE 2035*.

United States (2016), *Joint Operating Environment—JOE 2035*.

References

Brown, Drew. 2010. "Troops Seek to Replicate Gains Made in Afghan Village." *Stars and Stripes* (July 12). http://www.stripes.com/news/middle-east/afghanistan/troops-seek-to-replicate-gains-made-in-afghan-village-1.110764 (accessed February 21, 2016).

Canada. 2001-2014. *Canada's Engagement in Afghanistan.* http://www.international.gc.ca/afghanistan (accessed August 21, 2016).

Canada. Operation Athena. http://www.forces.gc.ca/en/operations-abroad-past/op-athena.page (accessed February 21, 2016).

Canada. 2005. *International Policy Statement (IPS).* http://publications.gc.ca/site/eng/274692/publication.html (accessed February 21, 2016).

Canada. 2008. *Canadian Forces—Counter-Insurgency Operations.* http://info.publicintelligence.net/CanadaCOIN.pdf (accessed August 21, 2016).

Canada. 2008. *Canadian Forces—Land Operations.* https://info.publicintelligence.net/CanadaLandOps.pdf (accessed August 21, 2016).

Canada. 2008. *Independent Commission on the Future of Canada in Afghanistan (The Manley Report).* http://dsp-psd.pwgsc.gc.ca/collection_2008/dfait-maeci/FR5-20-1-2008E.pdf (accessed February 21, 2016).

Canada. 2009. *Canada's Engagement in Afghanistan: Op Kantolo,* Roch Lacroix, GERFI—École Nationale d'Administration Publique.

http://enap.ca/enap/docs/GERFI/Photos_des_activites/ Presentation_Lacroix.pdf (accessed February 21, 2016).

Charmaz, K. 2006. *Constructing Grounded Theory: A Practical Guide through Qualitative Analysis.* Thousand Oaks, CA: SAGE Publications.

Christensen, Tom Per Lægreid (2007). "The Whole-of-Government Approach to Public Sector Reform." *Public Administration Review* 67, no. 6 (November/December): 1059–1066. http://onlinelibrary. wiley.com/doi/10.1111/j.1540-6210.2007.00797.x/abstract (accessed February 21, 2016).

Coombs, Howard G. 2012. *Canadian Whole of Government Operations.* Vimy Paper, Conference of Defence Association Institute. http:// www.cdainstitute.ca/images/CDAInstitute_WOG_Dec2012.pdf (accessed February 21, 2016).

De Coning, Cedric. 2008. *The United Nations and the Comprehensive Approach.* DIIS Report 2008, no. 14 (October). http://subweb.diis.dk/ graphics/Publications/Reports%202008/ Report-2008-14_The_United_Nations_and_the_Comprehensive_ Approach.pdf (accessed February 21, 2016).

Dion, Eric. 2014. "Canada's Comprehensive Approach in Afghanistan: A Critical Review of Literature, 2001–2011." *Defence Studies* 14, no. 2: 192–215. http://www.tandfonline.com/doi/abs/10.1080/1470243 6.2014.891854 (accessed February 21, 2016).

Dorronsoro, Gilles. 2009. *Running Out of Time: Arguments for a New Strategy in Afghanistan.* Center for International Policy Studies), Ottawa U (July). http://mercury.ethz.ch/serviceengine/Files/ISN/103579/ ipublicationdocument_singledocument/c0ff9f35-0e1b-4f25-bc4a-104b35e23fe8/en/CIPS_WP_Dorronsoro_July2009.pdf (accessed February 21, 2016).

European Union. 2010. *Comprehensive Approach.* Foresight Security Scenarios: Mapping Research to a Comprehensive Approach to

Exogenous EU Roles—FOCUS. http://www.focusproject.eu/web/focus/wiki/-/wiki/COMPREHENSIVE/FrontPage (accessed February 21, 2016).

Gammer, Nicholas. 2012. *Integrating Civilian-Military Operations: The Comprehensive Approach and the ATF Experience, 2008–2009.* Canadian Political Science Association. https://www.cpsa-acsp.ca/papers-2012/Gammer.pdf (accessed February 21, 2016).

George, Alexander L., Andrew Bennett. 2005. *Case Studies and Theory Development in the Social Sciences.* Belfer Center Studies in International Security. London: MIT Press (February).

Gizewski, Peter, Michael Rostek, Andrew Leslie. 2008. *Comprehensive Operations: Moving to a JIMP-capable Land Force.* Vanguard. http://www.vanguardcanada.com/2008/08/01/comprehensive-operations-moving-jimp-capable-land-force/ (accessed February 21, 2016).

Horn, Bernd and Tony Balasevicius, eds. 2007. *Casting Light on the Shadows: Canadian Perspectives on Special Operations Forces.* Toronto: CDA Press and Dundurn Press. https://www.dundurn.com/books/Casting-Light-Shadows (accessed February 21, 2016).

Johnson, Thomas H., M. Chris Mason. 2008. "All Counterinsurgency Is Local." *The Atlantic,* no. 3 (October), 302. http://www.theatlantic.com/magazine/archive/2008/10/all-counterinsurgency-is-local/306965/ (accessed February 21, 2016).

Lévi-Strauss, Claude. 1958. *Structural Anthropology,* revised edition. Basic Books, 1974.

Mintzberg, Henry. 1987. "The Strategy Concept: The Five Ps of Strategy." *California Management Review* (Fall).

Mulroney, David. 2007. *Common Narrative: Canada's Integrated Approach to Afghanistan.* Interview by Parkins and Thatcher, Vanguard, July. http://www.vanguardcanada.com/2007/08/01/

common-narrative-canadas-integrated-approach-afghanistan/ (accessed February 21, 2016).

NATO. 2006. *Comprehensive Political Guidance.* Endorsed by NATO Heads of State and Government, November 29. http://www.nato.int/cps/ en/natolive/official_texts_56425.htm (accessed February 21, 2016).

Patrick, Stewart, Kaysie Brown. 2007. *Greater Than the Sum of Its Parts? Assessing "Whole of Government" Approaches to Fragile States.* International Peace Academy. www.cgdev.org/ files/13935_file_Fragile_States.pdf (accessed February 21, 2016).

Pugliese, David. 2014. "'Whole of Government' Is Old Wine in a New Bottle." *Ottawa Citizen* (February 19). http://www.ottawacitizen. com/news/Whole+government+wine+bottle/9532284/story.html (accessed February 21, 2016).

Pugliese, David. 2016. "More Problems for the Dahla Dam—One of Canada's Afghan Signature Projects." *Ottawa Citizen* (February 26). http://ottawacitizen.com/news/national/defence-watch/more-problems-for-the-dahla-dam-one-of-canadas-signature-project-in-afghanistan (accessed February 21, 2016).

Rintakosi, Kristiina and Mikko Autti, eds. 2008. *Seminar Publication on Comprehensive Approach: Trends, Challenges and Possibilities for Cooperation in Crisis Prevention and Management.* Finland Comprehensive Approach Research Team. Seminar Publication. http://www.defmin.fi/files/1316/ Comprehensive_Approach_-_Trends_Challenges_and_ Possibilities_for_Cooperation_in_Crisis_Prevention_and_ Management.pdf (accessed February 21, 2016).

Ritchie, Robert T. 2010. *Stabilization in the Afghanistan Counter-Insurgency: Assessing the Comprehensive Approach in Kandahar Province.* Canadian Forces College (CFC)—Joint Command and Staff Programme (JCSP 36), February 26, 2010. http://www.cfc. forces.gc.ca/papers/csc/csc36/mds/Ritchie.pdf (accessed February 21, 2016).

Rothkopf, David. 2015. "Our Reaction to Terrorism Is More Dangerous Than the Terrorists." *Foreign Policy*. http://foreignpolicy.com/2015/11/25/our-reaction-to-terrorism-is-more-dangerous-than-the-terrorists-trump-obama-eu-isis/ (accessed February 21, 2016).

Sanders, Irene. 2002. "To Fight Terror, We Can't Think Straight." *The Washington Post* (May 5): B2. https://www.washingtonpost.com/archive/opinions/2002/05/05/to-fight-terror-we-cant-think-straight/c25c95a8-cdac-46c7-9ff4-c7f817d55579/?utm_term=.47d0215b26f2 (accessed February 21, 2016).

Sanders, Irene T. 2003. "What Is Complexity?" *Washington Center for Complexity and Public Policy*. http://www.complexsys.org/pdf/what_is_complexity.pdf (accessed February 21, 2016).

Smith, Gordon. 2007. *Canada in Afghanistan: Is It Working?* Prepared for the Canadian Defense and Foreign Affairs Institute (CDFAI). https://depot.erudit.org/bitstream/001776dd/1/Canada-Afg_is_it_working_2007-03-01_.pdf (accessed February 21, 2016).

St.-Louis, Michel-Henri. 2009. "The Strategic Advisory Team Afghanistan—Part of the Canadian Comprehensive Approach to Stability Operations." *Canadian Military Journal* 9, no. 3: 58–67. http://www.journal.forces.gc.ca/vo9/no3/doc/09-stlouis-eng.pdf (accessed February 21, 2016).

United Nations. 2006. *Integrated Missions Planning Process*. Guidelines Endorsed by the Secretary-General on June 13. https://docs.unocha.org/sites/dms/Documents/UN%20IMPP%20Guidelines%20(2006).pdf (accessed February 21, 2016).

UNHCR. 2015. *2015 UNHCR Subregional Operations Profile—Middle East*. http://www.unhcr.org/pages/49e45ade6.html (accessed February 21, 2016).

United Kingdom. 2010. *The Comprehensive Approach: The Point of War Is Not Just to Win but to Make a Better Peace*. House of Commons

Defence Committee, seventh report of session (2009–2010). http://www.publications.parliament.uk/pa/cm200910/cmselect/cmdfence/224/224.pdf (accessed February 21, 2016).

United States. 2008. *Stability Operations—Field Manual 3-07.* http://usacac.army.mil/cac2/repository/FM307/FM3-07.pdf (accessed February 21, 2016).

United States Combined Joint Task Force. Operation Inherent Resolve (CJTF–OIR), Central Command (CENTCOM). http://www.centcom.mil/en/news/articles/operation-inherent-resolve-airstrikes-proving-effective-in-iraq-syria (accessed February 21, 2016).

Unterganschnigg, K. 2011. "Canada's Whole of Government Mission in Afghanistan—Lessons Learned." *Canadian Military Journal* 13, no. 2. http://www.journal.forces.gc.ca/vol13/no2/images/Unterganschnigg-Pages816-eng.pdf (accessed February 21, 2016).

USAID. 2006. *Provincial Reconstruction Teams (PRTs) in Afghanistan: An Interagency Assessment.* http://pdf.usaid.gov/pdf docs/PNADG252.pdf (accessed February 21, 2016).

Van De Ven, A. H. 1989. "Nothing Is Quite so Practical as a Good Theory." *Academy of Management Review* 14, no. 4: 486–489. http://www.www.aom.org/uploadedFiles/Publications/AMR/VandeVenNothing.pdf (accessed February 21, 2016).

5

Synergy as Canada's Comprehensive Approach

Abstract

The comprehensive approach has been a key emerging theme in international security. As such, we are applying our previously developed synergistic model, which is composed of six dimensions: the situational context, the socioculture, the organisational structure, the strategic policies, the systemic processes and the synergy dynamics. This article takes our model a step forward in the field of management and makes key policy recommendations.

Explaining the methodology that led to our synergistic model of the comprehensive approach in a collaborative public strategic management perspective enables us to provide theoretically grounded recommendations for Canada's engagement in Iraq and the Levant.

Approaching the subject of the comprehensive approach from a collaborative public strategic management perspective provides for a pragmatic theoretical model explanation. What is found is that Canada could greatly benefit from applying such a synergistic model, and particularly from synchronising the management levers supporting the six dimensions. In doing so, an integrated perspective could emerge that would foster greater synergy.

Introduction

The comprehensive approach has been a key emerging theme in international security in light of the complex interdependencies of contemporary conflicts, requiring much greater integration. "The comprehensive approach not only makes sense—it is necessary,"[113] according to former NATO Secretary General Anders Fogh Rasmussen. It can be defined as "Commonly understood principles and collaborative processes that enhance the likelihood of favourable and enduring outcomes within a particular situation."[114] Indeed, the emphasis of the comprehensive approach is on those collaborative processes.

Instead of approaching the subject of comprehensive approach from a political science or from an international relations perspective, we approached it from a strategic management perspective, focusing more on how to actually make things work very pragmatically. Bozeman (1993) defines public management as being concretely concerned with prescription and prescriptive theory, indicating that some amount of interaction between academics and practitioners is to be expected (Pitts and Fernandez 2009, 402). This is precisely the endeavour this article embarks on by applying our synergistic model.

Indeed, following an extensive research on the subject, it appears that synergy is the central construct underlying the comprehensive approach, as reflected through its own discourse. Starting by explaining our methodology and leading to our synergistic model, we discuss the comprehensive approach and collaborative public strategic management in order to set the background to apply our synergistic model to Canada's engagement in Iraq and Levant.

Henceforth, this article demonstrates how such a synergistic model could be applied, as in the case of Canada's engagement in Iraq and the Levant, in order to foster more synergy.

---

[113] NATO, 2010, http://www.nato.int/cps/en/natohq/opinions_66727.htm (accessed January 16, 2016).

[114] UK, 2010, p. 9, http://www.publications.parliament.uk/pa/cm200910/cmselect/cmdfence/224/224.pdf

Methodology

According to Kurt Lewin (1952, 169), "There is nothing so practical as a good theory." Karl Weick (1989) states, "Theory construction is disciplined imagination." By employing the principles of grounded theory as outlined by Glaser and Strauss (1967) this research was designed in order to study the comprehensive approach as an executive management phenomenon. Indeed, in the absence of a model, a framework or a theory of the so-called *comprehensive approach* from a preceding systematic review of literature,[115] it was proposed to develop the basic constructs, concepts and categories for such an approach. In doing so, it was found that synergy was a better explanation for this comprehensive approach and that synergy better explains the dynamics of the whole system of systems.

In order to retain the literature reviewed, a keyword search was conducted on the literature for comprehensive approach, as well as its precursors: the 3Ds of defence, diplomacy and development and the whole-of-government approach. These integral expressions were used to constitute our original corpus. In total, over 615 files were saved in a database from which keyword searches were further conducted. This research followed the principles of grounded theory, and so there was no predetermined number of text to read; neither was there a predetermined body of literature on the subject. Indeed, as this study spiral developed, the main categories became significantly saturated to $\alpha = 0.01$. In the end, 178 texts were retained, 58 percent of which originated from Canada (where the search was conducted), while 15 percent originated from Europe (mainly the UK and Scandinavian countries), as well as 10 percent from the United States. The remainder came from the UN (8 percent) and NATO (6 percent), and 3 percent from Afghanistan. The following table presents those percentages, and the next figure represents the number of texts retained per year from 2001 to 2014.

---

[115] Dion, "Canada's Comprehensive Approach in Afghanistan," *Defence Studies,* 2014.

Table 2—Origin of Selected Texts

Origin	Count	Percent
Canada	104	58%
Europe and UK	26	15%
United States (US)	18	10%
NATO Alliance	15	8%
United Nations (UN)	10	6%
Afghanistan	5	3%
Total Count	**178**	**100%**

Figure 3—Number of Texts Retained per Year

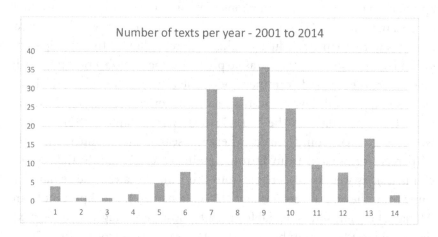

Although originating from a strategic sampling, these preliminary results tend to demonstrate that Canada was at the forefront of the *comprehensive approach*, and in particular between the years 2007–2010, when the vast majority of texts on the topic appeared within the literature. From this preliminary strategic sampling, a further keyword search was conducted using word-counting software.[116] This allowed for further discrimination on categorical keywords, refining and saturating the categories. Following

---

[116] Primitive Word Counter; available for free at www.primitivezone.com

an initial reading and interpretative analysis, each text was passed through the software, generating an automated count of all the words. This allowed for further keyword searches for the following concepts: situation, context, history, society, culture, people, structure, organisation, agency, strategy, policy, plan, system, function, process, synergy, dynamic and collaboration. The number of occurrences of each was extracted from the software and noted in a spreadsheet, and basic descriptive statistics were provided for each text. The goal was to achieve theoretical saturation of the main categories to construct a model.

It appeared that some concepts could be clustered into larger categories, and as such within the first 88 iterations of texts, it was apparent that the strategic dimension, the organisational structure and the systemic processes were well-established categories. As this grounded theory development scheme continued to develop, the further sociological dimension also appeared. Only after more iterations did it become apparent that the situational context dimension, as well as the synergy dimension, were significantly saturated as categories. In particular, the situational dimension appeared as a contextual consideration within texts, whereas the synergy dynamics dimension appeared as the most interesting of the other five categories, explaining the greater effects overall. By the end, at 178 documents read, all six dimensions proved significant to $\alpha = 0.01$. A synergistic model thus emerged that theoretically represents six management dimensions.

Synergistic Model

The proposition of a synergistic theoretical model to be employed for Canada's future engagements is based on six dimensions: the situational context, the socioculture, the organisational structure, the strategic policies, the systemic processes and the synergy dynamics. This article takes our theoretical model a step forward into strategic management. It is noteworthy, through our preceding review of literature, that no working model or theory of this comprehensive approach had been found, thus presenting a theoretical void. Actually, it was found that the comprehensive approach is a philosophy, according to the *Canadian Forces Manual on Land Operations* (2008, 5–14). Hence, we developed a synergistic model in order to support executive management in the case of future engagements needing to employ a comprehensive approach, like in Iraq. As such, it can help support executive management from planning to implementation.

By analysing a set of circumstances, strategically thinking with each of the six dimensions about their individual incidences and making strategic inferences thanks to their levers, a more integrated, comprehensive and synergistic framework can emerge for management that can then be pragmatically applied to assist executives in a comprehensive approach. In particular, when considering the intersections between these six dimensions, a more integrated perspective can ensue, and thus six degrees of integration are proposed. The crucial case of Afghanistan was used as the background for our theoretical developments.

Figure 8—Synergy: A Theoretical Model

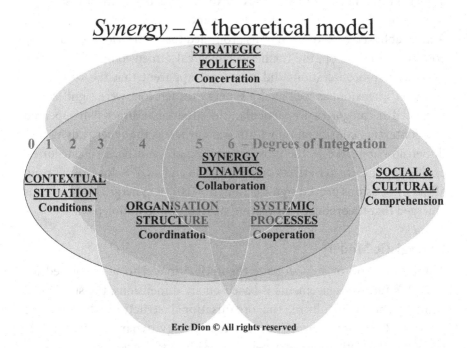

Theoretically speaking, our synergistic model would work something like the following: The situational context refers to the space and time conditions within which a given issue is situated, such as in Dand District of Kandahar Province in Afghanistan, and within a specific time frame and context, such as during the surge for Op Hamkari[117] in 2010.

---

[117] Carl Forsberg, *Counterinsurgency in Kandahar: Evaluating the 2010 Hamkari Campaign,* 2010.

The socio-culture refers to the shared comprehension that emerges between stakeholders, such as between military troops from the International Security Assistance Force, the Afghan National Army, the Government of the Islamic Republic of Afghanistan, the District Governor and the local Shura (the council of village elders and chiefs). Communication appears as the essential precondition to create a common understanding.

The organisational structure refers to the coordination that is required of all these institutional arrangements—for example, between ISAF, the ANA, GIRoA and the locals, which are all enabled to coordinate through provincial, district and community councils.

The strategic policies refers to the concertation that is formally (but more often informally) created, which brings to bear its strategic means in order to meet its ends—for example, through the community implementation of the Afghan National Development Strategy, which brought together elements of government defence, diplomacy and development.

The systemic processes refers to the cooperation that should exist, over and beyond the coordination of organisations and concertation of strategies, to ensure that operating processes work effectively, and ideally efficiently—for example to funnel funds for reconstruction.

Finally, the synergy dynamics refers to the collaboration that would arise from the close-working and networking interactions that are fostered by leveraging the conditions, the comprehension, the concertation and the coordination. For example when net effects are greater than the sum of their parts, as was the case in the Dand District of Kandahar, where Canadian troops employed a Key Village Approach[118] in order to work through the insurgency in 2010, ensure common understanding across all interested stakeholders, coordinate between the different organisations and create a new village-level concertation, they operated seamlessly within the network during the surge for Operation Hamkari in 2010. Thus a collaborative perspective emerges, creating greater effects than the sum of the parts.

---

[118] Drew Brown, "Troops Seek to Replicate Gains Made in Afghan Village," *Stars and Stripes*, 2010.

131

Eric Dion, CD, MBA, PhD

Henceforth, a more integrated model can be presented, outlining each of these dimensions in a holistic fashion, where the higher degrees of integration from one to six appear to be optimal where conditions, comprehension, coordination, concertation and cooperation interact in order to achieve a higher degree of collaboration for their management.

Indeed, theoretically the higher the degree of integration, the better chances of synergy. Benecke et al. (2010) define synergy as a "concept that describes the systemic processes whereby business units of diverse, complex organisations will generate greater value through working as one system than as separate entities" (p. 10)—that is, in a system of systems. "Synergy is the result of a number of individual physical, cybernetic and moral effects which when combined produces a total impact greater than the sum of individual effects."[119]

Each dimension within the model adds a degree of integration, and although lower degrees of integration are entirely possible, the higher the degree to six, the higher the chances for synergy. These degrees of integration have thus been proposed so that management executives can visualise the degree of consolidation a given configuration of dimensions provides in effect. Management executives would be senior commanding officers as well as governmental and non-governmental executives involved in Canada's current or future engagements requiring a comprehensive approach. As such, a given issue can be placed within the model, thus simplifying the inherent complexity and also illustrating the causal relations and interactions between an issue and its major dimensions. Moreover, the overlapping circles explain how such complexity interacts in between these six dimensions and their levers, providing a more holistic, synergistic and integrated visualisation.

What's more, leveraging the degrees of integration for the six dimensions can provide the basis for an operational research perspective to take shape. In support of the executive's decision-making process, a decision support system can be designed that would optimise different options according to their relative weight, through indicators in each dimension. For example, a given issue like reconstructing or retaking a major electrical dam, a key

---

[119] NATO, *COPD*, 2010, p. A20.

infrastructure, could be weighted in relative percentage against investing priority in clinics or schools in order to determine its overall effect on the root causes of an insurgency. A small operational research team armed with such a *synergistic model* could balance these options and optimise the executive management's strategic decision made in action, shifting the focus from the infrastructure for example to the social and cultural dimension. A decision-support software could be developed to create and sustain synergy in real-time and in action.

Synergy as Comprehensive Approach

The *comprehensive approach* is defined as "Commonly understood principles and collaborative processes that enhance the likelihood of favourable and enduring outcomes within a particular situation" (UK-JDN 4/2005, 15). This crucial definition talks more of managerial actions and collaborative processes than of strategic policies. Taking a management perspective in planning for and implementing an integrated *comprehensive approach* provides for a very innovative "theory as practice" contribution to management literature overall (Whittington 1996; Jarzabkowski 2004; Jarzabkowski and Spee 2009).

What's more, according to former NATO Secretary General Rasmussen, "The *comprehensive approach* not only makes sense—it is necessary."[120] This affirmation was made in the context of an important counterinsurgency campaign in Afghanistan in 2010. At the time, there was a common understanding amongst Allies that a much larger campaign than the military one was required in order to stabilise Afghanistan.[121] "It is widely believed that interventions cannot be limited to military action and that military force is simply the first step in a complex program of reform of the political, economic and social structures of the targeted state" (Jorgensen 2008, 5). Henceforth, coordination needed to be affected between the Allies, the coalition needed to be maintained and cooperation was essential to achieve a comprehension effect throughout this counterinsurgency campaign. Moreover, collaborative dynamics were also required and crucial. Indeed, it does not suffice to adopt a political science, international relations or

---

[120] NATO, "Comprehensive Approach."
[121] Canada, *Counter-Insurgency Operations—Canadian Forces Manual,* 2008.

strategic studies perspective in order to address the fundamental causes of insurgency and terrorism.

On August 22, 2001, then United Nations Secretary-General Kofi Annan suggested that the UN adopt a "comprehensive approach to ending Afghanistan conflict."[122] This was before the tragic events of September 11, 2001, which led to Operation Enduring Freedom. Although a surgical counterterrorism campaign was and is still required to neutralise core threats, the true measure of success in the coalition's contemporary engagements will come through reconstruction and rehabilitation while employing a comprehensive approach. In the case of current and future engagements such as in the Middle-East, the Levant and more specifically in the case of Canada's engagement in Iraq, taking on a comprehensive approach appears quintessential to address the roots causes of conflicts and insurgencies. Indeed, "Identification of the roots and causes of radicalism and terrorism have need for a comprehensive causal modelling" (Dawoody 2016, 142), as we have developed by proposing our six fundamental dimensions to consider a more synergistic approach. For example, root causes can be found in the sociocultural dimension such as alienation, in the systemic dimension such as in the lack of education, and in the strategic dimension such as a lack of governance, but all these issues require integration and collaboration.

The Marshall Plan, cited in Hrychuk and Gizewski (2008), is an excellent example of the successful collaborative effort on a huge scale. The Marshall Plan involved the United States providing aid to assist with the rebuilding of Europe after the end of World War II. Although not predominantly a military effort, this plan is often cited as "one of the seminal histories of postwar cooperation and development" (Hrychuk and Gizewski 2008, 5). Indeed, the Marshall Plan sought to address mainly the societal, structural and strategic dimensions and their levers, but it also considered the situation and the systems (and thus the synergy in a comprehensive approach), which at the time provided phenomenal leverage. This of course was before the contemporary comprehensive approach made its comeback.

---

[122] Relief Web, Kofi Annan speech, 2001, http://reliefweb.int/report/afghanistan/annan-suggests-un-adopt-comprehensive-approach-ending-afghanistan-conflict (accessed October 22, 2016)

One of the distinguishing features of the plan's implementation was that it received a strong endorsement from a number of different components that were initially governmental but then morphed into more public support. This core agreement amongst key players about the goals of the plan is cited as one of the main factors in its success (Hrychuk and Gizewski 2008). Henceforth, we could say that a Marshall Plan of sorts is required for the Middle East, which employs the comprehensive approach within a collaborative public management. Moreover, our synergistic theoretical model could help in such a comprehensive approach.

Collaborative Public Management

Agranoff and McGuire (2003) define collaborative public management (CPM) as a "Concept that describes the process of facilitating and operating in multi-organizational arrangements for solving problems that cannot be achieved, or achieved easily, by single organizations," thereby pointing to our own synergy dynamics as an important dimension. "Collaborative arrangements, in some cases, attain a 'collaborative advantage which is concerned with the potential for synergy from working collaboratively'" (Huxham 2003, 401)." "Collaborative Public Management is an endeavor in which 'administrators exchange information (system), seek knowledge (society), and work out problems (situations), programs (structures) and policies (strategy) across the boundaries of their agencies and their organisations' (Agranoff and Yildiz 2007, 319) by bringing together representatives from the public, private and not-for-profit sectors" (McGuire et al. 2011, 22)—that is, in synergy. As one can see in the parentheses, our synergistic model can find practical applications. "Synergy is not altruistic; it is mutually-beneficial win-win reciprocity" (Corning 2007), and as such it must be deliberately managed and maintained.

"Collaborative strategic management appears to be a more integrated and comprehensive approach making it possible to manage, but also to organise, the collaboration at the different stages of the development and implementation of partnership strategies" (Favoreu et al. 2016, 441). "Collaborative Public Management has become a major practice and research focus" (Bardach 1998; Bingham and O'Leary 2008; O'Leary and Bingham 2009). The resulting literature has paid substantial attention to management generally, but surprisingly little to collaborative strategic management specifically as an integrated (or comprehensive) approach, with partial exceptions including Huxham and Vangen (2005), Healey (2003), Agranoff (2007), Bryson et al. (2009) and Innes and Booher (2010). Hence, "Although a great deal of work has been done in the area of Collaborative Public Management, not much has been done on Collaborative Public Strategic Management" (Bryson et al. 2010, 505), where we foresee our synergistic model's key contribution.

Collaborative Public Strategic Management

"Strategic management is largely a matter of utilizing and coordinating all of the resources and venues at top management's disposal, enforcing a kind of 'omnidirectional alignment' among them in the interest of advancing the strategic agenda" (Poister and Van Slyke 2002). By representing a holistic decision support system-of-systems for executive management, our model is scalable to issues from the local-municipal to the global-international levels. Moreover, in the area of collaborative public strategic management, our model presents the favourable conditions under which synergy can be achieved and delivered for effects. "Despite the scepticism of researchers and practitioners, many public administrations ... have turned results based management and strategic planning into tools that make it possible to intelligently combine the purposes, objectives, means and resources required to steer states' administrations towards tangible results" (Mazouz et al. 2016, 412). Thus our synergistic model fits well with this key idea of comprehensive strategic management.

In a geostrategic perspective, this is akin to leveraging the elements of international power,[123] where "omnidirectional alignment" is provided through coalition's key leadership. "More than any other single approach in the public manager's tool kit, strategic management is the most fundamental, and the most critical, process for producing results in the challenging and increasingly competitive environment in which most public managers work" (Poister and Streib 1999, 324), such as in the *Contemporary Operating Environment* and the *Future Operating Environment 2035*,[124] where insurgencies flourish. Indeed, it does not suffice to have a stand-

---

[123] Elements of National Power or PEMSII: Political, Economic, Military, Society, Information and Infra.
[124] United Kingdom, *Future Operating Environment—FOE 2035*, 2015. United States, *Joint Operating Environment—JOE 2035*, 2016.

alone military strategy for the Middle East, but a more encompassing and comprehensive approach is required to be strategically managed. This starts with strategic planning, employing our synergistic model to its implementation.

By strategically leveraging each of the levers of dimensions—for example, by setting the conditions for common understanding and comprehension, for coordination, for concertation and for cooperation—a collaborative synergistic decision system is arrived at. Applying such a synergistic model can achieve greater effects than the sum of their parts. Indeed, by the virtue of collaboration and through operational synchronisation, synergy can thus be achieved by combining the six dimensions we have presented in our model. Each set of circumstances would thus present a unique configuration in terms of the relative weight afforded to each dimension individually, and in terms of their degree of integration. "The primary benefit from synchronisation is the ability to produce synergy and gain leverage by the imaginative creation and exploitation of desired conditions and effects."[125] As such, Canada's engagement in Iraq and the Levant can thus be used as a validating case where synergy can be fostered, but also where it can be deliberately strategically managed.

Canada's Engagement in Iraq and the Levant

Within a collaborative public strategic management perspective, it becomes interesting to apply our synergistic model to Canada's engagement in Iraq and the Levant. First off, Canada has handpicked the conditions of its engagement in space and in time by selecting to engage on the ground in Erbil, northern Iraq, in a training assistance mission until the government of Canada pleases or until February 8, 2019, to the end of three years. Canada has ensured a common understanding and comprehension surrounding its mission by communicating its intent clearly to Allies, as in the case of the cessation of airstrikes, as well as through its increased risk and participation within the training assistance mission. Canada has also coordinated its participation within the coalition and is also cooperating militarily, as well as collaborating within the alliance to bring all the stakeholders together, thus making the strategic leverage of the six dimensions presented in our synergistic model.

---

[125] NATO, *COPD*, 2010, p. A20.

Prime Minister Trudeau (2016) announced, "The Canadian government will spend more than $1.6 billion over the next three years on the mission as a whole, including on security, stabilization, humanitarian and development assistance in the region. That includes $840 million to provide water, shelter, health care, hygiene and sanitation, and $270 million to build capacity in countries helping refugees from the region"[126]—that is, in Jordan and Lebanon. But Canada has not made the synchronisation of its entire effort a crucial consideration, and it seems Canada has not learned from the hard-won lessons of ten years in Afghanistan.

"As the Canadian government looks forward towards involvement with other fractured and war-torn environments, like Iraq and Syria, as well as threats at home, it needs to heed the lessons identified by our contribution in southern Afghanistan and increase the effectiveness of its whole of government—WoG efforts overall" (Coombs 2015, 30). The Canadian government espoused the importance of whole of government approaches in its strategies and activities in Afghanistan, Haiti and Sudan (Patrick and Brown 2007). Moreover, a comprehensive approach is required, collaborating with non-governmental and international organisations, as well as the private sector, all working for reconstruction.

Indeed, although Canada has recently expanded its training assistance mission to Mosul in northern Iraq, this largely remains a special operation and does not have a wider mandate, which in a comprehensive and in a synergistic perspective should be much more integrated.

Working from an old military airbase in northern Iraq, Canada's whole-of-government team could enable a comprehensive approach to take shape in between now and 2019. Deploying a first Provincial Reconstruction Team would provide more common understanding and comprehension with the local population—for example, in Erbil Province. Coordinating amongst the military forces, non-governmental and international organisations would allow for a more comprehensive perspective to take root and facilitate a resolution, such as an overarching United Nations plan to stabilise the region and affect reconstruction. Indeed, if the top-down approach is

---

[126] Justin Trudeau, *Canada's New Approach to Addressing the Ongoing Crises in Iraq and Syria*, 2016.

hard to implement, a bottom-up one can better emerge, starting to work collaboratively at the local village level as was done with some success in Canada's engagement in Afghanistan, such as in Deh-e Bagh in the Dand District of Kandahar where the key village approach (KVA) was implemented.

Engaging with our Allies towards a comprehensive reconstruction and resettlement plan, starting with Northern Iraq and the strategic city of Mosul, would reinforce the concertation, respect Turkish sovereignty and preserve as much as possible Iraq and Syria's own sovereignty. But redefining the Sykes-Picot Agreement (1916) between the English and the French, to which Russia gave its assent, might be a necessary step to stabilise the entire region. Cooperating through the United Nations' system and ensuring due process and diligence would enable funding to be prioritised to assist the more than six million refugees[127] and internally displaced persons making the journey back home, stabilising the region. Collaborating with all stakeholders, including Russia and Iran, to find common ground is essential to leverage the comprehensive approach, and to foster much greater synergy. Indeed, collaboration must be comprehensive to ensure better comprehension so that the coalition secures the conditions for better structural coordination, as well as systemic cooperation. In essence, applying our synergistic model to Canada's engagement in Iraq and in the Levant is quintessential in order to achieve greater collaborative effects overall. Learning from the hard won lessons of over ten years in Afghanistan is crucial.

Conclusion

In the final analysis, synergy is only the servant of various human purposes, impulses and perceptions. The inescapable conclusion is that so long as the gains of collective violence are perceived to outweigh the costs, there will be no end to war (Corning 2007). "From 2008 to 2011, the intensive whole of government approach and focus on Kandahar led to considerable attention being paid to synergies within and across sectors, aiming to stabilize the province" (Canada 2015, 31). This should now be the case for Canada's engagement in Iraq and the Levant, which to start should be considered an engagement. Deploying Special Forces in Erbil and to Mosul, having

---

[127] UNHCR, *Subregional Operations Profile—Middle East*, 2015.

air forces covering the entire region, investing heavily $1.6 billion but not having an integrated approach is doomed for failure in the medium term, 5 to 10 years (Horizon 2).

On the contrary, engaging holistically, comprehensively and synergistically by leveraging our proposed model is more likely to lead to greater effects and more efficient results. The case of Afghanistan demonstrates that synergy was achieved by strategically managing the entire system of systems, albeit not at a national level but at the local and regional level. The key village approach applied in the Dand District of Kandahar Province in Afghanistan is a case in point and the stabilisation of Kandahar city through the surge is also noteworthy of successful synergy, although that was not the result of a model, as we have proposed. Replicating such results can be facilitated by leveraging our synergistic model as a whole.

A strategic Marshall Plan of sorts is required for the coalition to better coordinate and cooperate, as well as set conditions for a common understanding and comprehension amongst all stakeholders and collaborate synergistically in a comprehensive approach. Indeed, "An explicit synchronization mechanism must be derived and implemented in order to achieve such cross-cutting synergy" (Ritchie 2010, 65), such as in our model. As cited previously, in a strategic management perspective, an "omnidirectional alignment" is required not only for political leadership but also for strategic management integration.

As such, establishment of a Privy Council Task Force and of a Representative of Canada for Iraq and Syria (RoCIS), in allusion to our Canadian Rocky Mountains, and activation of the Stabilisation and Reconstruction Task Force to deploy civilian experts in Iraq and Syria to work collaboratively on a United Nations Middle East Marshall Plan, are thus required for Canada to focus on the overarching but missing plan. Such a comprehensive approach could be developed using our synergistic model, leveraging and synchronising each of the six dimensions in order to achieve greater effects. Thus, we presented a theoretical synergistic model that could be used by executives in the case of future engagements that require a comprehensive approach in a general sense. In essence, our synergistic model, or synergy, can become Canada's comprehensive approach. Synergy should be deliberately created and maintained by employing our model. Henceforth, and in many regards, Canada can demonstrate a synergistic leadership.

References

Agranoff, Robert, Michael McGuire. 2003. *Collaborative Public Management: New Strategies for Local Governments*. Georgetown University Press

Benecke, G., W. Schurink, G. Roodt. 2007. "Towards a Substantive Theory of Synergy." *South-African Journal of Human Resource Management* 5, no. 2: 9–19. http://www.sajhrm.co.za/index.php/sajhrm/article/viewFile/115/113 (accessed October 22, 2016).

Brown, Drew. 2010. "Troops Seek to Replicate Gains Made in Afghan Village." *Stars and Stripes* (July 12). http://www.stripes.com/news/middle-east/afghanistan/troops-seek-to-replicate-gains-made-in-afghan-village-1.110764 (accessed October 22, 2016).

Bryson, J. M., F. S. Berry, K. Yang. 2010. "The State of Public Strategic Management Research: A Selective Literature Review and Set of Future Directions." *American Review of Public Administration* 40, no. 5 (September): 495–521.

Canada. 2015. *Summative Evaluation of Canada's Afghanistan Development Program 2004–2005 to 2012–2013*, Department of Foreign Affairs, Trade and Development (DFATD), March. http://www.international.gc.ca/department-ministere/assets/pdfs/evaluation/2015/adp-pda-eng.pdf (accessed October 22, 2016).

Canada. 2008. *Counter-Insurgency Operations—Canadian Forces Manual*. http://info.publicintelligence.net/CanadaCOIN.pdf (accessed October 22, 2016).

Eric Dion, CD, MBA, PhD

Canada. 2008. *Land Operations*, B-GL-300-001/FP-001, Final Draft. http://armyapp.forces.gc.ca/olc/soh/SOH_Content/B-GL-300-001-FP-001-Eng_Land%20Ops%20%20-%20Final%20Draft%202008.pdf (accessed February 25, 2016).

Coombs, Howard. 2012. "Canadian Whole of Government Operations; Kandahar—Sept 2010 to July 2011." Conference of Defence Association Institute, Vimy Paper, December. http://www.cdainstitute.ca/images/CDAInstitute_WOG_Dec2012.pdf (accessed October 22, 2016).

Corning, Peter A. 2007. *Synergy Goes to War.* Institute for the Study of Complex Systems, Palo Alto, CA. http://complexsystems.org/publications/bioeconomic-theory-of-collective-violence (accessed October 22, 2016).

Dawoody, Alexander R. 2016. *Eradicating Terrorism from the Middle East: Policy and Administrative Approaches.* Springer.

Favoreu, Christophe, David Carassus, Christophe Maurel. 2016. "Strategic Management in the Public Sector: A Rational, Political or Collaborative Approach?" *International Review of Administrative Sciences* 82, no. 3 (September): 435–453.

Forsberg, Carl. 2010. *Counterinsurgency in Kandahar: Evaluating the 2010 Hamkari Campaign.* Institute for the Study of War, December. http://www.understandingwar.org/files/Afghanistan%20Report%207_15Dec.pdf (accessed October 22, 2016).

Glaser, B. G., A. L. Strauss. 1967. *The Discovery of Grounded Theory: Strategies for Qualitative Research.* Chicago: Aldine, 1999.

Hrychuk, Heather, Peter Gizewski. 2008. "The Comprehensive Approach: Historical Antecedents/Lessons Learned." DRDC CORA TN 2008-000.

Hrychuk, Heather. 2009. "Combating the Security Development Nexus? Lessons Learned from Afghanistan." *International Journal* 64, no.

3 (September): 825–842. http://ca.vlex.com/vid/combating-nexus-lessons-learned-afghanistan-69258137 (accessed October 22, 2016).

Huxham, Chris. 2003. "Theorizing Collaboration Practice." *Public Management Review* 5, no. 3: 401–423.

Jarzabkowski, P. 2004. "Strategy as Practice: Recursiveness, Adaptation and Practice-in-use." *Journal of Management Studies* 25, no. 4: 529–560.

Jarzabkowski, P., A. P. Spee. 2009. "Strategy as Practice: A Review and Future Direction of the Field." *International Journal of Management Reviews* 11, no. 1: 69–95.

Mazouz, Bachir, Anne Rousseau, Pierre-André Hudon. 2016. "Strategic Management in Public Administrations: A Results-based Approach to Strategic Public Management." *International Review of Administrative Sciences* 82, no. 3: 411–417.

McGuire, Michael, Robert Agranoff, Chris Silvia. 2011. "Putting the 'Public' Back into Collaborative Public Management." Paper presented at the Public Management Research Conference, Syracuse, NY, June 1–4. https://www.maxwell.syr.edu/uploadedFiles/conferences/pmrc/Files/McGuire_Putting%20the%20Public%20Back%20into%20Collaborative%20Public%20Management.pdf (accessed October 22, 2016).

North Atlantic Treaty Organisation. 2010. *Comprehensive Operational Planning Directive.* https://info.publicintelligence.net/NATO-COPD.pdf (accessed October 22, 2016).

North Atlantic Treaty Organisation. "Comprehensive Approach." http://www.nato.int/cps/en/natolive/topics_51633.htm (accessed October 22, 2016).

Patrick, Stewart, Kaysie Brown. 2007. *Greater Than the Sum of Its Parts? Assessing "Whole of Government" Approaches to Fragile States.* International Peace Academy. www.cgdev.org/files/13935_file_Fragile_States.pdf (accessed October 22, 2016).

Pitts, David, Sergio Fernandez. 2009. "The State of Public Management Research: An Analysis of Scope and Methodology." *International Public Management Journal* 12, no. 4 (December): 399–420.

Poister, T. H., G. D. Streib. 1999. "Strategic Management in the Public Sector: Concepts, Models, and Processes." *Public Productivity and Management Review* 22, no. 3 (March): 308–325.

Poister, Theodore H., David W. Pitts, Lauren Hamilton Edwards. 2010. "Strategic Management Research in the Public Sector: A Review, Synthesis, and Future Directions." *The American Review of Public Administration* 40, no. 5 (September): 522–545.

Ritchie, Robert T. 2010. "Stabilization in the Afghanistan Counter-Insurgency: Assessing the Comprehensive Approach in Kandahar Province." Canadian Forces College—Joint Command and Staff Programme (JCSP 36), February 26. http://www.cfc.forces.gc.ca/papers/csc/csc36/mds/Ritchie.pdf (accessed October 22, 2016).

Trudeau, Justin. 2016. "Canada's New Approach to Addressing the Ongoing Crises in Iraq and Syria and Impacts on the Region: Promoting Security and Stability." February 8. http://pm.gc.ca/eng/news/2016/02/08/canadas-new-approach-addressing-ongoing-crises-iraq-and-syria-and-impacts-region (accessed October 22, 2016).

United Kingdom. 2010. "The Comprehensive Approach: The Point of War Is Not Just to Win but to Make a Better Peace." House of Commons Defence Committee, seventh report of Session 2009–10. http://www.publications.parliament.uk/pa/cm200910/cmselect/cmdfence/224/224.pdf (accessed February 21, 2016).

United Nations High Commissioner for Refugees. 2015. *Sub-regional Operations Profile—Middle East.* http://www.unhcr.org/pages/49e45ade6.html (accessed October 22, 2016).

Whittington, R. 1996. "Strategy-as-practice." *Long Range Planning* 29, no. 5: 731–735.

6

Discussion on Synergy

Canada's engagement in Afghanistan from 2001 to 2014 has proven to be a real learning curve. Starting off with a small contingent of Special Operations Forces in October 2001 (Horn and Balasevicius 2007, 13–14), Canada's engagement rapidly grew into a full combat mission involving a battle group and later morphed into a 3D, but it stopped short of the whole-of-government approach and comprehensive approach. Indeed, as much as we like to look back and say, "We Canadians made a contribution, there never was a comprehensive plan" (Nelofer Pazira 2011; in Sachs 2011, A11). That does not neglect the real results that have been achieved but only serves to highlight the true potential, which has been missed by not leveraging this comprehensive approach.

> Canada's civilian and military efforts in Kandahar after just two years
> of close collaboration were starting to achieve some real operational
> synergy that would be difficult to replicate with forces from another
> country. (Manley Report 2008, 31)

This was Canada's distinctive edge, but faced with the weakness of current frameworks of the comprehensive approach, this research proposed what could be the building blocks for a theoretical model of synergy. It is believed synergy represents a more integrated, holistic and dynamic theoretical model of the comprehensive approach. Indeed, because the comprehensive approach never truly came to fruition in Afghanistan, shifting paradigms is quintessential. Moreover, our synergistic model presents a much more integrated, holistic, dynamic and fruitful approach. Synergy is the outcome of six dimensions presented in our synergistic model; it also answers each of the original subquestions we had laid out in introduction and within the first chapter's section on questions:

- ✓ Where and when is the comprehensive approach situated today?
- ✓ Who are the comprehensive approach's societal stakeholders?
- ✓ What is the comprehensive approach's organisation structures?
- ✓ How is the comprehensive approach systematically designed?
- ✓ Why is the comprehensive approach a new strategic paradigm?
- ✓ Is the comprehensive approach creating positive synergies?

Today, it is widely recognised that the military is only one of the pieces in a comprehensive approach that, ideally, should preemptively address the root causes of conflict within troubled regions. There is recognition that a multidimensional analysis to such issues is now fundamental, incorporating different prisms or perspectives within a more integrated and dynamic analysis overall. As such, following a systematic review of the 178 texts consisting of our empirical literature on both the subject of the comprehensive approach and on the object of Canada's engagement in Afghanistan, we found that six major threads best reflected on this topic: strategic planning, international security, counterinsurgency, emerging normative, efficiency assumption and intellectual complexity. In particular, the international relations, the efficiency assumption and the intellectual complexity represented three serious limitations within the comprehensive approach. Thus, constructing a theoretical model that would retain its strengths but also address these limitations was key for this research. The idea is that with such a theoretical model, executives in Canada's engagements can leverage a more synergistic approach and achieve greater effects and enduring outcomes from such a collaborative and dynamic view.

By employing the principles of grounded theory as outlined by Glaser and Strauss (1967), this research proposed to construct a theoretical model that could support executive decision making in the case of Canada's future unconventional engagements. Because there was no working model or theory of the comprehensive approach from which to start, one had to be pragmatically constructed from the literature. As this research design developed, systematically reading through literature, codes were clustered into the concepts and categories to provide an original model from which further theorisation spirals were then iterated. Doing so led to the selection of major keywords and to the realisation that Canada's engagement in Afghanistan was a crucial background to study the emergence of the comprehensive approach. Moreover, a unique opportunity for participation and observation presented itself as the author was deployed to Afghanistan in 2010, leading to many discussions and the collection of notes and memos. These were later used in the final analysis to serve as verification means along with a further meta-analysis of the codes, concepts and categories to extract their correlations and degree of validity. Following such a unique research design to study the comprehensive approach and propose a theoretical model, this research then presented three articles before discussing its overall contribution.

The first article was presented in the third chapter: "Canada's Comprehensive Approach in Afghanistan: A Critical Review of Literature, 2001–2011." As a refocus from the larger review of the empirical literature on the approach, it essentially presented the background's content analysis and similarly presented six threads that further highlighted the case: security apparatus, political strategy, emerging normative, efficiency assumption, international relations and intellectual complexity. Separately, each thread can be synthesised into management dimensions like strategic policies, organisational structure, socioculture, systemic processes, situational context and collaborative dynamics. From the review of the empirical literature on the comprehensive approach in Canada's engagement in Afghanistan, it can thus be said that these six dimensions best reflect the practice of the comprehensive approach, and as such they could constitute the basic building blocks for a grounded theory of this approach to be leveraged by management executives.

The fourth chapter presented our second article: "Constructing Canada's Synergistic Model: Lessons from Afghanistan." Following from our previous systematic review of literature of Canada's engagement in Afghanistan and the so-called comprehensive approach, it demonstrated that this approach has not been theorised or modelled in Afghanistan. This article thus proposed to theoretically model the comprehensive approach in order to provide the executive management with a more synergistic construct. Based on six dimensions—the situational context, the socioculture, the organisational structure, the strategic policies, the systemic processes and the synergy dynamics—this theoretical model allows us to tackle some of the fundamental lessons learned from Canada's engagement in Afghanistan with a view to applying them generally to Canada's current and future engagements. In particular, it is found that synergy is the central theme underlying the comprehensive approach, and that constructing a theoretical model from this dynamic dimension is crucial in order to provide greater effects as a system overall. This article also offers an answer to our question: What would be an applicable decision-making model of the comprehensive approach?

The fifth chapter presented our third article: "Synergy as Canada's Comprehensive Approach." Approaching the subject of the comprehensive approach from a collaborative public strategic management perspective provided for a pragmatic theoretical model explanation. Indeed, we applied our previously developed synergistic model composed of six dimensions: the situational context, the socioculture, the organisational structure, the strategic policies, the systemic processes and the synergy dynamics. This article thus took our model a step forward in the field of management and made key policy recommendations. Explaining the methodology which led to our synergistic model of the *comprehensive approach* in a collaborative public strategic management perspective enabled us to provide theoretically grounded recommendations for Canada's Engagement in Iraq and the Levant. We found that Canada could greatly benefit from applying such a synergistic model, and particularly from synchronising the management levers supporting the six dimensions. In doing so, an integrated perspective could emerge that would foster greater synergy. Synergy thus is the central theme, and it is now worth looking synthetically into this construct. In particular, it is worth looking into the important contributions of this doctoral research, followed by some limitations, before concluding.

On Synergy

Having systematically reviewed the empirical literature on the comprehensive approach and focused specifically on the empirical literature on Canada's engagement in Afghanistan—and this following the presentation of our research logic and research design employing grounded theory, following also upon the presentation of the three articles for this doctoral research—this book now turns into a discussion on synergy as a grounded theoretical model, having emerged from the corpus on the comprehensive approach employed in Afghanistan. By definition, synergy is the interaction of two or more agents or forces so that their combined effect is greater than the sum of their individual effects.[128] Henceforth, a dynamic notion of interactions is key as well as the greater combined effects, which are enhanced.

As such, for the purpose of this book, synergy can be understood simply as a phenomenon where the sum creates an effect that is greater than that of its parts. This phenomenon can be seen from natural sciences, as with life itself, to strategic management where synergies are achieved by strategically leveraging interactions and combining effects in a much larger one. Synergy does not happen in a vacuum, and this is where our proposed theoretical model finds its most useful contribution, being applied pragmatically by executive managers. Indeed, it does not suffice to simply state synergy exists; a theoretical model is quintessential to help explain the component parts of such synergy and demonstrate interdependency.

First, the situational-context dimension helps answer the where and when questions, locating decisions in space and time. This dimension is significant to a very high degree and is positively correlated to the other five dimensions, albeit to the medium level, only partially explaining the theoretical model. This situation relates to the counterinsurgency context and to the international relations aspect of the issue in Afghanistan, setting the background for the research. This dimension sets the space-time conditions in which synergy can emerge.

Second, the socio-cultural dimension helps answer the who and with whom questions, identifying major stakeholders. This sociocultural dimension is correlated positively but at a low level, providing little influence upon the other five dimensions. It relates to the emerging normative and to the narrative that surrounded the Afghan mission, and it speaks mostly to the

---

[128] *Oxford English Dictionary,* "Synergy," https://en.oxforddictionaries.com/definition/synergy

social and cultural comprehension such as underlying values and norms, which unfortunately are not taken to be major considerations.

Third, the organisational structure dimension helps answer the question of what, thus anchoring issues around a framework. By being highly positively correlated to other dimensions (save for society, to which it has medium correlation), the organisational structure dimension is also very significant. Discussion of the predominance of the defence outlook and of international security within the comprehensive approach often underscores the importance of this structural dimension. This dimension explains the coordination that exists.

Fourth, the strategic policies dimension generally answers the why question of strategic management and helps explicit key interests. It's very significant as dimension and is very positively correlated to other dimensions, in particular to synergy, structure and systems. The strategic dimension explains why the comprehensive approach is often associated with a political and strategic planning effort. In fact, the notable lack of an overarching strategic framework is a key weakness to the approach, and this is in spite of a significant overusage of strategy as a consideration for making decisions. This dimension speaks to a concertation of interests that strategically forms sometimes formally, but most often quite informally.

Fifth, the systemic processes dimension answers the how question in order to explicate the process by which decisions are reached and implemented. It's also very significant and highly correlated in a positive sense, but the systemic dimension is less important to explain the model as a whole. The systemic dimension is often understood as a systemic efficiency assumption, which remains undemonstrated within the comprehensive approach. As such, it seems to provide an ideal type. This dimension explains the cooperation that must exist.

Sixth and finally, the synergy dynamics dimension answers the so what question and captures the essence of total effects from the sum of the parts. It's very positively correlated to strategy, structure and systems; synergy is less correlated to situation and society. Associated with some intellectual complexity, synergy should be understood as the sum of its parts, which in theory provides a constructive and a pragmatic explanation for effects that are greater. Collaboration is thus its hallmark.

As such, the following figure represents these six dimensions in an integrated and holistic fashion. Each dimension is represented as a circle, overlapping other dimensions in significant ways, and as such degrees of integration are presented in red, indicating a level of interdependency. Under each dimension's title is its lever, which can be understood as the practical extension of the dimension in question: conditions, comprehension, coordination, concertation, cooperation and collaboration. These represent the practical executive management levers that can be constructively and pragmatically employed.

Figure 8—Synergy: A Theoretical Model

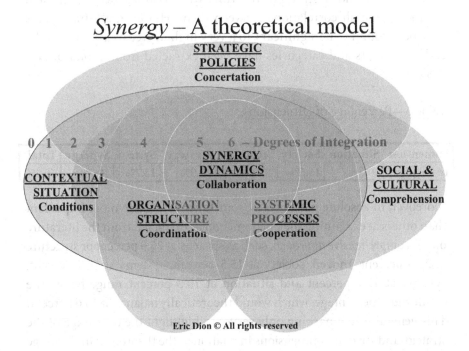

Synergy – A theoretical model

As discussed earlier, synergy theoretically emerges from being a crucial condition, not by being left to chance. A sociocultural comprehension with regards to synergy that fosters a sense of common understanding on the idea that the sum can be greater than its parts is required. An integrative coordination structure of some form is quintessential to anchor synergy on a given architecture as much as adding strategic value through concertation by employing the idea of synergy appears very important. Systemic cooperation and efficiency can be said to be either a requisite for synergy or indeed part of its effect in a holistic fashion, while collaborative dynamics are the most important effect from synergy. Together, these six strategic management dimensions represent an integrated, holistic and dynamic synergistic model that could be applied to different backgrounds.

In order to verify, a further meta-analysis was conducted after having established synergy as an overarching construct that includes many ontological and epistemological perspectives into a larger, more holistic and more dynamic worldview where sums are greater than their parts (Annex A). All dimensions are thus significant and positively correlated. Some dimensions, like socioculture and situation, presented low to medium correlations; strategy, structure, systems and synergy presented high to very high correlations between them. However, all dimensions have been found to be significant to a very high degree of $\alpha = 0.01$, as the codes, concepts and categories have been extracted from a total of N = 178 texts.

Table 6—Percentage of Dimensions

Dimension	Situation	Society	Structure	Strategy	System	Synergy	Total
In corpus	10.3%	15.5%	20.3%	26.9%	13.7%	12.7%	99.4%

Moreover, in absolute percentages, some dimensions are more important than others at explaining the phenomenon as extracted from the literature on the *comprehensive approach*, such as strategy at 26.9 percent or structure at 20.3 percent. Indeed, society at 15.5 percent, systems at 13.7 percent, synergy at 12.7 percent and situation at 10.3 percent range below the equilibrium percentage, which would theoretically balance at 16.6 percent. This general benchmarking only serves to highlight the overusage of the strategy and structure dimensions in relation to the theoretical underusage of context, systems and synergy, thus presenting an opportunity. The opportunity this research exploited was the theoretical void surrounding synergy, in particular because unlike the other five dimensions, synergy has no integrated body of theory, such as we propose in Annex A.

The next figure represents the configuration of the six dimensions according to the percentages extracted through our content analysis of 178 texts (in red) in comparison to a more theoretical balance of all six dimensions (in blue) and compared to our previous configuration of these same six dimensions at 108 texts (in green). As such, one can visually note the overusage of strategy and structure in comparison to the underusage of context, system and synergy, which led us to develop the synergy dimension. Moreover, one can note the relative similar configuration of our content analysis from 105 texts to 178 texts. This illustrates that a degree of saturation was already being achieved with 105 texts in that the configuration has only slightly shifted from the structural to the strategic dimension. In essence, the following figure graphically demonstrates the gap we analysed between what would be a balanced model (in blue) and the actual practice (in green and in red), as reflected through the discourse on the subject of the comprehensive approach.

Figure 9—Synergy: Reality versus Rhetoric Gap Analysis

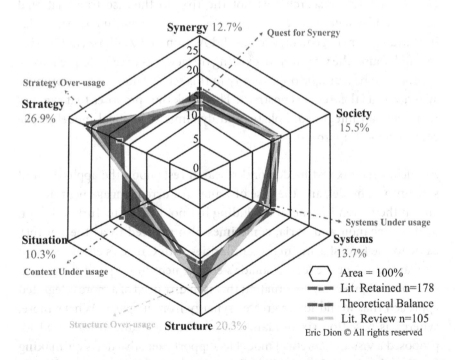

This doctoral research was simply unable to find a comprehensive approach model or theory, although some elements of a framework were in place, essentially based on precursor constructs like 3D, whole-of-government,

JIMP, CIMIC, NEO and more. However, in an integrated, holistic and constructive and pragmatic perspective, it is clear the comprehensive approach seems not to exist practically as we presented it, essentially remaining a philosophy for favourable enduring outcomes (CF Land Ops 2008, 5–14). By precisely following a grounded theory design, this research then turned to synergy as a valuable idea to explain the phenomenon found in the crucial case study of Canada's engagement in Afghanistan. This was found following the qualitative and quantitative saturation of codes and their categories, which yielded six significant fundamental executive management dimensions to be considered: the situational-context, the socioculture, the organisational structure, the strategic policies, the systemic processes and the synergy dynamics. All dimensions are positively correlated within our model, indicating that synergy in particular interacts with these categorical variables. It can thus be said with a high degree of certainty that synergy is a valid theoretical model for the comprehensive approach.

Henceforth, this research was not the first to theorise from national security and defence studies into executive management, and in particular into strategic management; such as did Allison and Zelikow (1999). This research found the weakness of existing frameworks of the comprehensive approach to be a unique opportunity in this sense, allowing us to propose synergy as its theoretical construct. This book thus proposes that synergy represents an integrated, holistic and dynamic theoretical model of the comprehensive approach.

As such, the crux of this doctoral research rests upon the application of synergy as a model, and the case of Canada's current engagement in Iraq and in the region in general (including but not limited to Turkey, Egypt, Jordan, Lebanon and Syria, sometimes also referred to as the Levant), came to the fore, sharing many similarities with Canada's engagement in Afghanistan. Not the least, Canada's engagement in Iraq and the Levant presents a highly complex situation that is in dire need of a more integrated approach that would foster greater synergy from its parts. What's more, synergy is based on six fundamental management dimensions, and we proposed a visual theoretical model to support executive decision-making for Canada, the UN, and Allied future engagements. It appears further general contributions can be found in strategic management, as well as in other fields.

On Contributions

In term of its contributions, this book makes a number of significant propositions. First and foremost, on the theoretical plane, we have presented a synergistic theoretical model as the main explanation for the comprehensive approach, which is an innovative contribution in itself. Furthermore, this book makes important contributions in the field of strategic management, namely with regards to strategic performance (strategy), strategic planning (structuration), strategic processes (systems) and collaborative strategic management (synergy). What's more, this book contributes to the international relations field by offering a more constructive, pragmatic, synergistic theoretical model to be applied in different contexts (situations). It also contributes to national security and defence, presenting an innovative managerial perspective for unconventional warfare (society). Altogether, these make a significant contribution to the field of collaborative public strategic management, particularly within national security and defence—a crucial innovation for the better holistic prevention and the pre-emption of conflicts, as well as for their resolution.

Moreover, through its proposition of a synergistic theoretical model, this book addresses some of the serious limitations that were identified following our systematic critical review of literature on the comprehensive approach. Indeed, by presenting an integrated dynamic perspective to decision makers, our model offers the potential for an optimised decision making and does not simply assume efficiency without a model. What's more, our model helps to simplify intellectual complexity in strategic management by presenting six key dimensions for strategic thinking and decision making. Finally, our model also considers the societal stakeholders as a fundamental dimension and thus expands the international relations perspective, which has been skewed by the dominating occidental view of others' own issues. Henceforth, our model addresses serious limitations we previously identified.

Strategic Management

Our synergistic theoretical model makes an added contribution to the subject of strategic performance by explaining that it is the outcome of a complex understanding, simplified by our explanation of synergy. In our perspective, performance is intimately tied to achieving a higher degree of integration from our six dimensions, which in theory would provide synergy through synchronising their combined effects, thanks to the six levers of actions we identified. In a more classic strategic management perspective, performance is often associated with effectiveness and efficiency (Weber 1921), based on the optimisation ideal (Pareto 1897). Performance is also understood as a strategic objective (Chandler 1962; Andrews 1971). More recently, the idea of the core competence (Hamel and Prahalad 1990) and the competitive advantage of nations (Porter 1999) have become central notions within the strategic management literature on performance where nations are in constant competition.

> Strategic management is not a linear process of planning, implementation, and evaluation. Rather, it entails managing a public agency from a strategic perspective on an ongoing basis to ensure that strategic plans are kept current and that they are effectively driving other management processes. (Poister and Streib 1999, 311)

What is fundamental are the six dimensions each with their lever, which can be activated. Such levers of action are, for example, the conditions of space and time, the comprehension or common understanding, the coordination, the concertation and the cooperation, which together lead to greater collaboration and thus foster synergy. Henceforth, explaining the strategic performance of organisations in such a holistic and dynamic perspective is a key contribution. The idea is to better position organisations (structures) within their external environment (situation) so that they meet their objectives (strategy) more effectively and efficiently (systems) as to achieve public value (society) and a higher return on investment (synergy). Our synergistic model thus offers a more integrated, holistic and dynamic view of performance, which is unlike any other offered thus far in the field of strategic management.

Bozeman (1993) defines public strategic management as being concretely concerned with prescription and prescriptive theory, indicating that some amount of interaction between academics and practitioners is to be expected (Pitts and Fernandez 2009, 402). In this perspective, our synergistic model can be used in a prescriptive fashion, as we have demonstrated with the case of Canada's engagement in Iraq and the Levant. "Strategic management is argued by some authors to be increasingly important for shaping performance of public organizations" (Andrews et al. 2012; Jesper and Ewan 2016, 2). "It is only more recently that strategic management has received attention within the public administration literature" (Ferlie 2003; Johansson 2009), and the field is still developing.

> In the past 25 years, public strategic management has evolved in theory, research, and seemingly in practice from a framework that focused largely on strategic planning to a more comprehensive, integrated, and interactive framework in which strategic planning significantly affects, while also being affected by, budgeting and related performance management efforts within a context of institutional, organizational, processual, stakeholder opportunities and constraints. (Bryson et al. 2010, 505)

On a macro level, strategic management, with emphasis on developing and implementing a strategic agenda, is synonymous with managing for results (Poister and Streib 1999, 323).

> More than any other single approach in the public manager's tool kit, strategic management is the most fundamental, and the most critical, process for producing results in the challenging and increasingly competitive environment in which most public managers work (Poister and Streib 1999, 324).

> Complementing this move to more holistic strategic management, we need to shift the emphasis of the performance movement from a principal concern with measurement to the more encompassing process of performance management over the coming decade in order to focus more proactively on achieving strategic goals and objectives. (Poister 2010, S246).

This is very much akin to the emergence of the *comprehensive approach*. As such, one of this book's contribution is to add the holistic notion of synergy to the strategic analysis of performance, meaning that performance is not simply the outcome of one or two dimensions but of a whole system-of-systems, which we presented as our synergistic model. This is very much in line with the new public governance movement (Lynn 2006), which we complement with our idea of synergy as being an integrative model for better strategic management as well as for performance optimisation that is 360 degrees in all six of our dimensions. However, with reason, some authors have questioned the strategic management field's fixation on performance as optimisation (March and Sutton 1997; Guérard et al. 2013). Moreover, others argued that strategic management fundamentally requires structured planning.

Structured Planning

For its part, strategic planning has been an important current in strategic management (Ansoff 1965), which has assumed that the rationalistic-comprehensive perspective dominates, as if all could be strategically planned (Mintzberg 1994). Strategic planning has been incorporated into legislation to ensure that public organisations follow its precepts, thus taking on the status of a dominant paradigm following from the new public management. It is notable, however, that such structured planning is skewed and limited to certain dimensions. Indeed, limited or bounded rationality (Simon 1991) explains how decisions are satisficing. As such, we have presented a more balanced perspective on strategic planning, where strategy does not dominate over other dimensions but works in harmony and in synchrony. Like the metaphor of the orchestra, one needs leadership at the head, but this strategy is also composed of categories of musical instruments, and each has its part to play in the harmony, i.e. in concertation.

"The point here is that strategic planning will become more meaningful as more agencies transition to comprehensive strategic management approaches that, among other things, drive their performance management systems forward" (Poister 2010, S252). As such, our synergistic model can be used as strategic planning and as a strategic management tool. Indeed, because it reflects a given corpus, it can greatly assist in explaining and predicting actions based on the six dimensions we have identified, serving as a dynamic thinking tool:

> It is hoped that public agencies will move further toward more comprehensive strategic management … as they not only see the value of good strategic planning, but also feel the need to use strategy

to drive decisions and actions to advance their strategic agendas effectively. (Vinzant and Vinzant 1996; in Poister 2010, S249)

Hence, our theoretical model is composed of six dimensions working together in synchrony: the situational context, the socioculture, the organisational structure, the strategic policies, the systemic processes and the synergy dynamics, which compose our metaphorical orchestra. If strategic planning does not account for these six dimensions, the perspective risks being skewed. For example, if strategic planning limits its thinking to only two or three of the six dimensions, leaving out the socioculture for example, it is obvious the perspective will be less than comprehensive in scope. Proposing a comprehensive approach thus requires a comprehensive strategic planning that is structured by the six dimensions we have identified. These six dimensions appear to be generic but will vary in relative weight and percentage. As such, taking into consideration our synergistic model for strategic planning offers better prospects for the structuration of planning itself, adding fundamental dimensions of analysis.

As with strategic performance, our theoretical model presents a more dynamic and holistic perspective to account for in structured planning. Planners should take into consideration the sociocultural dimension in the same manner as they do the strategic and structural ones. As much as context is understood as the external environment analysis in strategic planning, the systemic and synergic dimensions must also be understood as essential considerations. It thus appears that our synergistic model could structure a more integrated, strategic planning.

> Strategic planning isn't strategic thinking. One is analysis, and the other is synthesis.... Planners should make their greatest contribution around the strategy-making process rather than inside it.... Real strategic change requires inventing new categories, not rearranging old ones. (Minztberg 1994)

That is exactly what our synergistic model proposes, offering a comprehensive model and a new synergistic category for strategic planning. As such, "Strategic planning and many elements of a more comprehensive strategic management approach have become fairly ubiquitous in practice, although their actual impacts still remain unclear" (Bryson et al. 2010, 505).

> Making strategy more meaningful in the future will require transitioning from strategic planning to the broader process of strategic management, which involves managing an agency's overall strategic agenda on an ongoing rather than an episodic basis, as well as ensuring that strategies are implemented effectively. (Poister 2010, S246)

> Thus, strategic planning takes a "big picture" approach that blends futuristic thinking, objective analysis, and subjective evaluation of values, goals, and priorities to chart a future direction and courses of action to ensure an organization's vitality, effectiveness, and the ability to add public value. (Poister 2010, S247)

Here, such integrative structured planning is akin to a systemic comprehensive approach.

Systemic Processes

"Each organisation represents a resultant of complex forces, an empirical and complex entity" (Selznick 1948, 30). This dynamic perspective is now more appreciated than ever before. As of late, a strategic process perspective has appeared (Langley 1997), which better explains the mechanism by which strategy is achieved. Mintzberg (1994) had already talked of strategy as a plan (structure), a pattern (system), a position (situation), a perspective (society) and even a ploy (strategy) that reflects well upon our theoretical model dimensions in strategic management, which together foster synergy as a sixth phenomenon. This integrative, dynamic and holistic perspective presented by our synergistic model thus offers a whole new dimension to consider in a strategic process perspective, where strategy is formulated through a system-of-systems view, accounting for all six dimensions.

"There's a new kid on the block, a [public strategic] management that defines its task more broadly than do previous paradigms and achieves many of its purposes through a dynamic of network governance" (Stoker 2006, 43). "Substantively, the possible effects of alternative reforms need to be investigated, in particular whether they encourage the development of alternative cooperative or network-based forms of strategy" (Jesper and Ewan 2016, 15).

> Many governmental units and agencies have some of the pieces in place, but relatively few actually have developed full-fledged strategic management systems that truly integrate all major functions and management processes and direct them toward defining and advancing an organization's strategic agenda. (Poister and Streib 1999, 324)

That is to say, they are missing a synergistic theoretical model. As a strategic management system, our synergistic model is much like the balanced scorecard (Kaplan and Norton 1996) and can thus be understood as an integrated, holistic and dynamic tool. The scorecard did not propose dimensions for analysis and for management, as our synergistic theoretical model does. In a dynamic process perspective, where the environment is in constant evolution, taking on a more holistic, integrated and systemic perspective is key. Moreover, "None of the articles we found treated strategic planning and management as an iterative process in which, for example, difficulties arising in implementing a strategy may lead to reviewing and perhaps revising it" (Poister et al. 2010, 540) in a systemic way.

> Strategic management may be defined as "the appropriate and reasonable integration of strategic planning and implementation across an organization (or other entity) in an ongoing way to enhance the fulfillment of its mission, meeting of mandates, continuous learning, and sustained creation of public value." (Bryson et al. 2010, 495–496)

> Strategic management theory now emphasizes the development and *alignment* of an organization's mission, mandates, strategies, and operations, along with major strategic initiatives such as new policies, programs, or projects, while also paying careful attention to stakeholders seen as claimants on the organization's attention, resources, or outputs, or as affected by that output. (Bryson 2004a; Poister and Streib 1999; Bryson et al. 2010, 496)

That is as a system-of-systems view.

Eric Dion, CD, MBA, PhD

Synergic Collaboration

Collaborative Public Management has also become a major practice and research focus (Bardach 1998; Bingham and O'Leary 2008; O'Leary and Bingham 2009). Moreover, "The politics involved in strategic management for public purposes must be embraced and worked with, rather than simply decried" (Bloodworth 2001, 346). Nonetheless,

> The resulting literature has paid substantial attention to management generally, but surprisingly little to collaborative public strategic management specifically as an integrated approach, with partial exceptions including Huxham and Vangen (2005), Healey (2003), Agranoff (2007), Bryson et al. (2009), and Innes and Booher (2010). (Bryon 2010, 10).

As counterbalance, a collaborative strategic management current emerged that shapes the notion of performance and of strategic planning regarding collaboration with the others. Drucker's *Practice of Management* (1954) was the first to look at management as a whole. He considered the manager in context and regarded society, structure and strategy as crucial.

Indeed, achieving higher degrees of performance and better strategic planning must account for numerous perspectives and viewpoints, which together form a more integrated solution. Synergy can thus be defined by its levers of action and by its degrees of integration from one to six, the sixth degree forming the most integrated model and each dimension adding a degree of integration to the model, while percentages of each dimension present its level of intensity. The next breakthrough in strategy execution, *Alignment* by Kaplan and Norton (2006) shows how companies today can unlock unrealised value from these enterprise synergies.

However, *Alignment* is essentially based on the balanced scorecard as a strategic management system, whereas our synergistic model presents six dimensions for executive management, which when taken together as a whole offer a dynamic and integrated explanation of synergy. As such, synergic collaboration based on time-space conditions (situation), a common comprehension (socio-culture), a coordination of efforts (structure), a concertation of interests (strategy) and a cooperation of activities (system) can add value to a proposition. This integrated, holistic and dynamic management explanation for synergy presents a new contribution to the field, which can be leveraged by executives in many different perspectives. One such perspective is collaborative public strategic management as an emerging current.

Agranoff and McGuire (2003) define collaborative public management as a "Concept that describes the process of facilitating and operating in multi-organizational arrangements for solving problems that cannot be achieved, or achieved easily, by single organizations," thereby pointing to our own synergy dynamics as a fundamental and collaborative dimension. "Collaborative arrangements, in some cases, attain a 'collaborative advantage which is concerned with potential synergy from working collaboratively'" (Huxham 2003, 401).

> Collaborative public management is an endeavor in which "administrators exchange information (system), seek knowledge (society), and work out problems (situation), programs (structures) and policies (strategy) across the boundaries of their agencies and their organizations" (Agranoff and Yildiz 2007, 319) by bringing together representatives from the public, private, and/or not-for-profit sectors. (McGuire et al. 2011, 22)

This is akin to the comprehensive approach.

> The collaborative manager plays the role of mediator and stimulates interaction (Koppenjan and Klijn 2004). Network structuring, or "tinkering with the network" (p. 51), involves influencing formal policy (strategy), influencing interrelationships (system), influencing values and perceptions (society), mobilizing new coalitions (strategy), and managing by chaos (situation). (McGuire 2006, 37)

This type of management is much more integrative and requires a synergistic, collaborative approach to achieve a comprehensive one, as well as leadership, to champion such a comprehensive approach. However, "Practitioner-oriented guidance on how to engage in collaborative strategic planning and management is also surprisingly thin, with a few significant exceptions (e.g., Straus 2002, Winer and Ray 1994). (Bryson et al. 2010,

504)." "Collaboration and networking have become core concerns in public management. However, despite a growing empirical tradition, movement toward theorizing has not kept pace" (McGuire et al. 2011, 1). "Although a great deal of work has been done in the area of collaborative public management, not much has been done on collaborative public strategic management (Bryson et al. 2010, 505), where we thus foresee the main contribution of this doctoral research.

> Collaborative strategic management appears to be a more integrated and comprehensive approach, making it possible to manage, but also to organise, the collaboration at the different stages of the development and implementation of partnership strategies. Process models have thus been developed, comprising the major stages of the classical strategic management approach (Bryson et al. 2006; Clarke and Fuller 2011). (Favoreu et al. 2016, 441)

In essence, our own synergistic theoretical model offers contributions in the areas of strategic management, structured strategic planning, systemic processes and synergistic collaboration, which constitute the main, overarching dimensions of an executive management approach. It also offers contributions in the area of international relations and that of strategic studies, as we will see in the following two sections before we turn to some of its limitations.

Situational Relations

Our synergistic model also offers a contribution to the field of international relations per se. Many explain the behaviour of national government in terms of the rational actor model. However, alternative conceptual models labelled the organisational behaviour model and the governmental politics model provide more basis for improved explanation and predictions (Allison and Zelikow 1999, 2–5). Henceforth, according to our own theorisation, the rational actor model is represented by the situation and structure, the organisational behaviour model is represented by the socioculture and system and the governmental politics model is represented by the strategy and the synergy dimensions. As such, contrary to many studies following from Allison and Zelikow, which identified with either one of the three models studied, we have proposed through our synergistic model an integrated perspective that incorporates these three models within six management dimensions for decision making. "Fully incorporating politics into strategic planning and management is consistent with a practice perspective, because strategy-as-practice approach emphasizes the contextualization of actions by the strategy practitioners (Whittington, 2003)" (Bryson et al. 2010, 502).

> Strategic management must provide for the implementation of strategies through vehicles such as action plans, budgeting process, performance management system, changes in organizational structure, and program and project management. These and other "management levers" are used by effective strategic managers to drive macro-level strategies down into their organizations to ensure decisions are designed to advance these strategies or, at the very least, are consistent with them. (Poister and Streib 1999, 311)

Henceforth, an overarching architecture is thus quintessential. Indeed, the field of international relations is complex, due to pressures from the environment (situation), societal factors (socio-culture), the structuring forces of globalisation (structure), a chess game of interests (strategy) and operational considerations (system), which together represent truly complex interdependency (synergy). Henceforth, it appears as a more integrated, holistic and dynamic perspective, because the one proposed herein is needed to offer international relations executives a more pragmatic understanding of this field. Indeed, decision making is not limited to one or two dimensions such as presented through our analysis of Allison and Zelikow's (1999) three decision models. It is also noteworthy that the comprehensive approach emerged from the international relations, but these presented serious limitations—namely, in the fact they reflected the dominating view, as if the Westerner's perspective was the right one and thus needed to be enforced in places. We can think of different international regime change adventures as such serious limitations to harmonious, stable and perhaps evolutionary rather than revolutionary international relations. But without a holistic and synergistic decision-making model as we have proposed, the risk is the old antagonist and dominating Western perspective remains a self-fulfilling prophecy. Henceforth, a more integrated and synergistic decision-making model is thus truly required.

Eric Dion, CD, MBA, PhD

Societal Warfare

Finally, our synergistic theoretical model also presents a crucial contribution to the field of national security and defence studies, also called strategic studies, because of its ability to propose a more integrated, holistic and dynamic perspective on unconventional warfare. Indeed, warfare has moved from a primarily military affair to a larger societal perspective, where elements of war can be the environment, people, institutions, non-nations, cyber and space, even the economy and elections, reflecting well upon the six dimensions of our model. Such a perspective is offered namely through such work as *Unrestricted Warfare* (Liang and Xiangsui 1999), where warfare becomes a societal one by indirectly attacking the peoples.

Henceforth, countering such warfare becomes a matter of collaborative public management that goes well beyond the traditional understanding of war as primarily a military affair. Counterinsurgency such as in Afghanistan thus truly requires a comprehensive approach in order to be effective and efficient, and this is where our synergistic model really adds value. Countering global terrorism from Iraq and Syria also requires a comprehensive approach to be managed by executives who have understanding of its root causes and consequences, namely to prevent generational and more geopolitical warfare within nation-states. As such, employing our synergistic theoretical model, analysis and execution of actions in the public domain could have much greater leverage through synergic collaboration as a whole. This is also why we have presented policy recommendations to that effect in our third article, which also makes our synergistic theoretical model a pragmatic executive management tool.

"Strategic management is largely a matter of utilizing and coordinating all of the resources and venues at top management's disposal, enforcing a kind of 'omnidirectional alignment' among them in the interest of advancing the strategic agenda" (Poister and Van Slyke 2002). This is akin to strategically managing all the elements of national power for better alignment:

> Strategic management is the broader process of managing an organization in a strategic manner on a continuing basis. Strategic planning is a principal element of strategic management, which also involves resource management, implementation, and control and

evaluation. (Steiss, 1985; Vinzant and Vinzant, 1996b; in Poister et al. 2010, 524)

Comprehensive collaborative strategic management is required. However, none of the existing theories alone is sufficient to explain the root causes of conflict and terrorism, because each type of terrorism demonstrates a dissimilar pattern of causation. "This necessitates the development of a comprehensive causal model" (Dawoody 2016, 122). Henceforth, "Identification of the roots and causes of radicalism and terrorism have need of a comprehensive causal modelling" (Dawoody 2016, 142), and this is indirectly the venture this doctoral research project embarked on regarding synergy.

> Despite the scepticism of researchers and practitioners, many public administrations ... are now subject to legislation and regulations that have turned results based management and strategic planning into tools that make it possible to intelligently combine the purposes, objectives, means and resources required to steer states' administrations towards tangible results. (Mazouz et al. 2016, 412)

Beyond the theoretical understanding of our model lies more practical potential applications in the fields of strategic management, of international relations and unconventional warfare. We could think of strategic and artificial intelligence applications for decision making. Here, the essence is to understand the holistic implications and impacts of unconventional warfare's new and emerging forms, like illegal and illicit warfare, in order to better appreciate the effect that our synergistic model can have in an emerging, collaborative executive management perspective.

Steering all the elements of power towards a collaborative public strategic management approach has thus become a fundamental requirement in the face of the latest societal warfare that knows no limits or boundaries. Beyond the comprehensive approach, an integrated, holistic and dynamic understanding to counter such unrestricted warfare in a synergistic way is quintessential. Henceforth, synergy as we have presented it does offer great contributions. Beyond the public sector, applications can be foreseen in business intelligence. Of course, as with any research project, there are potential limitations to a study of this nature.

On Limitations

First and foremost is the unique background on which this whole endeavour is based: the case of Canada's engagement in Afghanistan from 2001 to 2014, with a particular focus on the comprehensive approach. Although this is a unique background—and so far the only one which has used the comprehensive approach—there is a healthy, critical, reflexive perspective to be maintained in its regards as a major combat, foreign affairs engagement for Canada. The argument could thus easily be made that this was an exception, a unique background, which nonetheless has merit to be studied like a crucial case, which we have thus researched. Indeed, the comprehensive approach has emerged out of Afghanistan, and so we have explained why this crucial background was important, although it has limitations—namely, the fact that as of yet, still no other engagement has adopted the comprehensive approach. This could be indicative of its complexity, or perhaps a unique case of the entire Afghan context, or further indication of the complexity of the whole comprehensive approach endeavour that simply has not been reattempted anywhere since.

What is more important, though, is the rigour with which this study has been conducted, unlike any other precedent study within the field of national security and defence management, where the focus has not been on the political science perspective but on the managerial perspective. Indeed, we have sought to outline the management view upon theories to propose a more holistic understanding of executive-level decision making, aiming for greater synergy as its outcome. We proposed a model based on the understanding of synergy, which can enrich the executive-level decision-making scheme, and we explained how these could be automated within decision support. As such, this study has clearly found that collaborative strategic management in national security and defence is indeed a lacking capability, but thanks to our grounded theorisation, we proposed important theoretical insights which could be leveraged.

Contrary to a more conventional academic approach, where a theory would first be selected and passed through the empirical case-study test, we have yet to find any one such theory that has been reliably employed empirically in testing the background of Canada's engagement in Afghanistan. This provides an important justification as to why this background was crucial, precisely because in spite of the significance of Canada's engagement in

Afghanistan, and of the comprehensive approach, there is an important theoretical void, but that has not prevented policy experts and practitioners from conducting real actions on the ground. Hence, a reverse methodology had to be employed, dwelling into the background to propose an inductive and more integrative theoretical model.

In terms of methodology, this research focused on a crucial background, Canada's engagement in Afghanistan from 2001 to 2014, which constituted the object of this research and also provided the unique background for this study of the comprehensive approach, which constituted its subject. This background is crucial, but not because any theory has either passed or failed empirical testing. Up to this point, through our literature review, no such comprehensive model or theory has yet been found supporting the comprehensive approach. This background is crucial because any theory on the comprehensive approach that would either pass or fail any empirical test through case-studying Canada's engagement in Afghanistan would prove itself to be central in explaining this key phenomenon as it is.

A final limitation is the fact that our synergistic theoretical model has not been tested on a different background or case study, and it has thus essentially emerged from a grounded theory. We would venture to say we are not the first to generalise into management from strategic studies, such as Graham Allison's study of the Cuban missile crisis, or the application of Sun Tzu's *Art of War*, or that of Machiavelli's *The Prince* to strategic management in general. What is particular about this study is its clear emphasis on the management rather than politics, on the *how to make things work* and the *so what* rather than on the *should* and *could*, on the constructive pragmatics. As such, we further venture to say that our study has found fruitful generalisations to the field of management by presenting a theoretical model, as well as some theory (<u>Annex A</u>) for executive and synergistic decision making. We believe we can find more applications in this field, thanks to imagination as well as pragmatic intelligence. As mentioned previously, our model could be leveraged thanks to artificial intelligence, and it could find practical applications in strategic intelligence and business intelligence in support of decision making.

Eric Dion, CD, MBA, PhD

Summary

In sum, chapter 6 consisted of a discussion on synergy, following from our systematic review of literature in chapter 1, from our research logic and research design in chapter 2 and from our three articles presented in chapters 3, 4 and 5, which have been published or submitted. Starting with a general discussion on this doctoral research, it went on to discuss synergy as a theoretical model composed of six dimensions that answer this book's original questions. Moreover, this discussion on synergy also answers this book's central question: What would be an applicable decision-making model of the comprehensive approach? We believe the answer rests with the possibility of presenting a synergistic theoretical model, as we've done.

This chapter then turned into a discussion of this book's contribution in six major areas: strategic management, structured planning, systemic processes and synergic collaboration, in an executive management perspective. In an international relations perspective, as well as in a strategic studies perspective, discussions of situational relations and societal war have also been key contributions of this book, presenting our synergistic theoretical model. In other words, synergy achieved by leveraging the six dimensions and levers we have presented should be the ultimate and optimal goal in all these crucial perspectives. This is also a reason why this book has adopted *Synergy—A Theoretical Model of Canada's Comprehensive Approach* as its title, precisely because it ensues from the model we presented. Moreover, thanks to our theoretical model, achieving synergy could become a norm, at least for Canada's current and future engagements, as well as Canada's allies and the UN. It would be a critical mistake to underestimate the potential of unconventional forms of warfare and to not think strategically with foresightedness about the potential applications of synergy.

Conclusion

Starting off with Canada's engagement in Afghanistan from 2001 to 2011 and then to 2014, and specifically with the study of the comprehensive approach, we have found that in fact synergy is a more fruitful theoretical model to explain this phenomenon. It was the constant quest for such synergy and better synchronicity that led the evolution from the three Ds of defence, diplomacy and development to the whole-of-government and comprehensive approach in the final instances of the mission. This has been demonstrated by using an axial-coding scheme from grounded theory combined with mixed methodology, including documentation review, content analysis, qualitative analysis and quantitative meta-analysis.

> The obvious question is whether the whole of government approach taken in Afghanistan can really offer a template for Canada's future, more modest whole of government operations in other parts of the world. And if the model as a whole is not applicable, are there elements that merit being replicated? (Buchan 2010, 75)

To answer such a question, a grounded theoretical approach made great sense, where the categories of the theory were defined for future decisions. This is precisely the venture this research embarked on regarding the comprehensive approach. What would be an applicable decision-making model of the comprehensive approach? We believe the answer rests in proposing a grounded theoretical model of synergy. To the question whether Canada's engagement in Afghanistan can be said to be a case of the comprehensive approach in practice, in theory we found it to be a quest for synergy.

Hence, faced with the weakness of the current frameworks, Canada's engagement in Afghanistan can hardly be said to be a case of the so-called comprehensive approach, and it appears from this research that the constant quest for synergy would be a better theory to explain actions in effect. However, without any model or theory of the comprehensive approach, problems remain intact: There cannot be feedback into the model in order to adjust actions as well as theories on actions, according to a double-hermeneutic loop.[129] This has been the fundamental problem underlying the comprehensive approach: the lack of a holistic, integrated, model and theory, which we proposed by developing synergy as theoretical model.

We have strived to answer each of the underlying *where/when, who* and *with whom, what, why, how* and *so what* questions. Indeed, the *where* and *when* are answered within the situational context dimension that speaks of synergy as being a crucial consideration in space and in time. The *who* and *with whom* questions are answered under the sociocultural dimension that speaks of synergy as being a comprehension, a way of seeing things, a worldview. As for the *what* question, it is answered through the organisational structure, which talks of required coordination for synergy. The important *why* question is answered through the strategic policies dimension, which further speaks of synergy as an essential value-adding concertation. The *how* question is answered by the systemic processes that operationalise efficiencies for cooperation in synergy. Finally the effects or the *so what* question is answered by collaborative dynamics, which are interdependent within synergy. In essence, all six underlying questions can be answered holistically through our proposed synergistic theoretical model, which better reflects upon Canada's comprehensive approach.

At the end of this doctoral research, six dimensions emerged from the retained corpus on the comprehensive approach. Each dimension adds a layer of explanation and adds value to our synergistic theoretical model within the field of strategic management for national security and defence. More complementary theoretical thoughts can be found in Annex A. As such, although emerging from the field of national security and defence, our constructive pragmatic model could find multiple applications such as in Iraq, Syria, Libya, Sudan, Mali, Somalia, Congo, Nigeria, Yemen, Haiti, the Arctic, narcotraffic or cyberwar.

---

[129] Double feedback loop is also known as double-hermeneutic, according to Argyris 1976 and Rennie 2000.

Moreover, what is most interesting are the potential general applications that such a theoretical model could find within the field of management at the strategic and the executive level. By employing our model of synergy, public administrations and businesses could leverage the insights generated by this holistic decision-support tool in order to gain a strategic, synergistic edge.

Such applications could generate the foundations for newer, faster and smarter synergy decisions offering the possibility of looking at issues in a holistic, dynamic and integrated perspective. Our theory of synergy and its adjoining model points to six crucial dimensions that have been developed throughout this research, which when taken as whole form a coherent integrated view. In essence, Canada's engagement in Afghanistan from 2001 to 2014 and its comprehensive approach together represent a case of the quest for more synergy. This book has ventured to propose a grounded theoretical model of this fundamental strategic management quest for *synergy* for the 21st century in general.

On Perspectives

If there is an academic out there willing to take up the challenges left out by this research, we suggest to start with a review of theories found in Annex A supporting our model to determine whether some have been left out and are missing in action, which would need to be further integrated into the model. We further suggest to empirically test our model on different case studies of the comprehensive approach in other backgrounds, perhaps looking at Canada's engagement in Haiti, which would have less of a national security and defence prism, thus offering a fresh start for the approach. Unconventional applications could also be found at the national level, such as in the Arctic, considering each of the dimensions relevant to a more synergistic decision-making scheme as well as in the case of major domestic events or crises.

Further perspectives for synergy as a theoretical model can also be foreseen. Applications could be developed, leveraging the operational planning process for example, and specifically for the Joint, Interagency, Multinational and Public domains, for civilian contributions to future engagements. Indeed, "Durable, comprehensive multi-disciplinary campaign plans must be developed to secure realistic and achievable solutions" (CF Ops 2005, 10-4). Within an integrated decision-making support model, consideration could be given to the situational-context, the socio-culture, the organisational structure, the strategic policies, the systemic processes and the synergy dynamics in order to propose an integrated executive decision scheme. Consideration for these six dimensions could be envisioned within policy recommendations and during implementation, in order to ensure an integrated synergy perspective is maintained throughout. In this perspective, conducting case studies would appear necessary. The further consideration of the notion of synchronisation would also appear very interesting.

As such, future research perspectives include looking into such a synergy decision-making theoretical model for the UN Department of Operations, particularly in the prevention and the resolution of conflicts as peace support operations. Applying and verifying synergy theory in such instances could prove an interesting research design by employing case studies. Analysing Canada's current and future engagements through our synergistic model can also prove an interesting research perspective, identifying areas that are clearly lacking to foster synergy. Finally, looking into NATO's Comprehensive Preparation of the Operational Environment (CPOE) could be an interesting way of integrating the idea of synergy within the process. See Slide 48 in Footnote.[130.]

In terms of future prospects, the grounded theory methodology has been very insightful and could be used for future research in circumstances where no clear theory appears to exist, and where more clarity is required from the ground. By employing the same ideas and principles (Guillemette and Luckerhoff 2009), a researcher could proceed through these general steps to create yet a newer theory. Developing theory in parallel to data collection, content analysis and meta-analysis requires a high degree of structuration, as Giddens would put it, but it also proves a very tight-knit way of producing a model that is as close to the ground as theoretically and technically possible. Future researchers starting off with a case study, but no clear theoretical insight, would find this grounded theory spiralling in

---

[130] NATO, NATO Operational Planning Process (OPP) and the Comprehensive Operations Planning Directive (COPD), Presentation, NATO School Oberammergau, 2013, slide 48, https://semanticu.files.wordpress.com/2014/09/02-1100-1200-nato-operational-planning-process-copd.pdf (accessed January 26, 2016).

development, and they would find its parallel methodology very useful in order to refine our theoretical model.

Not all the lessons that could be learned from this research have been learned, but we are confident that through our saturation of codes, concepts, categories and their correlations, we have highlighted the essence of the theoretical constructs present within the background. Such saturation was achieved thanks to axial coding and categorisation of quotations according to a constructive and pragmatic epistemology, as well as according to a strategic management and a systemic ontological perspective. These have been crucial in indicating what was worth money and what was not, from across the very extensive documentation, as well as from the literature. By employing a similar philosophy and approach, researchers could proceed to code quotations that are relevant to strategic management and a systemic perspective and extract their very essence, thus leveraging our synergistic model.

Figure 8—Synergy: A Theoretical Model

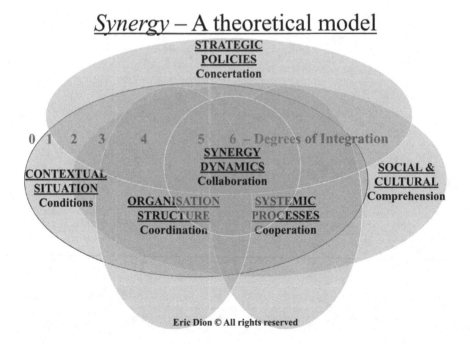

References

References Cited

Albert, Mathias, and Tanja Kopp-Malek. 2002. "The Pragmatism of Global and European Governance: Emerging Forms of the Political 'Beyond Westphalia.'" *Millennium—Journal of International Studies* 31, no. 3 (July): 453–471.

Albert, Mathias, and Tanja Kopp-Malek. 2002. "Pragmatism in International Relations Theory." *Millennium—Journal of International Studies* 31, no. 3. http://www.lse.ac.uk/internationalRelations/Journals/millenn/abstracts/31-3.aspx (accessed February 25, 2016).

Allison, Graham, and Philip Zelikow. 1999. *Essence of Decision: Explaining the Cuban Missile Crisis*, 2nd edition. http://www.amazon.fr/Essence-Decision-Explaining-Missile-Crisis/dp/0321013492 (accessed January 7, 2016).

Andrews, Kenneth Richmond. 1971. *The Concept of Corporate Strategy*.

Ansoff, H. Igor (1965). *Corporate Strategy: An Analytic Approach to Business Policy for Growth and Expansion*. New York: McGraw-Hill.

Ansoff, Igor. 1979. *Strategic Management*. Wiley, 2007.

Aupperle, Kenneth E. 1996. "Spontaneous Organisational Reconfiguration: A Historical Example Based on Xenophon's Anabasis." *Organisation Science* 7, no. 4: 445–460.

Argyris, Chris. 1976. "Single-Loop and Double-Loop Models in Research on Decision Making." *Administrative Science Quarterly* 21: 363–375.

Bellamy, Alex J. 2002. "Pragmatic Solidarism and the Dilemmas of Humanitarian Intervention." *Millennium—Journal of International Studies* 31, no. 3 (July): 473–497.

Benecke, G., W. Schurink, and G. Roodt. 2007. "Towards a Substantive Theory of Synergy." *South-African Journal of Human Resource Management* 5, no. 2: 9–19.

Bercq, Isabelle. 2005. *La Militarisation de l'Action Humanitaire en Afghanistan.* Note d'Analyse, Groupe de Recherche et d'Information sur la Paix et la Sécurité (9 mai): 2. http://www.grip.org/sites/grip.org/files/NOTES_ANALYSE/2005/NA_2005-05-06_FR_I-BERCQ.pdf (accessed February 2, 2016).

Biermann, Joachim, Pontus Hörling, and Lauro Snidaro. 2009. *Automated Support for Intelligence in Asymmetric Operations: Requirements and Experimental Results.* 12th International Conference on Information Fusion, July 6–9. http://users.dimi.uniud.it/~lauro.snidaro/Download/publications/JAIF.pdf (accessed February 20, 2016).

Blaikie, Norman. 2009. *Designing Social Research: The Logic of Anticipation.* Polity. http://books.google.je/books/about/Designing_Social_Research.html?id=lpCeLiDLZVYC (accessed February 25, 2016).

Bloodworth, Glenn. 2001. "From Strategic Planning to Strategic Management: A Manifesto." *Canadian Public Administration* 44, no. 3 (Fall): 346–354.

Bogdanor, Vernon. 2005. "Introduction." In *Joined-Up Government.* Oxford University Press, British Academy Occasional Papers, 15 September. https://global.oup.com/academic/product/joined-up-government-9780197263334?cc=ca&lang=en& (accessed February 25, 2016).

Bohman, James. 2002. "How to Make a Social Science Practical: Pragmatism, Critical Social Science and Multi-perspectival

Theory." *Millennium—Journal of International Studies* 31, no. 3 (July): 499–524.

Berger, Peter L., and Thomas Luckman. 1966. *The Social Construction of Reality: A Treatise in the Sociology of Knowledge.* Garden City, New York: Anchor Books. http://perflensburg.se/Berger%20social-construction-of-reality.pdf (accessed February 25, 2016).

Bryson, J. M., F. S. Berry, and K. Yang. 2010. "The State of Public Strategic Management Research: A Selective Literature Review and Set of Future Directions." *American Review of Public Administration* 40, no. 5 (September): 495–521.

Canada. 2005. *International Policy Statement.* http://www.isn.ethz.ch/Digital-Library/Publications/Detail/?lang=en&id=156830.

Canada. 2008. *Report of the Independent Panel on Canada's Future Role in Afghanistan,* (The Manley Panel). http://dsp-psd.pwgsc.gc.ca/collection_2008/dfait-maeci/FR5-20-1-2008E.pdf (accessed February 25, 2016).

Canada. 2008. *Land Operations.* B-GL-300-001/FP-001, final draft. http://armyapp.forces.gc.ca/olc/soh/SOH_Content/B-GL-300-001-FP-001-Eng_Land%20Ops%20%20-%20Final%20Draft%202008.pdf (accessed February 25, 2016).

CBC News. 2015. *David Mulroney Warns Canada Should Apply Afghanistan's Lessons to Iraq.* http://www.cbc.ca/news/politics/david-mulroney-warns-canada-should-apply-afghanistan-s-lessons-to-iraq-1.3002692 (accessed February 25, 2016).

Chandler, Alfred D. 1962. *Strategy and Structure: Chapters in the History of the American Enterprise.* Boston: MIT Press.

Chang, Yegmin M. 1990. "Synergy, Relatedness, and Organization Form in the Strategic Management of Diversification." Doctoral thesis. https://www.ideals.illinois.edu/handle/2142/22317 (accessed February 25, 2016).

Chapin, Paul, and George Petrolekas. 2012. *Canada Needs a National Security Strategy.* http://www.ipolitics.ca/2012/02/21/cda-institute-canada-needs-a-national-security-strategy/ (accessed February 25 2016).

Charmaz, K. 2006. *Constructing Grounded Theory: A Practical Guide through Qualitative Analysis.* Thousand Oaks, CA: SAGE Publications.

Christensen, Tom, and Per Laegreid. 2007. "The Whole of Government Approach to Public Sector Reform: Professors of Administration." *Public Administration Review* 67, no. 6 (Nov/Dec): 1059–1066. Also in *International Innovations* (Nov/Dec 2007), https://bora.uib.no/bitstream/1956/1893/1/N06-06%20Christensen-L%C3%A6greid.pdf (accessed February 25, 2016).

Christensson, S. Anders, Alexander E. R. Woodcock, Derek K. Hitchins, and Loren Cobb. 2004. "Modeling the Governance and Stability of Political Dynamical Systems." In Alexander Woodcock and David Davis, eds., *Analysis for Governance and Stability,* Cornwallis: Canadian Peacekeeping Press. http://www.ismor.com/cornwallis/cornwallis_2003/2003_1DavisFront-30Dec.pdf (accessed February 25, 2016).

Clark, Lynn Schofield. 1994. "Critical Theory and Constructivism." *International Hospitality Research Center.* Switzerland. http://www.ihrcs.ch/?p=92.

Coombs, Howard G. 2013. "Afghanistan 2010–2011: Counterinsurgency through Whole of Government." *Canadian Military Journal* 13, no. 3 (Summer): 16–24. http://www.journal.forces.gc.ca/vol13/no3/doc/Coombs-Pages1624-eng.pdf (accessed February 25, 2016).

Corning, P. A. 1983. *The Synergism Hypothesis: A Theory of Progressive Evolution.* New York: McGraw-Hill.

Corning, P. A. 1995. "Synergy and Self-Organization in the Evolution of Complex Systems." *Systems Research* 12, no. 2: 89–121.

Corning, P. A. 2003. *Nature's Magic: Synergy in Evolution and the Fate of Humankind.* Cambridge: Cambridge University Press.

Corning, P. A. 2007. *Synergy Goes to War.* Palo Alto, CA: Institute for the Study of Complex Systems. http://complexsystems.org/ publications/bioeconomic-theory-of-collective-violence/ (accessed February 25, 2016).

Corning, P. A. 2013. "Systems Theory and the Role of Synergy in the Evolution of Living Systems." *Systems Research and Behavioral Science* 31, no. 2 (March/April): 181–196. http://onlinelibrary.wiley. com/doi/10.1002/sres.2191/abstract (accessed February 25, 2016).

Cyert, R., and J. G. March. 1963. *Behavioural Theory of the Firm.* Wiley-Blackwell.

Davies, Martin Brett. 2007. *Doing a Successful Research Project: Using Qualitative or Quantitative Methods.* Palgrave Macmillan. http:// www.palgrave.com/sociology/davies/docs/chapter1.pdf (accessed February 25, 2016).

Dawoody, Alexander R. 2016. *Eradicating Terrorism from the Middle East: Policy and Administrative Approaches.* Springer.

De Coning, Cedric, Helge Lurås, Niels Nagelhus Schia, and Ståle Ulriksen. 2009. *Norway's Whole-of-Government Approach and Its Engagement with Afghanistan.* Security in Practice 8, NUPI Report. http://www.oecd.org/dac/evaluation/dcdndep/47107380. pdf (accessed February 25, 2016).

Denis, Jean-Louis, Ann Langley, and Viviane Sergi. 2012. "Leadership in the Plural." *The Academy of Management Annals* 6, no. 1: 211–283.

Denscombes, Martyn. 1998. *The Good Research Guide.* Open University Press.

Denzin, N. K., and Y. S. Lincoln, eds. 2003. *Collecting and Interpreting Qualitative Materials.* New York: Sage. http://www.amazon.

com/Collecting-Interpreting-Qualitative-Materials-Norman/
dp/145225804X (accessed February 25, 2016).

Denzin, N. K., and Y. S. Lincoln, eds. 2005. *The SAGE Handbook of Qualitative Research.* Thousand Oaks: Sage. https://us.sagepub. com/en-us/nam/the-sage-handbook-of-qualitative-research/ book233401 (accessed February 25, 2016).

Dewey, John, Larry Hickman, and Thomas M. Alexander. 1998. *The Essential Dewey: Pragmatism, Education, Democracy.*

Dodd, Lorraine, and Anthony Alston. 2009. *Complex Adaptive and "Inquiring" Systems Theory for Contemporary Military Operations: A Multi-perspective Approach.* Centre for Applied Systems Studies, Cranfield University, Defence Academy of the United Kingdom, Shrivenham. Presented at the Cornwallis Group XIV: Analysis of Societal Conflict and Counter-insurgency. http://www.ismor.com/ cornwallis/cornwallis_2009/10-Dodd-Alston-CXIV.pdf (accessed February 25, 2016).

Drucker, P. F. 1954. *The Practice of Management.* New York: Harper and Row.

El-Batal, Kamal. 2012. *La Gouvernance Synergique: Une Stratégie de Développement Local: Cas de Municipalités Régionales de Comté Québécoises.* Thèse, Université du Québec à Trois-Rivières.

Emanuelli, Claude. 1975. "Legal Aspects of Aerial Terrorism: The Piecemeal vs. the Comprehensive Approach." *Journal of International Law and Economics* 10: 503–515. http://droitcivil.uottawa.ca/ en/people/emanuelli-claude and http://heinonline.org/HOL/ LandingPage?handle=hein.journals/gwilr10&div=29&id=&page= (accessed February 23, 2016).

Emerson, Kirk, Tina Nabatchi, and Stephen Balogh. 2011. "An Integrative Framework for Collaborative Governance." *Journal of Public Administration Research and Theory* 22. http://jpart.oxfordjournals. org/content/22/1/1.full.pdf+html (accessed December 27, 2016).

Eisenhardt, Kathleen M. 1989. "Building Theories from Case Study Research." *The Academy of Management Review* 14, no. 4 (October): 532–550. http://www.jstor.org/stable/258557 (accessed February 25, 2016).

Eisenhardt, Kathleen M., and Melissa E. Graebner. 2007. "Theory Building from Cases: Opportunities and Challenges." *Academy of Management Journal* 50, no. 1: 25–32. https://aom.org/uploadedFiles/Publications/AMJ/Eisenhart.Graebner.2007.pdf (accessed February 25, 2016).

Ensign, P. C. 1998. "Interrelationships and Horizontal Strategy to Achieve Synergy and Competitive Advantage in the Diversified Firm." *Management Decision* 36, no. 10: 657–668.

European Union. 2010. *Thematic Evaluation of the European Commission Support to Conflict Prevention and Peace Building—Concept Study.* http://ec.europa.eu/europeaid/how/evaluation/evaluation_reports/reports/2010/1277_vol1_en.pdf.

Fair, Christine, and Seth Jones. 2009. *Securing Afghanistan: Getting on Track.* US Institute of Peace. http://www.usip.org/sites/default/files/February2009.pdf (accessed February 25, 2016).

Favoreu, Christophe, David Carassus, and Christophe Maurel. 2016. "Strategic Management in the Public Sector: A Rational, Political or Collaborative Approach?" *International Review of Administrative Sciences* 82, no. 3 (September): 435–453.

Finland. 2008. *Comprehensive Approach: Trends, Challenges and Possibilities for Cooperation in Crisis Prevention and Management.* Seminar publication, Comprehensive Approach Research Team, Helsinki, June 17. http://www.defmin.fi/files/1316/Comprehensive_Approach_-_Trends_Challenges_and_Possibilities_for_Cooperation_in_Crisis_Prevention_and_Management.pdf (accessed February 25, 2016).

Flyvbjerg, Bent. 2006. "Five Misunderstandings about Case Study Research." *Qualitative Inquiry* 12, no. 2 (April): 219–245. http://flyvbjerg.plan. aau.dk/Publications2006/0604FIVEMISPUBL2006.pdf and http:// poli.haifa.ac.il/~levi/res/fivemisunder.pdf (accessed February 25, 2016).

Fitz-Gerald, Ann M. 2004. "Addressing the Security-Development Nexus: Implications for Joined-Up Government." *Policy Matters* 5, no. 5 (September): 1–24. http://irpp.org/wp-content/uploads/assets/ research/defence-diplomacy-and-development/new-research-article-2/pmvol5no5.pdf (accessed February 25, 2016).

Flynn, T. 2011. "Sandals and Robes to Business Suits and Gulf Streams." *Special Warfare Journal* (April 20): 5–6. http://smallwarsjournal. com/blog/journal/docs-temp/739-flynn.pdf (accessed February 25, 2016).

Frederickson, George. 1971. *Toward a New Public Administration*. The Minnowbrook Perspective, Chandler Publishing Company.

Gagnon, Yves-Chantal. 2010. *The Case-Study as Research Method—Practical Handbook*. Les Presses de l'Université du Québec. http:// www.puq.ca/media/produits/documents/445_D2455_FPR.pdf (accessed February 25, 2016).

George, Alexander L., and Andrew Bennett. 2005. *Case Studies and Theory Development in the Social Sciences*. London: MIT Press. http:// mitpress.mit.edu/books/chapters/0262572222pref1.pdf and http:// mitpress.mit.edu/books/chapters/0262572222chap1.pdf (accessed August 12, 2016).

Gerring, John. 2006. *Case Study Research: Principles and Practices*. New York, Cambridge University Press. http://www.amazon.com/Case-Study-Research-Principles-Practices/dp/0521676568 (accessed February 25, 2016).

Giddens, Anthony. 1984. *The Constitution of Society: Outline of the Theory of Structuration*. Cambridge: Polity Press.

Golden, James L., Goodwin F. Berquist, William E. Coleman, and J. Michael Sproule. 2003. *The Rhetoric of Western Thought*, 8th edition. http://www.amazon.com/Rhetoric-Western-Thought-James-Golden/dp/0787299677 (accessed February 25, 2016).

Greneen, Harold. 1997. *The Synergy Myth*. St Martin's Press. http://www.amazon.com/The-Synergy-Myth-Ailments-Business/dp/0312147244 (accessed February 25, 2016).

Guérard, Stéphane, Ann Langley, and David Seidl. 2013. "Rethinking the Concept of Performance in Strategy Research." *Management* 16, no. 5: 566–578.

Guillemette, F., and J. Luckerhoff. 2009. "L'Induction en Méthodologie de la Théorisation Enracinée." *Recherches Qualitatives* 28, no. 2: 4–21.

Haas, Peter M., and Ernst B. Haas. 2002. "Pragmatic Constructivism and the Study of International Institutions." *Millennium—Journal of International Studies* 31, no. 3 (July): 573–601. http://mil.sagepub.com/cgi/content/abstract/31/3/573 and polsci.umass.edu/uploads/sites/main/Files/haas_haas.pdf (accessed February 25, 2016).

Hamel, G., and C. K. Prahalad. 1990. "The Core Competence of the Corporation." *Harvard Business Review* 68, no. 3: 79–93.

Hammes, Thomas X. 2006. "Four Generations of Warfare." *The Sling and the Stone: On War in the 21st Century*. St. Paul, MN. http://www.amazon.com/The-Sling-Stone-Military-Classics/dp/0760324077 (accessed February 25, 2016).

Hildebrand, David .2003. "The Neopragmatist Turn." *Southwest Philosophy Review* 19, no. 1 (January). http://www.davidhildebrand.org/media/uploads/files/2010/10/07/hildebrand_neopragmatist.pdf (accessed February 25, 2016).

Hildebrand, David. 2005. "Pragmatism, Neopragmatism, and Public Administration." *Administration and Society* 37, no. 3: 345–359.

http://aas.sagepub.com/cgi/content/abstract/37/3/345 (accessed February 25, 2016).

Hildebrand, David. 2008. "Public Administration as Pragmatic, Democratic, and Objective." *Public Administration Review* 68, no. 2 (March–April): 222–229. http://www3.interscience.wiley.com/journal/119395714/abstract?CRETRY=1&SRETRY=0 (accessed February 25, 2016).

Hoadley, Christopher M. 2004. "Methodological Alignment in Design-Based Research." *Educational Psychologist* 39, no. 4: 203–212. http://citeseerx.ist.psu.edu/viewdoc/download?doi=10.1.1.120.624&rep=rep1&type=pdf (accessed August 12, 2016).

Hofstede, G. 1983. "The Cultural Relativity of Organizational Practices and Theories." *Journal of International Business Studies* 14, no. 2 (Autumn): 75–89.

Horn, Col Bernd. 2010. *No Lack of Courage: Operation Medusa; Afghanistan.* Dundurn. https://www.dundurn.com/books/No-Lack-Courage (accessed February 20, 2016).

Horn, Bernd, and Tony Balasevicius, eds. 2007. *Casting Light on the Shadows: Canadian Perspectives on Special Operations Forces.* Toronto: CDA Press and Dundurn Press. https://www.dundurn.com/books/Casting-Light-Shadows (accessed February 21, 2016).

Hostovsky, Charles. 2006. "The Paradox of the Rational Comprehensive Model of Planning: Tales from Waste Management Planning in Ontario, Canada." *Journal of Planning Education and Research* 25: 382–395. http://individual.utoronto.ca/hostovsky/hostovsky2006jper.pdf (accessed February 23, 2016).

Huxham, Chris. 2003. "Theorizing Collaboration Practice." *Public Management Review* 5, no. 3: 401–423.

Hwang, Karl. 2010. *New Thinking in Measuring (Comprehensive) National Power.* WISC Second Global International Studies Conference, University of Ljubljana, Slovenia, July 23–26. http://www.wiscnetwork.org/ljubljana2008/papers/WISC_2008-137.pdf (accessed February 23, 2016).

Isacoff, Jonathan B. 2002. "On the Historical Imagination of International Relations: The Case for a 'Deweyan Reconstruction.'" *Millennium— Journal of International Studies* 31, no. 3 (July): 603–626.

Jacobs, Garry, and N. Asokan. Undated. "Toward a Comprehensive Theory." http://www.motherservice.org/Essays/toward_a_comprehensive_theory.htm (accessed February 23, 2016).

Jesper, Rosenberg Hansen, and Ferlie Ewan. 2016. "Applying Strategic Management Theories in Public Sector Organizations: Developing a Typology." *Public Management Review* 18, no. 1: 1–19.

Johnson, Thomas H., and M. Chris Mason. 2008. "All Counterinsurgency Is Local." *The Atlantic*, no. 3. http://www.theatlantic.com/magazine/archive/2008/10/all-counterinsurgency-is-local/306965/ (accessed February 25, 2016).

Johnson, B., and A. J. Onwuegbuzie. 2004. "Mixed Methods Research: A Research Paradigm Whose Time Has Come." *Educational Researcher* 33, no. 7: 14–26. http://www.d.umn.edu/~kgilbert/ened5560-1/Readings/Mixed%20MethodsResearch.pdf (accessed February 25, 2016).

Joyner. 2013. "Was Afghanistan Worth It?" *The National Interest* (March 6). http://nationalinterest.org/commentary/was-afghanistan-worth-it-8182 (accessed February 25, 2016).

Kaplan, Fred. 2014. *The Insurgents: David Petraeus and the Plot to Change the American Way of War.* http://www.amazon.com/The-Insurgents-Petraeus-Change-American/dp/1451642652 (accessed February 25, 2016).

Kaplan, Robert S., and D. P. Norton. 1996. *The Balanced Scorecard: Translating Strategy into Action*. Boston: Harvard Business School Press.

Kaplan, Robert S., and D. P. Norton. 1996. "Using the Balanced Scorecard as a Strategic Management System." *Harvard Business Review* (January–February). https://cours.etsmtl.ca/mti820/public_docs/lectures/UsingTheBalancedScoreCardAsStrategicManagementSystem.pdf (accessed November 22, 2016).

Kaplan, Robert S., and D. P. Norton. 2008. *The Execution Premium: Linking Strategy to Operations*. Boston: Harvard Business School Press.

Krulak, Charles C. 1999. "The Strategic Corporal: Leadership in the Three Block War." *Marines Magazine* (January). http://www.au.af.mil/au/awc/awcgate/usmc/strategic_corporal.htm (accessed February 25, 2016).

Lalumière M. 2006. *L'Approche Intégré 3D pour les Interventions à l'Étranger: Un pas Vers le Succès?* Toronto: Canadian Forces College, National Security Studies Course. http://www.cfc.forces.gc.ca/259/260/269/lalumiere.pdf (accessed January 28, 2016).

Langley, Ann. 1988. "The Roles of Formal Strategic Planning." *Long Range Planning* 21, no. 3 (June): 40–51. Langley, Ann. 1997. "L'Étude des Processus Stratégique: Défis Conceptuels et Analytiques." *Management International* 2, no. 1: 37–50.

Liang, Qao, and Wang Xiangsui. 1999. *Unrestricted Warfare*—超限战. Chinese People's Liberation Army Publishing Press.

Lind, Willam S. 2004. "Understanding Fourth Generation War." *Antiwar* (January 15). http://www.antiwar.com/lind/?articleid=1702 (accessed February 25, 2016).

Lynn, Jr., L. E. 2006. *Public Management: Old and New*. Routledge.

Machiavelli, Niccolo. 1984. *The Prince.* Oxford University Press, 1984. http://www.constitution.org/mac/prince.pdf (accessed February 25, 2016).

MacNamara, Don W. 2005. "Haiti: An Opportunity for Canada to Apply the '3-D.'" *Policy Options* (February). http://policyoptions.irpp.org/fr/issues/canada-in-the-world/haiti-an-opportunity-for-canada-to-apply-the-3-d-concept (accessed February 25, 2016).

Mäkinen, Kalevi. 2005. *A Constructivist Investigation of Critical Security and Strategic Organisational Learning Issues: Towards a Theory of Security Development.* Finnish National Defence College, Strategic Security, Publication Series 2, Research Report No. 15. http://www.defmin.fi/files/361/3021_3011_Kalevi_MAkinen_Strategic_Security.pdf (accessed February 25, 2016).

Maxcy, S. J. 2003. "Pragmatic Threads in Mixed Methods Research in the Social Sciences: The Search for Multiple Modes of Inquiry and the End of the Philosophy of Formalism." In A. Tashakkori and C. Teddlie, eds., *Handbook of Mixed Methods in Social and Behavioral Research,* Thousand Oaks, 51–89.

Mazouz, Bachir, Anne Rousseau, and Pierre-André Hudon. 2016. "Strategic Management in Public Administrations: A Results-based Approach to Strategic Public Management." *International Review of Administrative Sciences* 82, no. 3: 411–417.

McGuire, M. 2006, "Collaborative Public Management: Assessing What We Know and How We Know It." *Public Administration Review* 66, no. 1: 33–43. http://wiki.douglasbastien.comimages/1/1c/Collaborative_Public_Management-_Assessing_What_We_Know_and_How_We_Know_It.pdf.

McGuire, Michael, Robert Agranoff, and Chris Silvia. 2011. "Putting the "Public" Back into Collaborative Public Management." Paper presented at the Public Management Research Conference, Syracuse, NY, June 1–4. https://www.maxwell.syr.edu/

uploadedFiles/conferences/pmrc/Files/McGuire_Putting%20
the%20Public%20Back%20into%20Collaborative%20Public%20
Management.pdf.

McNemey, Michael J. 2006. "Stabilization and Reconstruction in
Afghanistan: Are PRTs a Model or a Muddle?" *Parameters* 35, no.
4 (Winter): 32–46. http://strategicstudiesinstitute.army.mil/pubs/
parameters/Articles/05winter/mcnerney.pdf (accessed January 31,
2016).

McWilliams, Spencer A. 2016. "Cultivating Constructivism: Inspiring
Intuition and Promoting Process and Pragmatism." *Journal of
Constructivist Psychology* 29, no. 1: 1–29. http://www.tandfonline.
com/doi/pdf/10.1080/10720537.2014.980871.

Miettinen, R., D. Samra-Fredericks, and D. Yanow. 2009. "Re-turn to
Practice: An Introductory Essay." *Organisation Science* 30, no. 12
(December): 1309–1327.

Mills, C. Wright. 1959. "On Intellectual Craftsmanship." Appendix
to *The Sociological Imagination*, Oxford University Press,
195–226. https://archivingthecity.files.wordpress.com/2011/01/
mills_on_intellctual_craftmanship.pdf (accessed February 25,
2016).

Mills, J., A. Bonner, and K. Francis. 2006. "The Development of
Constructivist Grounded Theory." *International Journal of
Qualitative Methods* 5, no. 1. http://www.ualberta.ca/~iiqm/
backissues/5_1/pdf/mills.pdf (accessed August 12, 2016).

Miller, John H., and Scott E. Page. 2007. *Complex Adaptive Systems: An
Introduction to Computational Models of Social Life*. Princeton
University Press. http://press.princeton.edu/titles/8429.html
(accessed February 25, 2016).

Mintzberg, Henry. 1979. *The Structuring of Organizations*. Englewood
Cliffs, NJ: Prentice-Hall.

Mintzberg, Henry. 1994. "The Fall and Rise of Strategic Planning." *Harvard Business Review* (January–February). https://hbr.org/1994/01/the-fall-and-rise-of-strategic-planning (accessed November 22, 2016).

Mintzberg, Henry. 1994. *The Rise and Fall of Strategic Planning.* Free Press.

Mintzberg, H. 2005. "Chapter 17: Developing Theory about the Development of Theory." In K. G. Smith and M. A. Hitt, *Great Minds in Management: The Process of Theory Development,* Oxford: Oxford University Press, 355–372.

Misak, Cheryl. 2004. *The Cambridge Companion to Peirce.* http://assets.cambridge.org/97805215/79100/excerpt/9780521579100_excerpt.pdf (accessed February 25, 2016).

Morse, Janice M., Michael Barrett, Maria Mayan, Karin Olson, and Jude Spiers. 2002. "Verification Strategies for Establishing Reliability and Validity in Qualitative Research." *International Journal of Qualitative Methods* 1, no. 2. http://ejournals.library.ualberta.ca/index.php/IJQM/article/viewArticle/4603 (accessed August 12, 2016).

NATO. 2003. *Civil-Military Cooperation (CIMIC),* Doctrine, 57 pp.: http://www.nato.int/ims/docu/ajp-9.pdf (accessed 25 Feb 2016)

Natsios, Andrew S. (2006), "The Nine Principles of Reconstruction and Development", *Parameters,* Vol. 35, No. 3, Autumn 2005-2006, pp. 4-20: http://strategicstudiesinstitute.army.mil/pubs/parameters/articles/05autumn/natsios.pdf (accessed 2 Feb 2016).

NATO. 2011. *Implementation of the Comprehensive Approach Action Plan and the Lisbon Summit Decisions on the Comprehensive Approach.* Private Office of the Secretary-General, November 30, Document PO(2011)0529. https://jadl.act.nato.int/NATO/data/NATO/lm data/lm 12820/999/objects/il 0 file 35471/20111130 NU NATO-IS-NSG-PO(2011)0529-Action-Plan-Comprehensive-Approach.pdf (accessed February 25, 2016).

NATO. 2013. *NATO Operational Planning Process (OPP) and the Comprehensive Operations Planning Directive (COPD)*. Presentation, NATO School Oberammergau. https://semanticu. files.wordpress.com/2014/09/02-1100-1200-nato-operational-planning-process-copd.pdf (accessed January 26, 2016).

Neumann, Iver B. 2002. "Returning Practice to the Linguistic Turn: The Case of Diplomacy." *Millennium—Journal of International Studies* 31, no. 3 (July): 627–651.

Norway. 2006. "A Comprehensive Approach to Peace-building Is Necessary in Afghanistan." Ambassador Johan L. Løvald, Speech to UN Security Council, March 14. http://www.norway-un.org/Statements/2006-/SecurityCouncil/20060314 securitycouncil afghanistan/ and http://www.un.org/press/en/2007/sc9143.doc.htm (accessed February 25, 2016).

Overton, Willis F. 2007. "A Coherent Metatheory for Dynamic Systems: Relational Organicism-Contextualism." *Human Development*, no. 50:154–159. http://www.karger.com/Article/PDF/100944 (accessed February 25, 2016).

Owen, David. 2002. "Re-orienting International Relations: On Pragmatism, Pluralism and Practical Reasoning." *Millennium—Journal of International Studies* 31, no. 3 (July): 653–673. http://mil.sagepub. com/content/31/3/653.abstract (accessed February 25, 2016).

Oxford. 2016. "Theoretical Model." https://en.oxforddictionaries.com/definition/theoretical model.

Pareto, Charles. 1897. "The New Theories of Economics." *Journal of Political Economy* 5: 485–502. http://www.econlib.org/library/Enc/bios/Pareto.html (accessed January 19, 2017).

Pestoff, V. A., T. Brandsen, and B. Verschuare. 2012. *New Public Governance—Third Sector and Co-production*. New York: Routledge.

Peters, Thomas, and Robert Waterman. 1980. *In Search of Excellence.* Dunod.

Pitts, David, and Sergio Fernandez. 2009. "The State of Public Management Research: An Analysis of Scope and Methodology." *International Public Management Journal* 12, no. 4 (December): 399–420.

Poister, T. H. 2010. "The Future of Strategic Planning in the Public Sector: Linking Strategic Management and Performance." *Public Administration Review* 70, no. 1: S246–S254.

Poister, T. H., and G. D. Streib. 1999. "Strategic Management in the Public Sector: Concepts, Models, and Processes." *Public Productivity and Management Review* 22, no. 3 (March): 308–325.

Poister, Theodore H., David W. Pitts, and Lauren Hamilton Edwards. 2010. "Strategic Management Research in the Public Sector: A Review, Synthesis, and Future Directions." *The American Review of Public Administration* 40, no. 5 (September): 522–545.

Porter, Michael. 1999. *The Competitive Advantage of Nations.* Free Press.

Rand. 2003. *America's Role in Nation-Building: From Germany to Iraq.* James Dobbins, John G. McGinn, Keith Crane, Seth G. Jones, Rollie Lal, Andrew Rathmell, Rachel Swanger, and Agna Timilsina, eds. http://www.rand.org/content/dam/rand/pubs/ monograph_reports/MR1753/MR1753.ch8.pdf (accessed January 28, 2016).

Reichertz, Jo. 2010. "Abduction: The Logic of Discovery of Grounded Theory." *Forum Qualitative Science* 11, no. 1 (January). http://www. qualitative-research.net/index.php/fqs/article/view/1412/2902 (accessed January 11, 2016).

Rennie, Dennis L. 2000. "Grounded Theory Methodology as Methodical Hermeneutics: Reconciling Realism and Relativism." *Theory and Psychology* 10 (August 2000): 481–502. http://tap.sagepub.com/ content/10/4/481.short (accessed February 25, 2016).

Ritzer, G. 2001. *Explorations in Social Theory: From Metatheorizing to Rationalization*. London: Sage. https://us.sagepub.com/en-us/nam/explorations-in-social-theory/book210230 (accessed February 25, 2016).

Russell, Stuart, and Peter Norvig. 2003. *Artificial Intelligence: A Modern Approach*, 2nd edition. http://coltech.vnu.edu.vn/~sonpb/AI/AIMA.pdf (accessed February 20, 2016).

Sachs, Susan. 2011. "Newsmakers 2011: In Their Own Words." *The Globe and Mail* (December 24): A11.

Salar, Mehmet. 2010. *NATO's Operational Planning Process: The COPD— Comprehensive Operations Planning Directive*, NATO School, Unclassified. https://pfpconsortium.org/system/files/02%201100%20-%201200%20NATO%20Operational%20Planning%20Process%20%2526%20COPD.pdf

Sanders, Irene T. 2002. "To Fight Terror, We Can't Think Straight." *The Washington Post* (May 5); B2. http://www.complexsys.org/downloads/washpostarticle.pdf (accessed February 25, 2016).

Sanders, Irene T. 2003. *What Is Complexity?* Washington Center for Complexity and Public Policy. http://www.complexsys.org/pdf/what_is_complexity.pdf (accessed February 25, 2016).

Savoie, Donald J. 1995. "What Is Wrong with the New Public Management?" *Canadian Public Administration* 38, no. 1: 112–121. http://onlinelibrary.wiley.com/doi/10.1111/j.1754-7121.1995.tb01132.x/abstract (accessed February 25, 2016).

Segal, Hugh. 2003. "A Grand Strategy for a Small Country." *Canadian Military Journal* 4, no. 3 (Autumn): 3–6. http://www.journal.forces.gc.ca/vo4/no3/doc/policy-police-eng.pdf (accessed February 25, 2016).

Selznick, Philip. 1948. "Foundations of the Theory of Organization." *American Sociological Review* 13, no. 1: 25–35.

Sen, Amartya. 1999. *Development as Freedom*. Oxford University Press.

Senlis Council. 2008. *US Policy in Afghanistan—Senlis Council Recommendations*. Development Recommendations II and III, February. http://www.icosgroup.net/static/reports/us_policy_recommendations.pdf.

Shields, Patricia M. 1998. "Pragmatism as Philosophy of Science: A Tool for Public Administration Research." *Public Administration* 4: 195–226. https://digital.library.txstate.edu/bitstream/handle/10877/3954/fulltext.pdf?sequence=1 (February 25, 2016).

Shields, Patricia M. 2003. "The Community of Inquiry: Classical Pragmatism and Public administration." *Administration and Society* 35, no. 5: 510–538. http://aas.sagepub.com/content/35/5/510.abstract (accessed February 25, 2016).

Shields, Patricia M. 2004. "Classical Pragmatism: Engaging Practitioner Experience." *Administration and Society* 36, no. 3: 351–361. http://aas.sagepub.com/content/36/3/351.extract (accessed February 25, 2016).

Shields, Patricia M. 2005. "Classical Pragmatism Does Not Need an Upgrade: Lessons for Public Administration." *Administration and Society* 37, no. 4 : 504–518. http://aas.sagepub.com/content/37/4/504.short (accessed February 25, 2016).

Shields, Patricia M. 2008. "Rediscovering the Taproot: Is Classical Pragmatism the Route to Renew Public Administration?" *Public administration Review* 68, no. 2 (March–April): 205–221. http://onlinelibrary.wiley.com/doi/10.1111/j.1540-6210.2007.00856.x/abstract (accessed February 25, 2016).

Simon, Herbert. 1957. *Models of Man, Social and Rational: Mathematical Essays on Rational Human Behavior in a Social Setting*. New York: Wiley.

Simon, Herbert. 1991. "Bounded Rationality and Organizational Learning." *Organization Science* 2, no. 1: 125–134.

Simon, Geza, and Muzaffer Duzenli. 2010. "The Comprehensive Operations Planning Directive (COPD)." *NRDC-ITA Magazine*, no. 16: 16–19. http://www.nato.int/nrdc-it/magazine/2009/0914/0914g.pdf (accessed January 19, 2016).

Singh, Jasjit. 2011. "Revolution in Human Affairs: The Root of Societal Violence." *CADMUS* 1, no. 2 (April). http://www.google.ca/url?sa=t&rct=j&q=&esrc=s&source=web&cd=1&ved=0ahUKEwi1k6WzutnKAhVKsIMKHY-bDKEQFggbMAA&url=http%3A%2F%2Fwww.cadmusjournal.org%2Ffiles%2Fguidelines%2FCADMUS-template.dot&usg=AFQjCNEnnuC-waLjjVVvkNF_ekgfhyqFpQ&bvm=bv.113034660,d.cWw (accessed February 2, 2016).

Smith K. G., and M. A. Mitt. 2007. *Great Minds in Management: The Process of Theory Development.* Oxford University Press.

Steptoe-Warren, Gail, Douglas Howat and Ian Hume. 2011. "Strategic Thinking and Decision Making: Literature Review." *Journal of Strategy and Management* 4, no. 3 (August): 238–250. http://www.deepdyve.com/lp/emerald-publishing/strategic-thinking-and-decision-making-literature-review-krb42ajJhV (accessed August 12, 2016).

Stevens, Christopher D. 1998. "Realism and Kelly's Pragmatic Constructivism." *Journal of Constructivist Psychology* 11, no. 4: 283–308. http://www.tandfonline.com/doi/abs/10.1080/10720539808405226?journalCode=upcy20 (accessed February 25, 2016).

Strogatz, Steven H. 2004. *Sync: How Order Emerges From Chaos in the Universe, Nature, and Daily Life.* Hachette Books. http://www.amazon.fr/Sync-Order-Emerges-Universe-Nature/dp/0786887214 (accessed February 25, 2016).

Sullivan, Gordon R., and Michael V. Harper. 1997. *Hope Is Not a Method.* Crown Business. http://www.amazon.com/Hope-Not-Method-Gordon-Sullivan/dp/076790060X (accessed January 22, 2016).

Svara, James H. 2001. "The Myth of the Dichotomy: Complementarity of Politics and Administration in the Past and Future of Public Administration." *Public Administration Review* 61, no. 2 (March–April): 176–183. http://onlinelibrary.wiley.com/doi/10.1111/0033-3352.00020/abstract (accessed February 25, 2016).

Svara, James H. 2006. "Complexity in Political-Administrative Relations and the Limits of the Dichotomy Concept." *Administrative Theory and Praxis* 28, no. 1: 121–139. http://www.jstor.org/stable/25610781 (accessed February 25, 2016).

Tamas, Andy. 2009. *Warriors and Nation Builders: Development and the Military in Afghanistan.* Kingston: Canadian Defence Academy Press. http://www.tamas.com/sites/default/files/Warriors%20and%20Nation%20Builders.pdf (accessed February 25, 2016).

Tan, Jin. 2010. "Grounded Theory in Practice: Issues and Discussion for New Qualitative Researchers." *Journal of Documentation* 66, no. 1: 93–112.

Tashakkori, Abbas, and Charles Teddlie. 1998. *Mixed Methodology: Combining Qualitative and Quantitative Approaches.* Sage Handbook, June 24. https://us.sagepub.com/en-us/nam/mixed-methodology/book6245 (accessed March 19 2016).

Toffler, Alvin, and Heidi Toffler. 1995. *War and Anti-War: Making Sense of Today's Global Chaos.* Grand Central Publishing. Book Review by Scott London: http://www.scottlondon.com/reviews/toffler.html (accessed January 19, 2017).

Travers, Patrick. 2008. "Between Metaphor and Strategy: Canada's Integrated Approach to Peacebuilding in Afghanistan." *International Journal—Canadian International Council* 63, no. 3 (June). http://ca.vlex.com/vid/metaphor-peacebuilding-afghanistan-60436286

and http://www.taylorowen.com/Articles/2008%20Travers%20&%20Owen%20-%20Between%20Metaphor%20an%20Strategy.pdf (accessed February 25, 2016).

United Nations. 2004. *A More Secure World: Our Shared Responsibility.* Report of the High-level Panel on Threats, Challenges and Changes, UN 59th General Assembly, December 2. http://www.un.org/en/peacebuilding/pdf/historical/hlp_more_secure_world.pdf (accessed February 20, 2016).

United States. 2008. *Stability Operations—Field Manual 3-07.* http://usacac.army.mil/cac2/repository/FM307/FM3-07.pdf (accessed February 21, 2016).

United States. 2008. *Operation Enduring Freedom (OEF): Tactics, Techniques and Procedures.* Handbook No. 02-8. http://www.globalsecurity.org/military/library/report/call/call_02-8_toc.htm (accessed February 25, 2016).

United States. 2011. *Integrated Civil-Military Campaign Plan.* http://nsarchive.gwu.edu/NSAEBB/NSAEBB370/docs/Document%209.pdf (accessed February 25, 2016).

United States Agency for International Development. 2006. *Provincial Reconstruction Teams (PRTs) in Afghanistan: An Interagency Assessment.* http://pdf.usaid.gov/pdf_docs/PNADG252.pdf (accessed February 25, 2016).

Unterganschnigg, Kimberley. 2011. "Canada's Whole of Government Mission in Afghanistan—Lessons Learned." *Canadian Military Journal* 13, no. 2. http://www.journal.forces.gc.ca/vol13/no2/page8-eng.asp (accessed February 25, 2016).

Van Edig, Helmut. 2005. "Nation-building: A Strategy for Regional Stabilization and Conflict Prevention." Chapter 12 in *Nation-Building: A Key Concept for Peaceful Conflict*, Jochen Hippler, ed., 151–163. http://www.jstor.org/stable/j.ctt18fs3tv (accessed January 28, 2016).

Višňovský, Emil. 2009. "The Global Potential of Pragmatism." *Human Affairs* 19, no. 11: 1–9. http://www.degruyter.com/view/j/humaff.2009.19.issue-1/v10023-009-0014-z/v10023-009-0014-z.xml (accessed February 25, 2016).

Weber, Maximillian. 1922. *Economy and Society: An Outline of Interpretive Sociology*. Guenther Roth and Claus Wittich, eds. Berkeley: University of California Press.

Whetten, D. A. 2002. "Chapter 3—Modelling-as-Theorizing: A Systematic Methodology for Theory Development." In D. Partington, *Essential Skills for Management Research*, Thousand Oaks: Sage, 45–71. http://sk.sagepub.com/books/essential-skills-for-management-research/n3.xml (accessed February 25, 2016).

Yin, Robert K. 2003. *Applications of Case Study Research*, 2nd edition. Thousand Oaks: Sage. http://www.amazon.com/Applications-Research-Edition-Applied-Methods/dp/0761925511 (accessed February 25, 2016).

Yin, Robert K. 2009. *Case Study Research: Design and Methods*, 4th edition. Newbury Park: Sage Publications. http://www.sagepub.in/books/Book237921 (accessed February 25, 2016).

References Dataset

Agency Coordinating Body for Afghan Relief. 2007. *ACBAR's Guide to the ANDS: A Comprehensive Guide to the Afghanistan National Development Strategy*. http://www.acbar.org/ACBAR%20Publications/The%20Ands%20Guide%20(FINAL%20DRAFT%20FOR%20PRINTING).pdf.

Agency Coordinating Body for Afghan Relief. 2006. *Afghan National Development Strategy (ANDS)*. Progress Report of ANDS/PRSP, prepared for IMF/World Bank Board of Directors (2006–2007). http://www.diplomatie.gouv.fr/fr/IMG/pdf/ANDS Progress Report IMFWB - English 2 .pdf.

Allan, Jr., Nigel. 2003. "Rethinking Governance in Afghanistan." *Journal of International Affairs* 56, no. 1: 193–202. http://lda.ucdavis.edu/old_site/faculty/allan/2003reth.pdf.

Asia Foundation. 2010. *Afghanistan: A Survey of Afghan People.* The Asia Foundation. https://asiafoundation.org/resources/pdfs/Afghanistanin2010survey.pdf.

Babcock, Sandra. 2005. *Policy Challenges in the Development of Integrated Network Enabled Operations in Canada.* Directorate Defence Analysis—National Defence Headquarters. http://www.dodccrp.org/events/10th_ICCRTS/CD/papers/193.pdf.

Baker, Jon. 2007. *"Quick Impact Projects: Towards a "Whole of Government" Approach." Paterson Review* 8. Norman Paterson School of International Affairs, Carleton University. http://www.diplomatonline.com/pdf_files/npsia/2007-08/1_QIPs_Jon%20Baker_FINAL.pdf.

Banerjee, Nipa. 2009. *Development for Afghans: Missing Measurements and Missed Opportunities.* Center for International Policy Studies, Policy Brief No. 4, February 2009. http://www.socialsciences.uottawa.ca/cepi-cips/eng/documents/CIPS_PolicyBrief_Banerjee_Feb2009.pdf.

Baumann, Andrea Barbara. 2010. *The UK's Approach to Stabilisation: The Comprehensive Approach in Action?* International Security Programme: Rapporteur Report, Oxford University, June 7, 2010. http://www.chathamhouse.org.uk/files/16973_0610baumann.pdf.

Bird, Tim. 2007. *Implications and Conclusions: A Comprehensive Approach Panel: New Approaches to Military Intervention for the Era of "Fourth Generation" Warfare.* International Studies Association Conference, Chicago; King's College, London, at the Joint Services Command and Staff College, UK. http://www.allacademic.com//meta/p_mla_apa_research_citation/1/8/0/5/4/pages180548/p180548-1.php.

Bisogniero, Amb Claudio. 2008. "Assisting Afghanistan: The Importance of a Comprehensive Approach." Keynote address by the NATO Deputy Secretary General at the GLOBSEC Conference, Bratislava, Slovakia, January 17, 2008. http://www.nato.int/docu/speech/2008/s080117a.html.

Black, Christina Leanne. 2013. "State-building in Afghanistan: A Gendered Human Security Perspective." Master's thesis, University of British Columbia. https://open.library.ubc.ca/cIRcle/collections/ubctheses/24/items/1.0074266.

Bleuer, Christian. 2010. *Afghan Analyst Bibliography*, 5th edition. http://easterncampaign.files.wordpress.com/2009/02/afghanistanbibliography2010.pdf.

Boucher, Jean-Christophe. 2009. "Selling Afghanistan: A Discourse Analysis of Canada's Military Intervention." *International Journal* 64, no. 3 (September): 717–733. http://ijx.sagepub.com/content/64/3/717.full.pdf+html.

Brown, Stephen. 2008. "CIDA under the Gun." in Jean Daudelin and Daniel Schwanen, eds., *Canada Among Nations 2007: What Room for Manoeuvre?* Montreal: McGill-Queen's University Press, 2008: 172–207. http://www.cpsa-acsp.ca/papers-2008/Brown.pdf and http://aix1.uottawa.ca/~brown/pages/Stephen_Brown_CAN07.pdf.

Brown, Andrea L., ad Barbara D. Adams. 2010. *Exploring the JIMP Concept: Literature Review.* Defence Research and Development Center (DRDC) CR-2010-021, February. http://www.dtic.mil/dtic/tr/fulltext/u2/a523224.pdf.

Buchan, Gavin. 2010. "Breaking Down the Silos: Managing the Whole of Government Effort in Afghanistan." *Canadian Military Journal* 10, no. 4 (Autumn): 75–79. http://www.journal.forces.gc.ca/vol10/no4/doc/13-buchan-eng.pdf.

Burtch, Andrew. 2013. "At the Limit of Acceptable Risk: The Canadian Operational Mentor and Liaison Team, 2006–2011." *International*

Journal 68, no. 2 (June): 314–330. http://ijx.sagepub.com/content/68/2/274.full.

Canada. 2005. *OPP—Operational Planning Process, Canadian Forces, Manual.* http://dsp-psd.pwgsc.gc.ca/collection_2010/forces/D2-252-500-2008-eng.pdf.

Canada. 2007. *Canadian Troops in Afghanistan: Taking a Hard Look at a Hard Mission.* An Interim Report of the Standing Senate Committee on National Security and Defence, February. http://www.parl.gc.ca/content/sen/committee/391/defe/rep/repfeb07-e.pdf.

Canada. 2007. *Canada First Defence Strategy.* http://www.forces.gc.ca/assets/FORCES_Internet/docs/en/about/CFDS-SDCD-eng.pdf and http://www.forces.gc.ca/en/about/canada-first-defence-strategy.page.

Canada. 2008. *Canada in Afghanistan.* Report of the Standing Committee on Foreign Affairs and International Development, House of Commons. http://publications.gc.ca/collections/collection_2008/parl/XC11-392-1-1-03E.pdf.

Canada. 2012. *The State of Readiness of the Canadian Forces.* Report of the Standing Committee on National Defence, 41st Parliament, First Session, December. http://www.parl.gc.ca/content/hoc/Committee/411/NDDN/Reports/RP5881736/nddnrp05/nddnrp05-e.pdf.

Canadian Forces. 2007. *Whole of Government (Comprehensive) Operations.* Canadian Forces Leadership Institute. http://www.cda-acd.forces.gc.ca/cfli-ilfc/Currentprojectsandactivities-eng.asp.

Capstick, Mike. 2008. "The Civil-Military Effort in Afghanistan: A Strategic Perspective." In Calgary Papers in Military and Strategic Studies, Volume 3, 2008: *Civil-Military Coordination: Challenges and Opportunities in Afghanistan and Beyond*, Center for Military and Strategic Studies, John Ferris, Lara Olson, Hrach Gregoria, eds.: 35–52. http://www.jmss.org/jmss/index.php/jmss/article/download/35/33.

Chandrasekaran, Rajiv. 2011. *Is NATO's Counterinsurgency Strategy Working in Afghanistan? A Case Study*. Center for International Policy Studies, Policy Brief No. 11, March 2011. http://www.socialsciences.uottawa.ca/cepi-cips/eng/documents/CIPS_PolicyBrief_Chandrasekaran_Mar2011.pdf.

Chapnik, Adams. 2002. "Collaborative Independence: Canadian-American Relations in Afghanistan." *International Journal* 57, no. 3 (Summer): 341–348. https://www.questia.com/library/journal/1P3-587688821/collaborative-independence-canadian-american-relations.

Christensen, T., and P. Lægreid. 2006. *Whole-of-Government Approach— Regulation, Performance, and Public-Sector Reform*. Working Paper N°6, Centre for Social Studies. https://bora.uib.no/bitstream/handle/1956/1893/N06-06%20Christensen-L?sequence=1.

Christensen, T., and P. Lægreid. 2007. "The *Whole-of-Government* Approach to Public Sector Reform." *Public Administration Review* 67, no. 6 (Nov/Dec): 1060.

Conference of Defence Associations Institute. 2013. The Strategic Outlook for Canada, Vimy Paper No. 6. http://www.cdainstitute.ca/images/Vimy_Paper_6_Strategic_Outlook_2013_EN.pdf.

Conliffe, Francis. 2009. "Military Development and Diplomacy in Afghanistan." *Canadian Military Journal* 9, no. 4. http://www.journal.dnd.ca/vo9/no4/doc/15-conliffe-eng.pdf.

Conrad, John. 2009. *What the Thunder Said: Reflections of a Canadian Officer in Kandahar*. Dundurn Press. http://www.amazon.ca/What-Thunder-Said-Reflections-Canadian/dp/155488408X/ref=pd_sim_b_15 and http://books.google.ca/books?id=3VElVkyY0eIC&source=gbs_similarbooks.

Coombs, Howard G. 2012. *Canadian Whole of Government Operations.* Vimy Paper, Conference of Defence Association Institute. http://www.cdainstitute.ca/images/CDAInstitute_WOG_Dec2012.pdf.

Coombs, Howard G., and Roger Cotton. 2010. "Helping Afghans Secure a Brighter Future; Roshana Sabah." Conference of Defence Association Institute, *On Track Magazine* 15, no. 3: 16–18. http://cda-cdai.ca/cdai/uploads/cdai/2008/12/ontrack15n3.pdf.

Cooper, David. 2012. "The Comprehensive Approach: Establishing a NATO Governance Support Team." *Canadian Military Journal* 12, no. 2 (Spring): 72–76. http://www.journal.forces.gc.ca/vol12/no2/doc/Cooper%20En%20page%2072-76.pdf.

Cornish, S., and M. Glad. 2009. *Civil-military Relations: No Room for Humanitarianism in Comprehensive Approaches.* CARE International, the Norwegian Atlantic Committee. http://www.google.ca/url?sa=t&rct=j&q=&esrc=s&source=web&cd=1&cad=rja&uact=8&ved=0ahUKEwjn1b3JmuvJAhVKXh4KHSDRA6MQFggeMAA&url=http%3A%2F%2Fwww.alnap.org%2Fpool%2Ffiles%2Fnorwegian-atlantic-committee-glad-cornish-civil-military-relations-no-room-for-humanitarianism-in-comprehensive-approaches-2008.pdf&usg=AFQjCNGpZ0aZVEphlz_pXZzR0Bv7hVil3Q.

Crawshaw, Mike, ed. 2007. "A Comprehensive Approach to Modern Conflict: Afghanistan and Beyond." *Connections Quarterly Journal* (Summer). https://pfpconsortium.org/journal-article/comprehensive-approach-modern-conflict-afghanistan-and-beyond.

Daxner, Michael. 2009. "Afghanistan: Graveyard of Good Intent." *World Policy Journal* 26, no. 2 (Summer): 13–23. http://wpj.sagepub.com/content/26/2/13.full.pdf+html.

Day, Adam. 2007. "Task Force Afghanistan: The Battle for the People." *Legion Magazine.* http://www.legionmagazine.com/features/militarymatters/07-01.asp#1.

Deconing, Cedric, Helge Lurås, Niels Nagelhus Schia, and Ståle Ulriksen. 2009. *Norway's Whole-of-Government Approach and Its Engagement with Afghanistan.* Security in Practice 8, NUPI Report. http:// www.oecd.org/dac/evaluation/dcdndep/47107380.pdf.

DeConing, Cedric. 2008. *The United Nations and the Comprehensive Approach.* DIIS Report 2008, No. 14, October 2008. http://www. diis.dk/graphics/Publications/Reports%202008/Report-2008-14 The United Nations and the Comprehensive Approach.pdf and http://se2.isn.ch/serviceengine/Files/EINIRAS/94608/ ipublicationdocument singledocument/F3B88F08-AE6F-47B2-8A03-C05EFDED49E2/en/2008-14.pdf.

DeConing, Cedric. 2009. *Implications of a Comprehensive or Integrated Approach for Training in United Nations and African Union Peace Operations.* Norwegian Institute of International Affairs, October 2009. http://www.ciaonet.org/wps/ nupi/0018119/f 0018119 15534.pdf.

DeConing, Cedric, and Karsten Friis. 2011. "Coherence and Coordination: The Limits of the Comprehensive Approach." *Journal of International Peacekeeping*, no. 15: 259–261. http://english. nupi.no/content/download/89823/294001/version/5/file/ CdC KF+Coherence+and+Coordination+FINAL.pdf.

DeHoop Schaeffer, and Amb Jaap. 2009. *Afghanistan: We Can Do Better.* North Atlantic Treaty Organisation (NATO), Secretary General of NATO, January 18. http://www.washingtonpost.com/wp-dyn/ content/article/2009/01/16/AR2009011603717.html.

DeHoop Scheffer, and Amb Jaap. 2007. *Managing Global Security and Risk.* Speech by the NATO Secretary General at the IISS Annual Conference, Geneva, Switzerland, September 7, 2007. http://www. nato.int/docu/speech/2007/s070907a.html.

DeHoop Scheffer, and Amb Jaap. 2009. *Transatlantic Leadership for a New Era.* Speech by the NATO Secretary General at the Security and

Defence Agenda, Brussels, Belgium, January 26, 2009. http://www.nato.int/docu/speech/2009/s090126a.html.

Dodd, Lorraine, and Anthony Alston. 2009. *Complex Adaptive and "Inquiring" Systems Theory for Contemporary Military Operations: A Multi-perspective Approach.* Centre for Applied Systems Studies, Cranfield University, Defence Academy of the United Kingdom, Shrivenham, United Kingdom. Presented at the Cornwallis Group XIV: Analysis of Societal Conflict and Counter-insurgency. http://www.thecornwallisgroup.org/cornwallis_2009/10-Dodd-Alston-CXIV.pdf.

Dorronsoro, Gilles. 2009. *Running Out of Time: Arguments for a New Strategy in Afghanistan.* Center for International Policy Studies (CIPS), working paper, July 2009. http://www.socialsciences.uottawa.ca/cepi-cips/eng/documents/CIPS_WP_Dorronsoro_July2009.pdf.

Environics. 2007. *Focus Afghanistan: 2007 Survey of Afghans.* Kabul: Environics Research Group Ltd. http://www.environicsinstitute.org/uploads/institute-projects/environics%20-%202007%20survey%20of%20afghans%20-%20summary%20report-%20english.pdf.

Finland. 2008. *Comprehensive Approach Research Team, Seminar Publication on Comprehensive Approach: Trends, Challenges and Possibilities for Cooperation in Crisis Prevention and Management.* Seminar Publication, Kristiina Rintakosi and Mikko Autti, eds. Helsinki, June 17, 2008. http://www.defmin.fi/files/1316/Comprehensive_Approach_-_Trends_Challenges_and_Possibilities_for_Cooperation_in_Crisis_Prevention_and_Management.pdf.

Finney, Nathan. 2010. "A Culture of Inclusion: Defense, Diplomacy, and Development as a Modern American Foreign Policy." *Small Wars Journal* (September 26, 2010). http://smallwarsjournal.com/blog/journal/docs-temp/553-finney.pdf.

Fitzgerald, Ronald J. 2009. *The Canadian Strategic Advisory Team to Afghanistan: A Possible Model for a Multinational Whole of Government Approach to Defeating an Insurgency.* School of Advanced Military Studies—United States Army Command and General Staff College, Fort Leavenworth, Kansas. http://www.dtic.mil/cgi-bin/GetTRDoc?Location=U2&doc=GetTRDoc.pdf&AD=ADA505221.

Fitzsimmons, Dan. 2013. "Canada, the North Atlantic Treaty Organization (NATO), and the International Security Assistance Force (ISAF) in Afghanistan." *International Journal* 68: 305–313. http://ijx.sagepub.com/content/68/2/305.full.pdf+html.

Flavelle, Ryan. 2013. *The Patrol: Seven Days in the Life of a Canadian Soldier in Afghanistan.* Harper Collins Canada, Kindle Edition.

Forsberg, Carl. 2010. *Counterinsurgency in Kandahar: Evaluating the 2010 HAMKARI Campaign.* Institute for the Study of War (ISW), December 2010. http://www.understandingwar.org/files/Afghanistan%20Report%207_15Dec.pdf.

Fraser, Andrew. 2009. "Deadly Ends: Canada, NATO and Suicide as a Weapon of War in Modern Afghanistan." *Canadian Army Journal* 12, no. 2. http://www.army.forces.gc.ca/caj/documents/vol_12/iss_2/CAJ_Vol12.2_09_e.pdf.

French, Nils N. 2008. "Learning from the Seven Soviet Wars: Lessons for Canada in Afghanistan." *Canadian Army Journal* 10, no. 4: 36–47. http://www.army.forces.gc.ca/caj/documents/vol_10/iss_4/CAJ_vol10.4_06_e.pdf.

Furey, Erik. 2010. "A Comprehensive Approach to Local Engagement in Afghanistan, That may also Mitigate IEDs." *Small Wars Journal* (October 24, 2010). http://smallwarsjournal.com/blog/journal/docs-temp/585-furey.pdf.

Gabriëlse, Robbert. 2007. *A 3D Approach to Security and Development.* Director for Conflict Prevention, Ministry of Foreign Affairs, the Netherlands, Summer 2007: 67–73. http://www.regjeringen. no/upload/UD/Vedlegg/FN/Multidimensional%20and%20 Integrated/A%203D%20Approach%20to%20Security%20and%20 Development.pdf.

Gammer. 2011. *The Afghanistan Task Force and Prime Ministerial Leadership*, Canadian Political Science Association. http://www. cpsa-acsp.ca/papers-2011/Gammer.pdf.

Gizewski, Peter, Michael Rostek, and Andrew Leslie. 2008. *Comprehensive Operations: Moving to a JIMP-capable Land Force*. Vanguard. http://www.vanguardcanada.com/2008/08/01/ comprehensive-operations-moving-jimp-capable-land-force.

Glad, Marit, et al. 2009. *Knowledge on Fire: Attacks on Education in Afghanistan: Risks and Measures for Successful Mitigation*. CARE Canada. Http://Www.Humansecuritygateway.Com/Documents/ Care_Knowledgeonfire_Attacksoneducationinafghanistan.Pdf.

Grandia, Mirjam. 2009. "The 3D Approach and Counterinsurgency. A Mix of Defence, Diplomacy and Development: The Case of Uruzgan." Master's thesis, University of Leiden, the Netherlands. http://www. cimic-coe.org/download/3DandCOIN.pdf.

Gravning, Veronica. 2008. *Afghanistan: Rethinking NATO's Approach*. The International Security Network, Security Watch, August 21, 2008.: http://www.isn.ethz.ch/isn/Current-Affairs/ Security-Watch/Detail/?ots591=4888CAA0-B3DB-1461-98B9- E20E7B9C13D4&lng=en&id=90338.

Greenspon, Edward. 2010. *Open Canada: A Global Positioning Strategy for a Networked Age*. June. http://wp.opencanada.org/reports/ opencanada.

Hamzo, George, and Ernie Regehr. 2008. "Canadian Peace and Security Spending: An Update on the 5 Ds." *The Ploughshares Monitor* 29, no. 3 (Autumn). http://www.ploughshares.ca/libraries/monitor/ mons08b.pdf.

Havard. 2012. *Aid Explorer—The Structure and Dynamics of International Development Assistance.* http://aidxp.atlas.cid.harvard.edu/media/aidxp/pdf/aidexplorer.pdf.

Henry, B. 2008. *Whole of Government Approach Applied to Canadian National Security.* Canadian Forces College—Joint Command and Staff Program 34. http://www.cfc.forces.gc.ca/papers/csc/csc34/mds/henry.pdf.

Hochwart, Michael A. 2008. *The Provincial Reconstruction Teams in Afghanistan—A Model for Future Nation Building Operations.* School of Advanced Military Studies, United States Army Command and General Staff College, Fort Leavenworth, Kansas. https://jko.harmonieweb.org/coi/iwt/IWed/Document%20Library/The%20Provincial%20Reconstruction%20Teams%20in%20Afghanistan-%20A%20Model%20for%20Future%20Nation%20Building%20Operations.pdf.

Hoffmann, Hubertus. 2010. *Afghanistan and Pakistan: A New and Comprehensive NATO Double-Track Decision Is Needed.* World Security Network, January 22, 10. http://www.worldsecuritynetwork.com/showArticle3.cfm?article_id=18190&topicID=42.

Holland, Kenneth, and Christopher Kirkey, eds. 2010. "Special Issue Introduction: Canada's Commitment to Afghanistan." *American Review of Canadian Studies* 40, no. 2 (June): 167–304. http://www.tandfonline.com/toc/rarc20/40/2 and http://www.informaworld.com/smpp/title~db=all~content=g922521129.

Horn, Bernd. 2009. *Fortune Favours the Brave: Tales of Courage and Tenacity in Canadian Military History.* Dundurn and Canadian Defence Academy Press, Kindle Edition.

Horn, Col Bernd. 2010. *No Lack of Courage: Operation Medusa, Afghanistan.* Dundurn and Canadian Defence Academy Press, Kindle Edition.

Howard, Michael. 2009. *A Comprehensive Approach to Bring Security in Afghanistan: The Tactical Level.* SHAPE—NATO. http://www.mil. be/rdc/viewdoc.asp?LAN=fr&FILE=doc&ID=2238.

Hrychuk, Heather. 2009. "Combating the Security Development Nexus? Lessons Learned from Afghanistan." *International Journal* 64, no. 3 (September): 825–842. http:// internationaljournal.ca/internationaljournal.ca/Home/ Entries/2009/9/16 Volume 64 Issue 3 summer 2009New perspectives on Canadian security studies.html and http:// ijx.sagepub.com/content/64/3/825.full.pdf+html and http://ca.vlex. com/vid/combating-nexus-lessons-learned-afghanistan-69258137.

Hwang, Karl. 2008. *New Thinking in Measuring National Power.* WISC Second Global International Studies Conference, University of Ljubljana, Slovenia, July 2008.

Ince, Matthew. 2011. "Counterinsurgency: Falling Short of the *Comprehensive Approach* in Afghanistan." *Small Wars Journal* (January 23). http://smallwarsjournal.com/blog/journal/docs-temp/653-ince.pdf.

Jakobsen, Peter Viggo. 2008. *NATO's Comprehensive Approach to Crisis Response Operations: A Work in Slow Progress.* DIIS Report, October 15, 2008. http://subweb. diis.dk/graphics/Publications/Reports%202008/Report 2008-15 NATO Comprehensive Approach Crisis Response Operations.pdf.

Jakobsen, Peter Viggo. 2010. *Right Strategy, Wrong Place-Why NATO's Comprehensive Approach Will Fail in Afghanistan.* University of Copenhagen, Department of Political Science, UNISCI Discussion Papers, N° 22, January. http://www.ucm.es/info/unisci/revistas/ UNISCI%20DP%2022%20-%20JAKOBSEN.pdf and http://www. airforce.forces.gc.ca/CFAWC/Contemporary Studies/2010/2010-Jan/2010-08-11 Right Strategy Wrong Place-Why Natos Comprehensive Approach Will Fail In Afghanistan e.asp.

Jeffery, Mike. 2005. Speaking Notes, Conference of Defence Associations Institute—2005 Seminar: Panel on Defence, Diplomacy, and Development—Canada's Need for Global Reach, March 3. http://www.cda-cdai.ca/cdai/uploads/cdai/2009/04/2005jeffery.pdf.

Jenny, J. 2001. "Civil-military Cooperation in Complex Emergencies: Finding Ways to Make It Work." *European Security* 10, no. 2: 23–33. http://pdfserve.informaworld.com/758889_731515095_783178853.pdf.

Jockel, Joseph, and Joel Sokolsky. 2008. "Canada and the War in Afghanistan: NATO's Odd Man Out Steps Forward." *Journal of Transatlantic Studies* 6, no. 1: 100–115. http://www.informaworld.com/smpp/content~content=a791385344~db=all~jumptype=rss.

Johnson, Chris, and Jolyon Leslie. 2002. "Afghans Have Their Memories: A Reflection on the Recent Experience of Assistance in Afghanistan." *Third World Quarterly* 23, no. 5: 861–874. http://www.jstor.org/stable/pdfplus/3993392.pdf.

Jones, Ann Engelhardt. 2009. "Everything That Happens in Afghanistan Is Based on Lies or Illusion." *Truthout* (July 18, 2009). http://original.antiwar.com/engelhardt/2009/07/16/everything-that-happens-in-afghanistan-is-based-on-lies-or-illusions and http://www.commondreams.org/view/2009/07/16-5.

Jorgensen, M. P. 2008. *A Strategy for Effective Peace-Building: Canada's Whole-of-Government Approach in Afghanistan.* Canadian Forces College—National Security Studies Program 10, Toronto, May 20, 2008. http://www.cfc.forces.gc.ca/papers/nssc/nssc10/jorgensen.pdf and http://www.cmp-cpm.forces.gc.ca/dsa-dns/sa-ns/ab/sobv-vbos-eng.asp?maction=view&mbiographyid=192.

Kelly, Patrick. 2007. *Hole in Whole of Government: Examining the Merits of Applying Systemic Operational Design to Whole of Government Campaign Planning.* Canadian Forces College—Advanced Military Studies Program 10. http://www.cfc.forces.gc.ca/papers/amsc/amsc10/kelly.pdf.

Klassen, Jerome. 2009. "Afghanistan and the Social Sciences." review essay. *Socialist Studies* 5, no. 2 (Fall): 123–132. http://socialiststudies.com/article/download/23729/17613.

Klassen, Jerome Greg Albo. 2012. *Empire's Ally: Canada and the War in Afghanistan.* University of Toronto Press, Scholarly Publishing Division. http://www.amazon.ca/Empires-Ally-Canada-War-Afghanistan/dp/1442613041/ref=pd_sim_sbs_b_2/183-5092720-3954150.

Kobieracki, Adam. 2007. "A Comprehensive Approach to Modern Conflict: Afghanistan and Beyond." *Connections Quarterly Journal* (Summer). https://pfpconsortium.org/journal-article/comprehensive-approach-modern-conflict-afghanistan-and-beyond.

Kraemer, Peter Andrew. 2010. "Towards State Legitimacy in Afghanistan." *International Journal* 65, no. 3: 637–651. http://ijx.sagepub.com/content/65/3/637.full.pdf+html.

Labonté, Nathalie. 2014. "Contradictions of Counter-Insurgency and Peacebuilding: The Canadian Stabilization Efforts in Kandahar." Chapter 7 of *Potentia*, 104–110: http://www.google.ca/url?sa=t&rct=j&q=&esrc=s&source=web&cd=2&cad=rja&uact=8&ved=0ahUKEwiVlZyHnf3JAhWJo4MKHXuZAGQQFggdMAE&url=http%3A%2F%2Fmercury.ethz.ch%2Fserviceengine%2FFiles%2FISN%2F185449%2Fichaptersection_singledocument%2Fcc718503-1fc6-4670-8ef7-832b6a45a5a9%2Fen%2FChapter%2B7.pdf&usg=AFQjCNFmqlSRqoEPoBFSqQXUWentovL6Gw.

Lacombe, Sid. 2007. "Bring the Troops Home Now: Why a Military Mission Will Not Bring Peace to Afghanistan." *Canadian Peace Alliance* (February 16, 2007). http://www.acp-cpa.ca/en/BringTheTroopsHomeNow.pdf.

Leprince, Caroline. 2013. "The Canadian-led Kandahar Provincial Reconstruction Team: A Success Story?" *International Journal*

68 (June): 359–377. http://ijx.sagepub.com/content/68/2/359.full. pdf+html.

Lerhe, Eric. 2006. *Is the 3D Construct at Work in Kandahar or Are We Kidding Ourselves?* Dispatch, Canadian Defence and Foreign Affairs Institute Newsletter, Fall 2006. http://www.cdfai.org/ newsletters/newsletterfall2006.htm#Article: Is the 3-D Construct at work in Kandahar or are we kidding ourselves.

Leslie, Andrew, Peter Gizewski, and Michael Rostek. 2009. "Developing a Comprehensive Approach to Canadian Forces Operations." *Canadian Military Journal* 9, no. 1: 11–20. http://www.journal. dnd.ca/vo9/no1/doc/04-leslie-eng.pdf.

Levasseur, Jean-Pascal. 2009. *Approche Compréhensive du Canada en Afghanistan: "As Good as It Gets."* Canadian Forces College—Joint Command and Staff Program 34. http://www.cfc.forces.gc.ca/ papers/csc/csc35/mds/levasseur.pdf.

Lindley-French, Julian. 2010. "Operationalizing the Comprehensive Approach." *The Atltantic Council*, Strategic Advisors Group. http:// www.atlanticcouncil.org/images/files/publication_pdfs/403/ ComprehensiveApproach_SAGIssueBrief.PDF.

Lipohar, P. J. 2007. *Whole of Government Support to Afghanistan: Is Defence on the Right Track?* Canadian Forces College—Joint Command and Staff Program 34. http://www.cfc.forces.gc.ca/papers/csc/ csc34/exnh/lipohar.pdf.

Lombardi, Ben. 2009. *Talking to the Enemy: Some Thoughts on What That Means.* Defence Research and Development Center. http://pubs. drdc.gc.ca/PDFS/unc88/p531831.pdf.

MacDonald, George. 2009. *The Canada First Defence Strategy— One Year Later.* Canadian Defence and Foreign Affairs Institute. https://d3n8a8pro7vhmx.cloudfront.net/ cdfai/pages/41/attachments/original/1413661707/

The Canada First Defence Strategy - One Year Later. pdf?1413661707.

Maloney, Sean M. 2007. *Enduring the Freedom: A Rogue Historian in Afghanistan.* Potomac Books Inc. http://www.amazon. ca/Enduring-Freedom-Rogue-Historian-Afghanistan/ dp/1597970492/ref=pd_sim_b_2.

Maloney, Sean M. 2011. *Fighting for Afghanistan: A Rogue Historian at War.* US Naval Institute Press. http://www.amazon.ca/ Fighting-Afghanistan-Rogue-Historian-War/dp/1591145090/ ref=pd_sim_b_6.

Maloney, Sean M. 2009. *Confronting the Chaos: A Rogue Military Historian Returns to Afghanistan.* US Naval Institute Press. http://www. amazon.ca/Confronting-Chaos-Military-Historian-Afghanistan/ dp/1591145082/ref=pd_sim_b_5.

Manley, John. 2010. "Canada's New Role in Afghanistan: Leading Rather Than Following Public Opinion." Institute for Research on Public Policy—Policy Options, December 2010. http://www.irpp.org/po/ archive/dec10/manley.pdf.

Mann, Sloan. 2008. "Taking Interagency Stability Operations to a New Level: The Integration of Special Operation Forces and USAID in Afghanistan." *Small Wars Journal.* http://smallwarsjournal.com/ documents/79-mann.pdf.

Mansager, Tucker B. 2006. "Interagency Lessons Learned in Afghanistan." *Joint Forces Quarterly*, no. 40 (1st Quarter): 80–84. http://www.dtic.mil/cgi-bin/GetTRDoc?AD=ADA521754& Location=U2&doc=GetTRDoc.pdf.

Manwaring, Max G. 2006. *Defense, Development, and Diplomacy (3D): Canadian and US Military Perspectives.* Colloquium Brief, Strategic Studies Institute—US Army War College, Queens University, and the Canadian Land Forces Doctrine and Training

System held in Kingston, Ontario, Canada, June 21–23. www. strategicstudiesinstitute.army.mil/pdffiles/pub732.pdf.

Massie, Justin. 2009. "Making Sense of Canada's 'Irrational' International Security Policy: A Tale of Three Strategic Cultures." *International Journal* 64, no. 3 (September): 625–645. http://ijx.sagepub.com/content/64/3/625.full.pdf+html.

Massie, Justin. 2013. "Canada's War for Prestige in Afghanistan: A Realist Paradox?" *International Journal* 68, no. 2 (June): 274–288. http://ijx.sagepub.com/content/68/2/274.full.

McChrystal, Stanley, and Amb Eikenberry. 2009. *United States Government Integrated Civilian–Military Campaign Plan for Support to Afghanistan.* August 10, 2009. http://info.publicintelligence.net/0908eikenberryandmcchrystal.pdf.

McCutcheon, Richard, and John Derksen. 2007. "Canada's Role in Afghanistan: Submissions to the Manley Panel." *Peace Research— The Canadian Journal of Peace and Conflict Studies* 39, no. 1–2: 94–149. http://www.peaceresearch.ca/pdf/39/McCutcheon.pdf.

McDonough, David S. 2007. "The Paradox of Afghanistan: Stability Operations and the Renewal of Canada's International Security Policy?" *International Journal* 62, no. 3 (Summer): 620–642. http://internationaljournal.ca/internationaljournal.ca/Home/Entries/2007/8/27 Volume 62 Issue 3 Summer 2007 What kind of security Afghanistan and beyond.html.

McDonough, David S. 2012. "Afghanistan and Renewing Canadian Leadership: Panacea or Hubris?" *International Journal* 64, no. 3 (September): 647–665/ http://ijx.sagepub.com/content/64/3/647.full.pdf+html.

McIllroy, Rob. 2008. "The Strategic Think Tank—Restructuring the Canadian Forces College to Achieve an Integrated Culture and to Provide an Enhanced Strategic Planning Resource." *Canadian*

Military Journal (Winter 2007–2008). http://www.journal.dnd.ca/vo8/no4/doc/mcilroy-eng.pdf.

MacNamara, Don. 2010. "'Comprehensive' National Security." Canadian Association of Defence Institute. *OnTrack Magazine*, republished in *Frontline Magazine*, Defence Issue 6, 2010. http://www.frontline-canada.com/downloads/10-6_Security_Macnamara.pdf.

McNerney, Michael J. 2005. "Stabilization and Reconstruction in Afghanistan: Are PRTs a Model or a Muddle?" *Parameters* (Winter 2005–2006): 32–46. http://humanitariantraining.org/McNerney.doc.

Moens, Alexander. 2008. "Afghanistan and the Revolution in Canadian Foreign Policy." *International Journal* 63, no. 1 (September): 569–586. http://ijx.sagepub.com/content/63/3/569.full.pdf+html.

Neumann, Ronald. 2009. *Afghanistan: Looking Forward*. Center for International Policy Studies, working paper, June 2009. http://www.socialsciences.uottawa.ca/cepi-cips/eng/documents/CIPS_WP_Neumann_June2009.pdf.

North Atlantic Treaty Organisation. 2008. *From Comprehensive Approach to Comprehensive Capability*. Friis Arne Petersen and Hans Binnendijk, NATO Review. http://www.nato.int/docu/review/2008/03/ART7/EN/index.htm.

North Atlantic Treaty Organisation. 2010. *Comprehensive Political Guidance*. http://www.nato.int/cps/en/natohq/topics_49176.htm.

Olson, Lara, Hrach Gregorian. 2007. "Civil-Military Coordination: Challenges and Opportunities in Afghanistan and Beyond." *Journal of Military and Strategic Studies* 10, no. 1 (Fall). www.jmss.org/jmss/index.php/jmss/article/download/34/32.

O'Reilly, Neil. 2010. *Canadian Forces Civil-military Cooperation (CIMIC) Operations—1990–2010: An Annotated Bibliography*. DRDC–CORA CR 2010-275, December. http://www.google.ca/

url?sa=t&rct=j&q=&esrc=s&source=web&cd=
1&ved=0CCAQFjAA&url=http%3A%2F%2Fwww.dtic.
mil%2Fcgi-bin%2FGetTRDoc%3FAD%3DADA
535091&ei=Ch5mVb fK4mKsAXh0I
HICQ&usg=AFQjCNFCVWYZ6W7mKQT1FclTXS
FulZPQug&sig2=vPpeGpjm3 HovzzSJAON-Q.

Pamplin, Richard A. 2007. *Making Whole-of-Government Work: Identifying Effective Governance in Canada's Approach to Foreign Policy Implementation.* Canadian Forces College—Joint Command and Staff Program 34. http://www.cfc.forces.gc.ca/papers/csc/csc34/mds/pamplin.pdf.

Paris, Roland. 2009. *Scaling Back Expectations in Afghanistan.* Center for International Policy Studies, Policy Brief No. 2, February 2009. http://www.socialsciences.uottawa.ca/cepi-cips/eng/documents/CIPS PolicyBrief Paris Feb2009 001.pdf.

Paris, Roland. 2013. "Afghanistan: What Went Wrong?" *Perspectives on Politics* 11, no. 2: 538–548. http://journals.cambridge.org/action/displayAbstract?fromPage=online&aid=8923724&fileId=S1537592713000911.

Patterson, Kevin, and Jane Warren. 2010. *Outside the Wire: The War in Afghanistan in the Words of Its Participants.* Random House of Canada, Kindle Edition. http://www.amazon.ca/Outside-Wire-Afghanistan-Words-Participants/dp/0307356310.

Patrick, Stewart, and Kaysie Brown. 2007. *Greater Than the Sum of Its Parts? Assessing "Whole of Government" Approaches to Fragile States.* International Peace Academy. www.cgdev.org/files/13935 file Fragile States.pdf.

Perry, David. 2009. "The Privatization of the Canadian Military: Afghanistan and Beyond." *International Journal* 64, no. 3 (September_: 687–702. http://ijx.sagepub.com/content/64/3/687.full.pdf+html.

Perry, David. 2008. "Canada's Seven Billion Dollar War." *International Journal* 63, no. 3: 703–725. http://ijx.sagepub.com/content/63/3/703. full.pdf+html.

Petersen, Friis Arne, and Hans Binnendijk. 2007. *The Comprehensive Approach Initiative: Future Options for NATO.* Defense Horizons, Center for Technology and National Security Policy—National Defense University, September 2007, no. 58. http://www.dtic.mil/cgi-bin/ GetTRDoc?AD=ADA473211&Location=U2&doc=GetTRDoc.pdf.

Petersen, Friis Arne, and Hans Binnendijk. 2008. *From Comprehensive Approach to Comprehensive Capability.* NATO Review, March 2008. http://www.nato.int/docu/review/2008/03/ART7/EN/ index.htm.

Pigott, Peter. 2007. *Canada in Afghanistan: The War So Far.* Dundurn and Canadian Defence Academy Press. https://www.dundurn.com/ books/Canada-Afghanistan.

Regehr, Ernie. 2007. "Canada Is Ignoring Its Own Advice." *Inroads Journal,* no. 20. http://www.inroadsjournal.ca/archives/inroads 20/ Inroads 20 afghanistan nepal.pdf.

Riphenburg, Carol J. 2006. "Afghanistan: Out of the Globalisation Mainstream?" *Third World Quarterly* 27, no. 3: 507–524. http:// www.jstor.org/stable/pdfplus/4017767.pdf?acceptTC=true.

Ritchie, Robert T. 2010. *Stabilization in the Afghanistan Counter-Insurgency: Assessing the Comprehensive Approach in Kandahar Province.* Canadian Forces College—Joint Command and Staff Programme 36, February 26, 2010. http://www.cfc.forces.gc.ca/papers/csc/ csc36/mds/Ritchie.pdf.

Ritchie, Holly. 2006. *Aid Effectiveness in Afghanistan at a Crossroads.* ABCAR Briefing Paper. www.reliefweb.int/library/document/2006.acbar- afg-oinov.pdf.

Rotmann, Phillip. 2010. *Built on Shaky Grounds: NATO Comprehensive Approach.* NATO Defence College, Research Paper No. 63, December. http://www.ndc.nato.int/download/downloads.php?icode=231.

Runger, Peter. 2009. "The Provincial Reconstruction Teams in Afghanistan: Role Model for Civil-military Relations?" Bonn International Center for Conversion, Occasional Paper IV, October 2009. http://www.bicc.de/uploads/pdf/publications/papers/occ_paper_04/occasional_paper_IV_11_09.pdf.

Schetter, von Conrad. 2002. *"The 'Bazaar Economy' of Afghanistan: A Comprehensive Approach." Südasien-Informationen,* no. 3 (February 2004). http://archiv.ub.uni-heidelberg.de/savifadok/volltexte/2007/68/pdf/nr3_bazaar.pdf.

Schirch, Lisa. 2010. *The Civil Society-Military Relationship in Afghanistan.* United States Institute of Peace, Peace Brief, September 24, 2010. http://www.usip.org/files/resources/PB%2056%20The%20Civil%20Society-Military%20Relationship%20in%20Afghanistan.pdf.

Schnaubelt, Christopher M. 2011. *Towards a Comprehensive Approach: Integrating Civilian and Military Concepts of Strategy.* NATO Defence College—Research Division Forum Paper No. 15, Rome, March 2011. http://www.operationspaix.net/IMG/pdf/OTAN_Towards_a_Comprehensive_Approach-Integrating_Civilian_and_Military_Concepts_of_Strategy_march_2011_.pdf.

Sedra, Mark. 2012. "Diagnosing the Failings of Security Sector Reform in Afghanistan." *Afghanistan in the Balance: Counterinsurgency, Comprehensive Approach, and Political Order,* no. 169 (July). http://mqup.mcgill.ca/book.php?bookid=2834.

Senlis Council. 2007. *Poppy for Medicine; Afghanistan Case Study.* London. http://www.poppyformedicine.net/documents/Poppy_for_medicine_in_Afghanistan.

Shae, Jamie. 2009. *NATO Strategy—Building the Comprehensive Approach in Afghanistan: Now You See Me?* IDEAS Strategic Update 001, March 2009. http://www2.lse.ac.uk/IDEAS/publications/reports/pdf/SU001/shea.pdf.

Shahrani, M. Nazif. 2009. *Afghanistan's Alternatives for Peace, Governance and Development: Transforming Subjects to Citizens and Rulers to Civil Servants.* Center for International Policy Studies (CIPS), working paper, August 2009. http://www.socialsciences.uottawa.ca/cepi-cips/eng/documents/CIPS_WP_Shahrani_August2009.pdf.

Smith, Graeme. 2013. *The Dogs Are Eating Them Now: Our War in Afghanistan.* Knopf Canada. http://www.amazon.ca/The-Dogs-Are-Eating-Them/dp/0307397807.

Smith, Gordon. 2007. *Canada in Afghanistan: Is It Working?* Prepared for the Canadian Defense and Foreign Affairs Institute. http://www.cdfai.org/PDF/Canada%20in%20Afghanistan%20Is%20it%20Working.pdf.

Smith-Windsor, Brooke. 2008. *Hasten Slowly: NATO's Effects Based and Comprehensive Approach to Operations.* NATO Defence College—Research Paper, Rome, No. 38, July 2008. http://se2.isn.ch/serviceengine/Files/ESDP/92060/ipublicationdocument_singledocument/E3C6789A-1821-4029-B200-56176A1FF520/en/rp_38en.pdf.

Staples, Steven, and Bill Robinson. 2005. "It's Never Enough: Canada's Alarming Rise in Military Spending." *The Polaris Institute* (October 25, 2005): 3. http://www.ipb.org/Canada's%20Alarming%20Rise%20in%20Military%20Spending.pdf.

Stavridis, James G. 2011. "The Comprehensive Approach in Afghanistan." *PRISM Journal* 2, no. 2. http://www.ndu.edu/press/lib/images/prism2-2/Prism_65-76_Stavridis.pdf.

St.-Louis, Michel-Henri. 2009. "The Strategic Advisory Team in Afghanistan—Part of the Canadian Comprehensive Approach to

Stability Operations." *Canadian Military Journal* 9, no. 3. http://www.journal.dnd.ca/vo9/no3/doc/09-stlouis-eng.pdf.

Tchantouridzé, Lasha. 2013. "Counterinsurgency in Afghanistan: Comparing Canadian and Soviet Efforts." *International Journal* 68: 331–345. http://ijx.sagepub.com/content/68/2/331.full.pdf+html.

Temple, T. J. 2004. *Conflict Resolution: The Need For a Coherent and Comprehensive Approach.* Canadian Forces College, Advanced Military Studies Course 7. http://www.cfc.forces.gc.ca/259/260/267/temple.pdf.

Thomson, M. H., C. D. T. Hall, and B. A. Adams. 2010. *Canadian Forces Education and Training for Interagency Operational Contexts.* DRDC Toronto CR 2010-013. http://pubs.drdc.gc.ca/PDFS/unc00/p533160_A1b.pdf.

Thomson, M. H., Barbara D. Adams, Courtney D. Hall, and Craig Flear. 2010. *Collaboration within the JIMP (Joint, Interagency, Multinational, Public) Environment.* DRDC Toronto CR 2010-136, August. http://cradpdf.drdc-rddc.gc.ca/PDFS/unc104/p534320_A1b.pdf.

Thruelsen, Peter Dahl. 2008. *"Counterinsurgency and a Comprehensive Approach: Helmand Province, Afghanistan."* Small Wars Journal. http://smallwarsjournal.com/mag/docs-temp/100-thruelsen.pdf.

Travers, Patrick, and Taylor Owen. 2008. "Canada in Afghanistan: Between Metaphor and Strategy." *The International Journal:* 682–702. http://www.taylorowen.com/Articles/2008%20Travers%20&%20Owen%20-%20Between%20Metaphor%20an%20Strategy.pdf.

Tvinnereim, Frode. 2010. *Provincial Reconstruction Teams and Counter-Insurgency Warfare Theory: A Perfect Match?* Joint Command and Staff College 36—Canadian Forces College, April 19, 2010. http://www.cfc.forces.gc.ca/papers/csc/csc36/mds/Tvinnereim.pdf.

UNDOC. 2011. *UN Drugs Chief Urges Comprehensive, Proactive and Humane Approach to Supply and Demand in Drug Control.* United

Nations Office on Drugs and Crimes, March 21, 2011. http://www.unodc.org/unodc/en/press/releases/2011/March/un-drugs-chief-urges-comprehensive-proactive-and-humane-approach-to-supply-and-demand-in-drug-control.html.

United Kingdom. 2010. *The Comprehensive Approach: The Point of War Is Not Just to Win but to Make a Better Peace.* House of Commons—Parliament Defence Committee. http://www.publications.parliament.uk/pa/cm200910/cmselect/cmdfence/224/224.pdf.

United Nations. 2004. "A More Secure World: Our Shared Responsibility." Report of the High-level Panel on Threats, Challenges and Changes, UN 59th General Assembly, Dec ember 2. http://www.un.org/en/peacebuilding/pdf/historical/hlp more secure world.pdf (accessed February 20, 2016).

United Nations Assistance Mission in Afghanistan. 2006. *The Afghanistan Compact.* London. http://unama.unmissions.org/Portals/UNAMA/Documents/AfghanistanCompact-English.pdf.

United Nations Development Program. 2001. *The Integration of Biodiversity into National Environmental Assessment Procedures.* Prepared by: Abdul Wajid Adil, the Society for Afghanistan Viable Environment (SAVE), September 2001. http://www.cbd.int/impact/case-studies/cs-impact-ibneap-af-en.pdf.

United Nations Security Council. 2001. "Comprehensive Approach Needed to End Afghanistan Conflict." Speech by Secretary General Kofi Annan, August 22, 2001. http://www.un.org/apps/news/storyAr.asp?NewsID=1165&Cr=Afghanistan&Cr1http://books.google.ca/books?id=i2ERY7ymj0kC&printsec=frontcover&dq=comprehensive+approach&source=bl&ots=bszIceqYaM&sig=ufQC4r6QxerManPJWc9emLwwD9U&hl=en&ei=dqM-TZyjIsH2gAeayNzdCA&sa=X&oi=book result&ct=result&resnum=10&ved=0CEkQ6AEwCTge - v=onepage&q&f=false.

United States. 2013. *Interorganizational Coordination During Joint Operations*, US Joint Publication 3-08. http://www.dtic.mil/ doctrine/new_pubs/jp3_08.pdf.

Vandahl, E. S. 2007. *No More Leading from Behind: Implementing a JIMP Strategy to Compliment the Canadian Whole of Government Initiative*. Canadian Forces College—Joint Command and Staff Program 33. http://www.cfc.forces.gc.ca/papers/csc/csc33/exnh/ vandahl.pdf.

Veilleux-Lepage, Yannick. 2013. "Implications of the Sunk Cost Effect and Regional Proximity for Public Support for Canada's Mission in Kandahar." *International Journal* 68: 346–358. http://ijx.sagepub. com/content/68/2/346.full.pdf+html.

Vincent, Etienne, Philip Eles, and Boris Vasiliez. 2007. *Opinion Polling in Support of Counterinsurgency*. Canadian Expeditionary Forces Command Operational Research Team, Centre for Operational Research and Analysis Defence Research and Development Canada, Ottawa, Ontario. http://www.thecornwallisgroup.org/ cornwallis_2009/7-Vincent_etal-CXIV.pdf.

Waddell, Christopher. 2009. "Inside the Wire: The Limited but Important Story Told by Embedded Journalism." *Canadian Literary Review*. http://reviewcanada.ca/reviews/2009/04/01/inside-the-wire.

Ward, Christopher, David Mansfield, Peter Oldham, and William Byrd. 2008. *Afghanistan: Economic Incentives and Development Initiatives to Reduce Opium Production*. The World Bank and the Department for International Development, February 2008. http://siteresources.worldbank.org/SOUTHASIAEXT/ Resources/223546-1202156192201/4638255-1202156207051/ fullreportAfghanistanOpiumIncentives.pdf.

Watson, John. 2005. *The Three Legged Stool*. Conference of Defence Associations Institute—2005 Seminar: Panel on Defence, Diplomacy, and Development, March 3. http://www.cda-cdai.ca/ cdai/uploads/cdai/2009/04/2005watson.pdf.

Welle, Joshua W. 2010. "Civil-Military Integration in Afghanistan: Creating Unity of Command." *Joint Forces Quarterly,* no. 56 (1st Quarter): 54–59. http://ndupress.ndu.edu/portals/68/Documents/jfq/jfq-56.pdf.

Williams, M. J. 2011. "Empire Lite Revisited: NATO, the Comprehensive Approach and State-building in Afghanistan." *International Peacekeeping* 18, no. 1: 64–78. http://www.informaworld.com/smpp/content~db=all~content=a932809680.

Wittkowsky, Andreas, and Ulrich Wittkampf. 2013. *Pioneering the Comprehensive Approach: How Germany's Partners Do It.* Policy briefing, Working Group on the Comprehensive Approach, ZIF. http://www.zif-berlin.org/fileadmin/uploads/analyse/dokumente/veroeffentlichungen/ZIF Policy Briefing Andreas Wittkowsky Ulrich Wittkampf Jan 2013.pdf.

Woodcock, Alexander E. R., Anders Christensson, and John Dockery. 2008. *A Systemic Approach Is Needed for Fully-Integrated Civilian-Military Policy- and Decision-Making.* Cornwallis XIII. http://www.thecornwallisgroup.org/pdf/CXIII 9 WoodcockChristenssonDockery.pdf.

Woolard, Catherine. 2013. *The EU and the Comprehensive Approach.* European Peacebuilding Liaison Office. http://www.eplo.org/assets/files/2.%20Activities/Civil%20Society%20Dialogue%20Network/Policy%20Meetings/Comprehensive%20Approach/EPLO CSDN ComprehensiveApproach DiscussionPoints.pdf.

World Bank. 2014. *Afghanistan.* Publications and Reports. http://www.worldbank.org/en/country/afghanistan.

Zyla, Benjamin. 2013. "Explaining Canada's Practices of Burden-sharing in the International Security Assistance Force (ISAF) through Its Norm of 'External Responsibility.'" *International Journal* 68 (June): 289–304. http://ijx.sagepub.com/content/68/2/289.full.pdf+html.

Annex A—More On Synergy

This annex discusses synergy as a grounded theory of Canada's comprehensive approach, based on the practical and crucial background of Canada's engagement in Afghanistan from 2001–2014. Indeed the comprehensive approach tries to achieve synchronisation (Crawshaw 2008, 46). This has little to do with the policies and everything to do with the management and execution. This is based on the hypothesis that although the comprehensive approach had been widely accepted as modus operandi for a coalition of 43 nations engaged within Afghanistan,[131] without a working framework, a model or theory supporting such an emerging holistic policy, it is most likely that complexity remained as a Gordian knot unable to solve its root causes, thereby focusing more on symptoms through disintegrated but well-intended courses of actions. Faced with the weakness of current frameworks of the approach, there can be no feedback into the model in order to challenge the fundamental assumptions so that optimal results can be expected.

Because "Hope is not a method,"[132] this doctoral research proposed that synergy may be an applicable and reliable theoretical construct to support strategic thinking and executive decision making in the case of Canadian or Allied future engagements in unconventional or in fourth-generation warfare.[133] Indeed, venturing strategically and internationally abroad in the context of unconventional wars is, as Clemenceau noted,[134] a matter

---

[131] See NATO, Comprehensive Approach website, 2014, http://natolibguides.info/comprehensiveapproach

[132] Sullivan and Harper, "Hope Is Not a Method," 1997.

[133] Lind, *Understanding Fourth Generation War*, 2004; Hammes 2006, 293.

[134] Georges Clemenceau was French prime minister twice during World War I, from 1906–1909 and from 1917–1920. For more on Clemenceau, see http://www.firstworldwar.com/bio/clemenceau.htm

too important to be entrusted solely to the military requiring all aspects of what Chinese call comprehensive national power[135] to be leveraged pre-emptively. Conversely, this also presents new threats or opportunities for multidimensional and unrestricted warfare[136] in rather emerging fields of war such as the economy, environment, cyber, space, law and even elections. This is no longer the prerogative of strategic studies and has become a public management issue. Henceforth, there is great use to be made of an integrative theory of synergy to support executive decision making in national security and defence regarding Canada, the UN or Allied future engagements.

Introduction

This complementary annex starts with the review of synergy literature. It was found that an integrative theory of synergy seems not to exist, but the topic has been used variably and parsimoniously within two streams: in complexity and biomedical sciences, as well as in management particularly to discuss mergers and acquisitions and cross-business activities. Only more recently, since about 2004, has synergy appeared within military studies as the idea that the sum can be greater than its parts. However, the conditions of this emergence of synergy in practice, and in theory has not been well developed in an integrated fashion.

This annex discusses theoretical answers to some of our original questioning, looking into synergy as a phenomenon. In order to become more than a simple philosophy for actions, it was found that according to our grounded theorisation, six dimensions would allow for synergy to emerge and become a reality in terms of effects. First, synergy must become a key consideration in time and space, and not be left to chance. Second, synergy must become a collective comprehension over and beyond

---

[135] "Chinese analysts have developed their own extensive index systems and equations for assessing Comprehensive National Power (CNP) or *zonghe guoli*—综合国力. Chinese assessments of CNP are done both qualitatively, in general discussions of country strengths and weaknesses, as well as quantitatively, through the use of formulas to calculate numerical values of CNP. China's forecasts of CNP reject using gross national product (GNP) indexes or measurement methods of national power used in the US" http://www.fas.org/nuke/guide/china/doctrine/pills2/part08.htm

[136] Qao Liang and Wang Xiangsui, *Unrestricted Warfare*—超限战, 1999.

an emerging narrative. Third, an integrative coordination must serve as key architecture for synergy to become realistic. Fourth, synergy must add strategic value in a significant measurable way in concertation beyond simply stating policies. Fifth, synergy must strive for cooperation and systemic efficiencies beyond simple effectiveness. And sixth, synergy must foster collaborative dynamics for parts to become greater than the sum. Following discussion of these theoretically grounded dimensions, and of their potential applications, this annex then turns to synergy as a theory. Indeed, because synergy is based on already well-established dimensions, such as organisational structure, strategic policies, systemic processes and socioculture and situational context, each with their own theoretical corpus, it can thus be said that synergy is a unifying theory.

Presenting summarily the fundamentals of such a theory, as well as the matrix representing linkages to other existing theories and ontologies, this annex then turns to present our meta-analysis. Having meta-analysed the coded data from a population of N = 178 texts (see References Dataset) in order to extract the six categories or dimensions of management (which have all been proven significant to $\alpha = 0.01$), this annex concludes that all categories are positively correlated, from low to very high degrees. In particular, it thus appears that synergy is highly correlated to structure, strategy and systems, and society and the situation are less positively correlated dimensions within the integrated model. This is also consistent with our qualitative, multidimensional analysis. Henceforth, it appears possible to propose an integrated and "comprehensive" theory of synergy that could be the basis for further theorisation research, or be applied practically in the field in support of executive decision making, as in Canada's current and future engagements.

Synergy Literature

Synergy is often associated with the simple cliché "The whole is greater than the sum of its parts," which dates back to Aristotle,[137] but this is actually a very narrow definition. Synergy is the outcome of a whole system of systems (SoS), beyond the sum of its integral parts. By definition, synergy is: (1) The interaction of two or more agents or forces so their combined effect is greater than the sum of their individual effects, and (2)

---

[137] See Aristotle, *Metaphysics*, http://classics.mit.edu/Aristotle/metaphysics.mb.txt

Cooperative interaction among groups, especially amongst the acquired subsidiaries or the merged parts of a corporation, that creates an enhanced combined effect. In particular, synergy has had two main applications since it was quite popular in the 1980s and early 1990s, the first within biology and medicine, and the second within the merger and acquisition literature to explain positive effects. Lately, synergy has resurfaced within the military operational literature with the same intent, which is to explain greater effects from the sum of their parts.

In medicine, as in psychology, the coordinated action of many organs, the association of many functions and many factors concurrently form a unique action and effect. Synergy can thus be translated as "an association of many organs to accomplish a function" (Belotti 2005, 13). In physics, synergy is associated with the behaviour of atoms and subatomic particles, as well as with superconductivity, synchronous light emissions (lasers) and esoteric molecular phenomena such as scale effects. Biochemistry and molecular biology are also rife with synergy. In the social sciences, synergy can be found in many of the phenomena studied by economists—from market dynamics (demand-supply relationships) to economies of scale, division of labour and, of course, the influence of technology. The computer sciences are also grounded in synergy. For example, massively parallel computers, which in effect exploit the synergies associated with a division of labour and hierarchical control, offer performance improvements of many orders of magnitude greater than what can be achieved by conventional sequential processing technology. In natural sciences in particular, synergy has been treated as a solvable equation for years, but it seems the missing elements have yet to be found. Synergy is thus often explained in terms of a black box, as a yet unknown and still intractable phenomenon that nonetheless creates greater effects overall.

Complexity Literature

The notion of science in this perspective is important. Indeed, synergy in general has often been understood as an equation, almost in a positivist perspective, as the sum of its parts, as if this sum was somehow the subject of a mathematical theorem yet to be fully developed. Complexity science, a very systemic way of looking at complexity and attempting to circumvent the chaos inherent in most if not all natural phenomena, has championed an approach whereby synergy, for example, was considered as a black box, an intractable part of the whole equation perhaps still unsolved, whereby synergy was simply assumed to be a higher order phenomena from a more positivist perspective. Although this equation has always composed an element of irrationality that has confronted modern science, in that the sum is actually greater than its parts, a more constructivist perspective allows for the consideration of other intangible, non-mathematical factors to the equation, thereby opening up possibility of an integrative definition of synergy. In this pragmatic perspective, synergy can thus be understood as sciences and arts, combining objectivity with subjectivity, positivism with interpretativism, to achieve a greater perspective, as in the very notion of synergy itself where the sum is greater than its parts. Thus an opened ontology is crucial.

As we progress deeper into the 21st century, the political, economic, social, technological, legal and educational environment (PESTLE) becomes increasingly complex. However, much of our leadership and management thinking is still based on linearity and is dominated by the classical Newtonian paradigm. There is much to do to generate new theories and empirical research into new models of leadership and management that can embrace and focus on those complex adaptive dynamics, on the networks of intelligence sources and on the unpredictability of the fast-changing world.[138] Synergistic effects of various kinds have been a primary cause of the observed trend towards more complex, multifunctional, multilevelled, hierarchically organised systems. This same synergistic effect is applicable both to biological complexification and to the evolution of complex human societies—though quite obviously the sources of innovation and the selective processes involved differ in some important respects. The most significant thing about organisation, however it arises, is the synergy it produces. Thus, synergy is found at the heart of the self-organising phenomena. Synergy may be the functional bridge that connects self-organisation and natural selection in complex systems (Corning 1995, 111–112). In other words, synergy is complex but real.

---

[138] See *International Journal of Complexity in Leadership and Management*'s description: http://www.inderscience.com/browse/index.php?journalCODE=ijclm

Biomedical Literature

Within the biomedical literature, synergy has been used specifically to describe a wide range of combined effects from molecular biology to pharmaceutical drug interactions and much more. The synergism hypothesis, originally proposed in 1983 by Peter A. Corning, addresses the evolution of cooperative phenomena in nature and why there has been a secular trend over time towards increased complexity in living systems. This theory highlights the functional synergy—adaptively significant combined effects that are interdependent and otherwise unattainable—in shaping the progressive emergence of complex living systems. The synergism hypothesis has recently gained scientific support, and there is growing appreciation for the role of various kind of synergy within the evolutionary process (Corning 2013). Indeed, synergy of various kinds has played a significant, creative role in evolution; it has been a prodigious source of evolutionary novelty. Elsewhere, it has been proposed that the functional advantages associated with various forms of synergistic phenomena have been an important cause of the progressive evolution of complex systems in time (Corning 2005).

What's more, synergy is not only a ubiquitous effect in nature, but it has played a key casual role within the evolutionary process. It has been at once the fountainhead and the raison d'être for the progressive increase in complexity over the broad span of evolutionary history. Complexity in nature and human societies alike is not the product of some inexorable force, mechanism or law. It has been shaped by the immediate functional advantages—the payoffs—arising from various forms of synergy. In other words, synergy is not altruistic at all, but it is a mutually beneficial, win-win reciprocity (Corning 2007). Synergy occurs when one entity that behaves in one way and another entity that behaves in another way merge into a third entity that starts behaving in an entirely new way (Greneen 1997, xiii).

It has always seemed ironic that we are surrounded and sustained by synergistic phenomena, combined (or cooperative) effects that can only be produced by two or more component parts, elements or individuals—yet most of us do not seem to appreciate its importance and take its routine miracles for granted. Neither do evolutionists, for the most part, seem to recognise the important causal role of synergy in the evolutionary process, despite the fact that we do depend upon it in a myriad of ways for our survival and reproductive success, and so do all other living things. Thus, synergy is literally everywhere around and in us; it is unavoidable (Corning 1995, 1) yet unrecognised. Indeed, contemporary management literature seems to have forgotten the subject of synergy altogether (Knoll 2006, 4).

Management Literature

Since the late 1990s, synergy became very popular within the strategic management literature in particular as it related to mergers and acquisitions, as well as to cross-business synergies. Ansoff (1965) introduced the concept of synergy into strategic management. He employed the term synergy to describe the effect that the combined return of a whole is greater than the sum of the returns from the individual parts. Since Igor Ansoff introduced the concept of synergy, it has been applied in several research streams within strategic management. Synergy has been discussed in the context of mergers and acquisitions (Larsson and Finkelstein 1998), alliances (Das and Teng 2000; Harrison et al. 2001), and multibusiness firms (Ansoff 1965; Porter 1985; Martin and Eisenhardt 2001; Martin 2002; Knoll 2006), 14–15).

In the 1960s and the 1970s, companies were looking for innovative ways to achieve growth (Ensign 1998). Synergy was used as one of the key components of various strategy formulation frameworks and was especially used for motivating corporate growth through diversification (Juga 1996). Diversification was seen as a way of ensuring profitability. This explains why most synergy research has been focusing on diversification (Ensign 1998). In particular, Chang (1990) studied the empirical relationship between synergy and diversification and proposed that synergy is achieved by sharing of resources amongst the business units within a diversified firm. According to him, the existence of synergy can be explained in terms of the relatedness between an organisation's business units, the particular strengths of the diversified organisation and the organisation's structure (Benecke et al. 2007, 10). Porter (in Ensign 1998) suggested that a way to achieve such a competitive advantage is to develop interrelationships between business units that will lead to effective resource sharing and synergy in executing value-chain activities. Hence, synergy is not new.

But Ansoff (1965) differentiated between sales synergy, operating synergy, investment synergy and managerial synergy as types of cross-business synergies. Adler (1997) for his part described cultural synergy as the process in which the managers shape the organisational strategies, policies, structures and practices based upon the cultural patterns of individual organisation members and clients. Knoll (2006) distinguished between operative synergies, market power synergies, financial synergies and corporate management synergies as types of cross-business synergies. Knoll went on to discuss growth synergy. Synergy thus describes the benefits a business experiences by strategically organising itself to maximise cooperation and innovation. In simple terms, a synergistic organisation achieves more as a group than its parts could by being isolated. Juga identifies synergism as "the co-operative action of discrete agencies in such a way that the total effect is greater than the sum of the effects taken independently" (Juga 1996, 51). Several streams of literature ranging from industrial economics to financial theory and strategic management refer to the concept of cross-business synergies. However, theoretically grounded typologies of cross-business synergies are largely absent from the literature (Knoll 2006, 24).

Increasing synergy requires a careful analysis of an organisation's current strategies to identify better ways of doing business.[139] When people say *synergy*, they usually mean productive use of assets or efficient allocation of manpower and resources. That requires sitting down and studying the situation—looking at all the steps within a process and either improving them, eliminating them or combining them. And that requires hard work, determination and strategic thinking—in a word, strong management (Greneen 1997, xiv). In the mergers and acquisitions literature, synergy usually refers to financial synergy that is gained through the merging of conglomerates (Chang 1990). In the industrial economics literature, synergy features in the context of economies of scale that lead to cost savings. Harris (2004) contends that synergy represents a dynamic process, involves adaptation and learning, creates an integrated solution, entails joint action by many in which the total effect is greater than the sum of the

---

[139] See "Synergy Approach to Strategic Analysis," http://smallbusiness.chron.com/Synergy-approach-strategic-analysis-35341.html

effects when acting independently, does not signify compromise and thus facilitates the release of team energies (Benecke 2007, 9).

Knoll's (2006) study of growth synergy realisation suggests that studies at the intersection of transaction cost theory, the resourced-based view and the converging theories of dynamic capabilities and co-evolutionary theory may be a fruitful starting point for research (p. 333). Itamic and Roehl (in Juga 1996) are of the opinion that synergy results from the process of making better use of resources, including physical assets such as manufacturing facilities, and invisible property like the brand name, customer knowledge, technological expertise and corporate culture. When the organisation exploits these unique resources, it achieves synergy by combining the situational, structural, systemic, sociocultural and strategic dimensions all together, as we have presented them within our synergistic model in this book.

For its part, the synergic governance model proposed by El-Batal (2012) aims to advise the decision makers on the values, attitudes and social behaviours, both organisational and political, which compose all the dynamic governance networks within public organisations (p. 414). His model, however, is limited to three dimensions: the sociocultural, the organisational structure and political strategic dimensions. He leaves out the situational context, the functional systemic and synergy dynamics as the outcome of working together collaboratively.[140] Moreover, Adler (1997) described cultural synergy as "the process in which the managers shape organisational strategies, policies, structures, and practices based upon the cultural patterns of individual organisation members and their clients," and this is consistent with management theory that leverages the preceding dimensions of strategy, structure, systems and socioculture in a situation, in order to achieve much greater synergy.

As the foregoing suggests, synergy can produce a variety of measurable, quantifiable benefits: economies of scale, increased efficiency, improved cost-benefit ratios, the melding of functional complementarities, reduction or spreading of costs and risks, augmentation effects, threshold effects and the emergence of novel functional effects (Corning 1995, 108). Amongst

---

[140] Strogatz, *Sync*, 2004.

other things, there have been (1) synergies of scale, (2) cost and risk sharing, (3) a division of labour (or better said, a combination of labour), (4) functional complementarities, (5) information sharing and collective intelligence and (6) tool and technology symbioses (Corning 2007). The synergy concept suggests that advantages are created when economies of scale and speed are combined with administrative coordination (Krumm et al. 1998). Chang's (1990) study found that synergy is a function of competitive advantage derived from shared resources. Waco and Wery (2004) argue that a key enabler of lasting synergies lies in approaching the diversified company in terms of the division of labour, management responsibilities and the development of common processes across business units and regions. Ensign (1998) argues that understanding interrelationships in diverse organisations is important for understanding synergy, an argument supported by Chang (1990). Separately, the management literature on synergy thus recognises our six different management dimensions but generally addresses them not in an integrated fashion.

Moreover, there is such thing as a synergy bias within the literature. Indeed, the bias stems from the perceived need of corporate managers to justify the existence of their corporations to their capital markets. Because the realisation of operative synergies is increasingly demanded by the investors, many corporate executives frequently engage in wishful thinking and see valuable synergies where there are none. This obviously leads to failing synergy projects (Goold and Campbell 1998; Eisenhardt and Galunic 2000). For a while, people were putting together conglomerates that weren't conglomerates; they were holding companies that resulted from stock deals. They were run as a loose collection of businesses, not a tight-knit group with an integrated management (Greneen 1997, xvi).

From the review of the management literature, it thus appears that synergy is a fruitful avenue for more grounded theorisation. Synergy underscores the other dimensions of management that are the situational context, the socioculture, the organisational structure, the strategic policies and the systemic functions, leveraging their respective contributions in order to form yet a more holistic and integrated understanding. This review of the management literature on synergy thus tends to confirm the validity and reliability of our synergistic model as presented within this book (see Figure 12), thereby leveraging each of the six dimensions.

Military Literature

Of late, the idea of synergy has been parsimoniously cited within the military literature. Contemporary military operations present a major challenge to command and control (C2) theory as they tend to be carried out in theatres and environments where there are increasing degrees of open-endedness (particularly in terms of the extent of effects and consequences of actions) and complexity (in terms of unpredictability and social diversity). In 2009, General Sir John Kiszely summarised the challenges facing governments and characterised them by four things in particular: "Complexity, ambiguity, uncertainty and volatility and by the fact that they all tend to be 'wicked problems'—problems that are intractable and circular with complex inter-dependencies—where solving one problem can create further problems and/or make the whole problem that greater."[141] Indeed, within the military literature, the idea of synergy has been present since about 2004, and this synergy has been defined as an ideal type of collaboration resulting in greater effects. Hence: "Synergy is the result of a number of individual physical, cybernetic and moral effects which when combined produces a total impact on the adversaries or factions that is greater than the sum of the individual effects."[142]

For Corning (2007), synergistic functional effects of various kinds thus have been an important (a necessary, though not sufficient) causal agency underlying all the manifold forms of collective violence in nature. To repeat, his claim is that synergy is a "common denominator" of warfare. One additional ingredient that must be added to the causal package is functional synergy. The functional benefits, or the payoffs, that can be generated by collective action are the necessary additional cause, without which collective violence will most likely not occur. That is, synergy is the "difference that makes a difference," to use the mantra of anthropologist Gregory Bateson. It is synergy of various kinds that determines the cost-effectiveness of collective violence, and the very fact that collective violence is so often contingent is closely related to the ebb and flow of various

---

[141] Lorraine Dodd and Anthony Alston, *Complex Adaptive and "Inquiring" Systems Theory for Contemporary Military Operations: A Multi-perspective Approach*, 2009, p. 149.
[142] NATO, *Comprehensive Operational Planning Directive*, 2010, p. A20.

kinds of functional synergy in a given situation. Synergy is not a unitary phenomenon, however. There are many different kinds of synergy. Indeed, as already noted, there can be negative synergy[143] as well as positive synergy (Corning 2003).

Most important, the incidence of collective violence—in nature and human societies alike—is greatly influenced by synergies of various kinds, which shape the bio-economic benefits, costs and risks. Synergy is a necessary (but insufficient) causal agency. This does not mean humans are killer apes, with a reflexive blood-lust or an aggressive drive. The biological, psychological and cultural underpinnings of collective violence are far more subtle and complex (Corning 2007, 1). Corning's theory of warfare (2007), in a nutshell, is that various forms of functional synergy are a major causal agency that is necessary but certainly not sufficient in precipitating collective violence in nature and humankind alike. Synergy is a universal denominator, often a major inducement and driver for these behaviours.

Tools and weapons also represent a major form of synergy, a cooperative effect (or effects) that are not otherwise attainable. Amongst other things, weapons can increase the force or reach of a blow, or enable the user to strike a blow from a distance, as well as providing the ability to cut or penetrate the flesh of an adversary. Likewise, technologies that are designed to protect the user against the blows of an adversary (like a shield or body armour) represent important defensive weapons (Corning 2007). Such tools are the processes used to make planning for war and its execution more effective and efficient, such as the Operational Planning Process. Indeed, unity of effort is often referred to as *"Planned Joint and Combined Synergy*: Establishing unity of effort across the components is fundamental to joint and combined Ops and constitutes the first step in ensuring a truly joint and combined approach" (*CF OPP Manual* 2002, 2–8). Henceforth, the most

---

[143] For example: "Drug traffickers have a symbiotic relationship with insurgents and terrorist groups such as the Taliban and al-Qaeda. Instability makes opium cultivation possible; opium buys protection and pays for weapons and foot soldiers, and these in turn create an environment in which drug lords, insurgents and terrorists can operate with impunity. Opium is the glue that holds this murky relationship together." UNODC Director Costa (2007), "An Opium Market Mystery," *Washington Post* (April 25), http://www.csdp.org/news/news/post_costa_042507.htm

important variable in coalition operations is unified action. The synergistic application of all the instruments of national and multinational power involving non-military and international organisations, governmental and military forces. But in order to achieve unified action, interoperability between multinational forces is characterised by the seamless exchange and sharing of information at the strategic, operational and tactical levels (Lewis 2009, 1).

Collaboration between military and civilian actors must lead to a civil-military integration. Such integration must be clearly understood and cannot only take place upstream. Rather, it must involve every level of intervention and requires integrated planning, as well as integrated reports with joint goals and operations. All these actions must be managed in synergy (Howard 2009). To this effect, synchronisation of military operations has become the mantra by which synergy is achieved. Synchronisation is the arrangement of actions and their effects within time and space, and the purpose to achieve maximum advantage and most favourable conditions. Operational planners will therefore make full use of all effects available to them (e.g., precision attack, decisive manoeuvre, information, psychological operations and civil-military cooperation) in order to achieve desired conditions and effects. The primary benefit from synchronisation is the ability to produce synergy and gain leverage by the imaginative creation and exploitation of the desired conditions and effects throughout the operations area using different resources.[144] Henceforth, synergy is operationalised through synchronisation.

On the other hand, fostering development and improving governance cannot proceed without security. Canada's civilian and military efforts in Kandahar, after just two years of close collaboration, were starting to achieve some real operational synergy that would be difficult to replicate quickly with the forces of another country (Manley Report 2008, 31). Moreover, ad hoc "just in time" coordination of efforts will never fully develop potential synergy between the interagency process and the military towards national objectives. The absence of a strategic vision and the lack of an integrated planning approach impel decision makers to focus on parts of the system (i.e., nodes) while ignoring the system as a whole. This approach

---

[144] NATO, *Comprehensive Operational Planning Directive*, 2010, p. A20.

expands the gap between diplomats and war fighters as they each fail to understand the other's core competencies and to maximise the effects of their integration (Zippwald 2006, 5). It has been recommended to strive for flexibility regarding personnel and funding: secondments of key staff between different ministries and international organisations can greatly help to develop shared understanding of the synergy between defence, diplomacy and development. In addition, synergy can be improved by making political and development advisors cooperate closely with military commanders in the field, and by joint training of personnel from different departments. To support such synergistic action, financial instruments and other systemic processes also need to be flexible.

Notwithstanding the importance of the military contribution to our international role, only by achieving the synergy of a true "Team Canada" approach within the Canadian international community can we have an impact as a nation (Jeffery 2005, 7). Simplified and isolated departmental approaches thus suffer from tunnel vision, failing to achieve synergy through vertical and horizontal coordination.[145] In many cases, it seems one of the obstacles to interdepartmental synergy has been a lack of intradepartmental synergy within the Canadian Forces. Intelligence and operations staffs are closely related and must ensure that their cooperative activities result in the highest level of operational synergy to support decision making at all levels of command (CF Ops 2005, 15–17). Unified leadership, or unity of command, has been amongst the most frequently cited requirements for greater synergy between the civilian and military efforts. Beyond this generic assertion, however, there is little agreement on an appropriate model. The instinctive association of unity of effort with unity of command within the military mindset makes it particularly difficult for the military to consider alternatives to a hierarchically organised chain of command, with a single decision-maker at the top (Baumann 2008, 72). Thus, shifting paradigms becomes key.

More fundamentally and as a corollary to this approach, the debate on aggregate power has begun to address how military power can be brought to bear on non-military issues. That debate must now turn the problem around and address how non-military economic or other types of power

---

[145] Christensen and Lægreid 2007, 1060.

may be used in a military or law-enforcement context. Operations will achieve strategic clarity and maximum effectiveness as a result of integrating both horizontal and vertical planning and implementations processes from the outset. That is, the organisational integration of horizontal (i.e., multinational/multilateral) political-military planning and operations with vertical national (e.g., interagency) political-military planning operations must be implemented to achieve synergy towards the achievement of an agreed political vision (Manwaring 2006, 4). Hence, we need a comprehensive approach, which represents new thinking, but the nature of the challenges is not new. Afghanistan is where NATO has been engaged for the first time in true ground combat operations. We must anticipate similar complexity in future operations (Crawshaw 2007, 14). Indeed, synergy is a common denominator in collective violence. It is a major culprit. Yet in the final analysis, synergy is only the subservant of various human purposes, impulses and perceptions, and the inescapable conclusion is that so long as the gains of collective violence are perceived to outweigh costs, there will unfortunately be no end to war (Corning 2007).

Synergy Theory

Henceforth, synergy is clearly not a peripheral phenomenon associated only with drug interactions or corporate mergers. Though it often travels in disguise, synergy can be found in the subject matter of most, if not of all, of the academic disciplines (Corning 1995, 90). Synergy exists in so many different forms that it defies efforts to develop an exhaustive typology (Corning 1995, 105). Synergy is a holistic phenomenon that cannot be described by linear, mono-causal reasoning. And whichever element on some particular level is chosen for investigation, it must be considered within context involving other levels, with circularly causal relations in between them (Grössing 2000, 2).

In essence, synergy is the outcome of a whole system of systems (SoS), which is greater than its parts. Used within the complexity literature in this perspective, the idea of synergy also found fruitful explanation within the biomedical and life sciences. The management literature has variously used the idea as well, in particular regarding mergers and acquisitions and for cross-business activities. Finally, within the military literature, synergy has been used only recently, and explicitly to point to the necessity of greater civil-military integration in order to achieve more dynamic and integrated effects on the ground. From this, synergy thus appears to be a very valid idea for further theorisation as well as for further theory integration.

Fundamental Theory

Indeed, in the absence of an empirical and theoretical model of the comprehensive approach, constructing one from available and applicable theories requires a meta-theoretical construct, taking strength from each theory in order to counterbalance the weaknesses of other theories. Henceforth, considering all management theories as potential parts of the solution is crucial for an integrated meta-theory to emerge and serve as umbrella for different management theories. In this, it may be seen that the greater diversity will lead to greater strength and the many will lead to the one, just as the success of one theory leads to greater diversity in application. Our ability to advance a meta-theory is founded on our ability to meet multiple requirements in an integrated way, not simply one or two (Wallis 2010, 109), and thus to construct a theory. From this integrative perspective, it can be seen that theories may be more or less applicable to a given situation, while nonetheless explaining parts of the whole phenomenon in its complexity. It is through integration that synergy creates greater effects.

A key consideration is to recognise the implicit requirement for coordination between the various power instruments. Consequently, an explicit synchronisation mechanism must be derived and implemented in order to achieve cross-cutting synergy (Ritchie 2010, 65). Indeed, synergy cannot and does not happen in a vacuum, and in fact because synergy is the combination of effects from the sum of its parts, as a dependent variable it is very much dependant on its components. These parts, we argue, are composed of other key dimensions—namely, the situational context, the socioculture, the organisational structure, the strategic policies and the systemic processes—all of which contribute to some extent to creating a larger phenomenon, which we have identified as synergy that is integrative, holistic and dynamic.

Theory Integration

As such, synergy does not happen in a vacuum. In fact, synergy is only the combined effect of the six dimensions we have presented. This is why also degrees of integration have been presented within our synergistic model, with each degree representing the effect of one to six dimensions, where six appears to be the more integrated synergy dimension. Achieving real leverage from synergy thus requires theory integration where different theoretical insights combine into a larger theoretical phenomenon that is synergy. The following section presents these theoretical linkages in between the six dimensions of our synergistic model, which helps better appreciate the theoretical integration of these different strategic management theories. Indeed, if a collaborative perspective is required, then collaborative theory integration is fundamental so that theories can come together and create real leverage.

First, the situational dimension is often linked to contingency theory, where decisions are contingent on a specific context and situation. The link between the situational-strategic dimensions is best reflected through the resource dependence theory, which explains how resources enter the strategic calculus based on a set of conditions. The situational-structural link for its part is explained through organisational ecology theory, where organisations adapt to the particular conditions of their external environment. And finally, the situational-systemic link is developed through evolutionary theory and how such a specific context conditions evolution. Together, these four theories help sustain the situational context dimension and its conditions, which are often context specific.

The sociocultural dimension for its part is best reflected through seven major theories. Indeed, the human relations theory helps understand who and with whom interrelations develop to sustain human comprehension. This can take two forms: The rationalistic one, which is based on social cognitive theory, and the emotional one, which is based on behavioural theory, both of which seek to explain common understanding from two standpoints. The link between the sociocultural-strategic dimensions is for its part best represented through the organisation culture theory, where organisational culture is a strategic lever for more comprehension. The sociocultural-structural link is explained through agency action theory, distinguishing the principal from the agent as people in action. The sociocultural-systemic link is supported by critical social theory, which accounts for unconventional views and perspectives within comprehension. Finally, the sociocultural-synergic link is represented by social dynamics theory, which explains the complexity that ensues from dynamic interactions.

The structural dimension for its part is supported by the classical institutional theory, and the linkage between structural-situational dimensions is best explained through neo-institutional theory, adapting the premises of institutional theory to the contemporary environment. The structural-systemic link is reflected through structuration theory, where social systems are constructed based on the analysis of structure and agents. As for the structural-strategic linkage, it is explained thanks to punctuated-equilibrium theory, which explains what forms organisations take in equilibrium according to their own strategies.

For the important strategic dimension, three theories help develop its corpus in relation to three dimensions. First, the strategic-structural linkage is often the subject of strategic management theory, which attempts to shift the organisation according to strategy. Secondly, the strategic-systemic link for its part is best reflected through new public management as a paradigm that seeks to adopt a more systemic management approach. Third and finally for the strategic dimension, the strategic-sociocultural linkage is represented through leadership theory, which explains how leaders influence society in line with their strategic objectives. These three theories and paradigms are well-recognised.

Fifth is the systemic dimension which itself is based on systems approach theory, which takes on a process perspective to explaining issues. Two crucial linkages are explicated: the systemic-structural one through complexity and chaos theory, which addresses how systems impact organisations, and the systemic-sociocultural one through double loop (or feedback) theory, which addresses how society impacts on systems by retroaction.

Sixth and finally is the synergy dynamics dimension, which explains greater effects. There is no substantive theory of *synergy*, which this book's annex proposes as additional contribution. The synergic-structural link is related to organisational learning theory, where these organisations adopt a learning culture that leverages lessons learned for better collaboration. The synergic-strategic link is explicated through the knowledge creation theory that explains the competitive edge gained by strategically creating different knowledge. And the synergic-systemic link is defined by dynamic capabilities theory, where the systemic integration of capabilities leverages the whole system and creates positive synergy.

Henceforth, synergy provides for an integrative theoretical framework, touching upon the six dimensions of our synergistic model and providing a meta-theory for the most commonly known strategic management theories to come together in a much stronger way. As such, the following table presents the general theoretical linkages to other management theories with a view to synthesizing some of the main dimensions according to their major theories. What this table presents is striking in its theoretical integration of numerous existing theories.

Table 7—Theoretical Matrix

Dimensions	Theoretical Linkages	Ontological Linkages
1. Situational Context (Where? When?) Conditions		Archaeology, Agriculture, Geography, History, Ecology, Environmental and Earth Sciences,
Situational	Contingency Theory (CT)	Situation
Situational-Strategic	Resource Dependence Theory (RDT)	Resources
Situational-Structural	Organisational Ecology Theory (OET)	Adaptation
Situational-Systemic	Evolutionary Theory (ET)	Evolution
Dimensions	Theoretical Linkages	Ontological Linkages
2. Sociocultural (Who?) Comprehension		Anthropology, Ethnology, Arts Communications Studies, Psychology, Humanities, Literature, Social Studies, Sociology, Religion

Sociocultural	Human Relations Theory (HRT)	Humans
Sociocultural-rational	Social Cognitive Theory (SCT)	Cognition
Sociocultural-emotional	Behavioural Theory (BT)	Behaviour
Sociocultural-Strategic	Organisation Culture Theory (OCT)	Criticism
Sociocultural-Structural	Agency (Action) Theory (AAT)	Society
Sociocultural-Systemic	Critical (Social) Theory (CST)	Agency
Sociocultural-Synergic	Social Dynamics Theory (SDT)	Culture

Dimensions	Theoretical linkages	Ontological linkages
3. Organisational Structure (What?) Coordination		Architecture and Design Sciences, Chemistry, Engineering, Physics, Organisation Studies, Urbanism
Structural	Institutional Theory (IT)	Institutions
Structural-Situational	Neo-Institutional Theory (NIT)	Organisations
Structural-Systemic	Structuration Theory (ST)	Structuration
Structural-Strategic	Punctuated-Equilibrium Theory (PET)	Equilibrium
Dimensions	Theoretical Linkages	Ontological Linkages
4. Strategic Policy (Why?) Concertation		Political Science, Strategic Studies, Management Science, Leadership Studies, Philosophy
Strategic-Structural	Management Theory (MT)	Managers

Strategic-Systemic	New Public Management (NPM)	Efficiency
Strategic-Sociocultural	Leadership Theory (LT)	Leadership
Dimensions	**Theoretical Linkages**	**Ontological Linkages**
5. Systemic Functional (How?) Cooperation		Biology, Medical Sciences and Health, Economics, Linguistics, Earth and Space Sciences, Law and Security Studies, Mathematics, Business and Public Administration
Systemic	Systems (Approach) Theory (SAT)	Systems
Systemic-Structural	Complexity and Chaos Theory (CCT)	Complexity
Systemic-Sociocultural	Double Loop (or Feedback) Theory (DLT)	Feedback
Dimensions	**Theoretical Linkages**	**Ontological Linkages**
6. Dynamic Synergy (So what?) Collaboration		Artificial Intelligence, Computing Sciences and Informatics, Logics, Education, Operations, Statistics, Systems Science, Cybernetics
Synergic-Structural	Organisational Learning Theory (OLT)	Learning
Synergic-Strategic	Knowledge Creation Theory (KCT)	Knowledge
Synergic-Systemic	Dynamic Capabilities Theory (DCT)	Dynamism

Meta-Theory

Meta-theories in general are complex and often implicitly (if not explicitly) recognise such complexity in the phenomenon of study by leveraging various theories to explain the whole, or the meta, linking theories together under a subject and its object. In our case, because we are aiming to construct theory for the comprehensive approach due to a lack of an actual model, theory or framework, as noted from the review of literature on this subject (see <u>Chapter 1</u>), meta-theory is important. It helps us position all relevant theories in a comprehensive way while referring to a management ontology, thus leveraging the respective strengths of individual theories and offsetting their weaknesses within an integrated meta-theory.

There are many important features of meta-theories, including the fact that they are ubiquitous (all theories and methods are formulated and operate within a meta-theory) and often reside quietly and unrecognised in the background of our day-to-day empirical science. An essential and sometimes unrecognised feature of meta-theories is that they emerge and operate at several levels of analysis. Meta-theories, sometimes also referred to as models or paradigms, tend to form a hierarchy in terms of increasing generality of their application. The hierarchical dimension of any given set of meta-theoretical ideas also forms a coherently interrelated system of ideas, and the model operating at the pinnacle of this hierarchy is usually termed as a world view. Thus, world views are composed of coherent interlocking sets of epistemological (i.e., issues of knowing) and ontological (i.e., issues of reality) principles (Overton 2007, 154). Moreover, the analysis of theory is an inherently meta-theoretical exercise (Ritzer 2001, 18); it occurs more frequently than most imagine. For example, every academic paper involves the implicit or explicit examination of extant theories—that is, a consideration of which theories (or parts thereof) might be suitable for advancing a new theory (Wallis 2010, 88).

A meta-theory is the philosophy behind theory, the fundamental set of ideas about how the phenomenon of interest in a field should be thought about or researched. Scientific meta-theories transcend theories as well as methods in the sense that they define the context in which both the theoretical and the methodological concepts are constructed. Although theories and methods refer directly to the empirical world, meta-theories refer to the theories and the methods themselves (Overton 2007, 154). Hence, meta-theory can be viewed as a theory of theories. In the case of synergy, because it is composed of numerous dimensions, each with its very own corpus of literature found within different disciplines (such as international relations, sociology, organisational studies, strategic management, systems approach and decision-making), all these theories combine into a theory of theories, which we underwrite as synergy.

Situational Dimension

History, geography, the physical environment and global context still have bearing today, so the first dimension is the situational context, which becomes the starting point of any holistic analysis. From a theoretical standpoint, this accounts for the contingency theory (relativism to the environmental analysis), as well as evolutionary theory (evolution over time), resource dependence theory (dependency on resources) and organisational ecology theory (adaptation to the physical as well as metaphysical environment). All of these theories adopt an outward look upon their situated and contextual environment as a crucial determinant. Identifying those imperatives, such as the actual physical environment (mountains and deserts, oceans and rivers), and the past history of them becomes the first order for any multidimensional analysis.

Contingency Theory

Contingency theorists suggest that previous theories, such as Taylor's scientific management and Weber's bureaucracy, are insufficient because they neglect the influence of various aspects of the environment on which decisions are very often contingent. Contingency theory thus represents the introduction of relativism into management with its well-known maxim: It depends! "The main assumption of the contingency theory is that the structural components of the organisation must be integrated for the organisations to survive. Therefore change, in one element must be followed by adaptive changes in other elements to maintain coherence" (Demers 2007, 4). This theory explains the situational context dimension.

Resource-Dependence Theory

Along the lines of the contingency theory is the resource dependence theory wherein according to Pfeffer and Salancik (1978), managers adjust resources depending on their environment and shape this environment as much as it shapes them. "There are important environmental and contingent factors in and around Public Service Organisations, which militate against innovative activity within them" (Osborne 2005, 171). "Within the logic of change programmes, it is often assumed that there is an embedded rational and strategic response to changing environment. However, political and contextual factors often play significant part in the adoption of particular types of change agenda" (Osborne 2005, 103). Many influential theories assumed that organisations are relatively malleable and able to adapt when circumstances change (e.g., Thompson 1967), which according to many other scholars may not always be the case and is thus limited by the other considerations, namely resources. "Global economic changes mean Public Service Organisations can no longer rely on steady incremental growth, and have to focus on efficient-effective use of increasingly scarce resources" (Osborne 2005, 4). This theory thus illustrates the strategic linkages that exist with a specific situation.

Organisational Ecology Theory

Hannan and Freeman's organisation ecology theory (1989) examines the immediate environment in which organisations compete, and it attempts to identify the key processes of natural selection. It is more deterministic than contingency theory, but it nonetheless considers change evolutionary. "Organisational ecology utilizes insights from biology, economics, and sociology, and employs statistical analysis to understand conditions under which organisations emerge, grow, and die." Henceforth, organisational ecology, also known as the organic adaptation approach (Demers 2007), is thus characterised as "An adaptively rational system rather than an omnisciently rational system" (Cyert and March 1963, 99), meaning that some rationality can be applied to understand how, within a given ecology of population for example, such a type of organisation may emerge. Therefore it has a key tenet: "Social change is evolutionary—path-dependent, yet contingent, shaped by legacies and affected by contingently related processes and conditions" (Sayer 2000, 26). Theories of organisational ecology help explain the linkage between the situation and the structure.

Evolutionary Theory

"Some authors also view the evolutionary perspective as an overarching framework within which other organisational theories, including the neo-institutional, cultural-interpretative, and learning schools, can be included" (Demers 2007, 135). Indeed, "We need an organisation that is very adaptive, that is very agile and quick. Instead of having cycles that

take years, we need cycles that take months, because the threat changes"
(Dunleavy 2006, 485).

> The emphasis is [today] on a shift from older, more imperative
> methods of managerial fiat, based on prescription, command, and
> control, to empowerment, teamwork, and networked relations.
> These it is argued, are more suited to the postmodern world as one
> of instability and fragmentation, where both the product and service
> markets, as well as systems that sustain them, change at a bewildering
> rate compared to the old certainties of industrial mass-production
> and mass-marketing. (Clegg 2003, 558)

Evolutionary theory explicit the linkage between a given situational context
and the systems-processes dimension.

Sociocultural Dimension

Secondly, accounting for human activities and specifically for the social and
cultural dimension of human activity in all things, comes the sociocultural
dimension. Theoretically, this covers the human relations theory (social
cognitive and behavioural social psychology), as well as organisation
culture theory, agency (action) theory, critical (social) theory (e.g., Marxist
and feminist studies) and social dynamics theory. This social and cultural
dimension represents the theories that have as their main driver the human
within organisations, whether at an individual, collective or organisational
unit of analysis. For each theory, their linkages are explained as follows.

Human Relations Theories

The Hawthorne studies (1924–1932) examined productivity through social
relations, motivation and employee satisfaction. "The hallmark of the
human-relation theories is the primacy given to organisations considered
as human cooperative systems, rather than mechanical contraptions."
These theories posit that individuals within organisations are somewhat
independent entities that collectively contribute to the organisational goal
but that moreover satisfy their own. Human relations theories explain the
sociocultural dimension and include the social cognitive theory as well as
the behavioural theory.

Eric Dion, CD, MBA, PhD

Social Cognitive Theory

The social cognitive theory posits that knowledge acquisition can be cognitive—that is, it's related to observing others within the context of social interactions, experiences, and media influences. Coming from psychological studies, the cognitive theory is premised on the foundations of the human relations school of thought, who studied the behaviour of people within organisations. Thus, research on managerial cognition in particular offers the possibility to examine the link between the way managers interpret information, the resulting mental frames and organisational adaptation. The second (subjective-interpretative) perspective, on the other hand, sees cognition as a meaning creation process that constructs organisational reality.

What is sometimes called the interpretative turn within organisation studies parallels an earlier movement in the social sciences (Reed 1992). This second perspective in particular, contrary to the first (which relates mainly to an objective-functionalist view), is fundamental from a constructive epistemology for, as Demers explains, "Organisations that were traditionally viewed as objective, concrete entities were now conceived [cognitively] as inter-subjective, symbolic constructions" (Demers 2007, 61).

Behavioral Theory

In the behavioural or adaptive learning approach developed by March and his colleagues (Cyert and March 1963; March 1981, 1991; Levinthal and March 1993), the generative mechanism is behaviour modification as a result of experience. In contrast to the cognitive approach presented above, which describes organisational learning as a change in the dominant coalition's mental frameworks, organisations are conceived as adaptive systems that learn from trial and error and that encode and retain that learning in routines (Holmqvist 2003; in Demers 2007, 121). Whereas cognitive theory considered a triad of personal and behavioural determinants in relation to environmental determinants, behavioural theory is primarily focused on explaining individual behaviour as opposed to human cognition.

Organisation Culture Theory

"While organisational culture has been an important concept and popular topic for several years, it is becoming increasingly evident that it is a key element of global competition" (Aupperle 1996, 447). Organisational culture can be defined as a pattern of shared basic assumptions that the group learned as it solved its problems of external adaptation and internal integration that has worked well enough to be considered valid and therefore be taught to new members as the correct way you perceive, think, and feel in relation to those problems (Schein 1993, 374). In short, organisational culture can be thought of as the way things get done around here, which encompasses the cultural traits, norms and values of people in an organisation. "To create and sustain any new organisational paradigm, a key ingredient is required: Culture. In the ever renewing society what matures is a system or framework within which continuous innovation, renewal and rebirth can thus occur" (Gardner 1963; in Aupperle 1996, 457). This theory links socioculture to the structure.

Agency (Action) Theory

Agency theory is directed at the ubiquitous agency relationship, in which one party (principal) delegates work to another (agent), who performs that work. Agency theory is concerned with resolving two problems that can occur in agency relationships. The first is the agency problem that arises when (a): the desires or goals of the principal and agent conflict; and (b): it is difficult or expensive for the principle to verify what the agent is actually doing. The problem here is that the principal cannot verify that the agent has behaved appropriately. The second is the problem of risk sharing that arises when the principal and agent have different attitudes towards risk. The problem here is that the principal and agent may prefer different actions because of the different risk preferences. (Eisenhardt 1989, 57)

One such analysis, based on the agency theory, is the stakeholder analysis. A stakeholder is usually defined as anyone who has interest in a particular organisation (or structure). "Stakeholder analysis is a systematic approach to identify these key stakeholders for a particular interest and seeking to influence them" (Osborne 2005, 205). This theory explains organisational linkages that exist between structure and sociocultural dimensions.

Critical (Social) Theory

Originating from the Frankfurt School of Sociology, and in particular from Horkheimer (1937), critical social theory sought not only to explain sociocultural phenomena, but also to challenge and change society, taking a critical stance on industrial and corporate capitalism as well as the political-economic system in general. Unlike Marxism, however, critical social theory does not view mankind as a struggle between social classes, but rather as a self-reflective stance that allows one to see through the effects of structural and systemic domination or dependence. "Critical thinking is that mode of thinking—about any subject, content, or problem—in which the thinker improves the quality of his or her thinking by skilfully taking charge of the structures inherent in thinking and imposing intellectual standards upon them" (Paul and Elder 2006, 1). Henceforth, critical social theory provides the requisite critical reflexivity that is required within an integrated model and more specifically highlights the linkage between the systemic and societal dimensions.

Social Dynamics Theory

Finally, social dynamics theory, akin to agency theory, assumes a larger unit of analysis than the individual or group scale organisational psychologists have most often focused upon, probably by professional deformation. Approaches in the social dynamics stream generally present a more sophisticated and diversified picture of agency. On the other hand, in the social dynamics tradition, context and history are socially constructed, and it is the way they are interpreted and used by actors in the construction of their world that is of interest (Demers 2007, 226). From this perspective, social dynamics theory does not assume a positivist epistemology, as behavioural theorists have done in the past. Rather, it assumes an interpretative and most often a constructive epistemology that refers not to how theorists perceive dynamics but, more to the point, how interrelations within a group unfold in a given context. This theory illustrates the key linkages with the synergy dimension.

Structural Dimension

The third dimension to consider is that of the organisational structure, which is internal. This dimension is concerned with organisations from an institutional management perspective, namely through institutional theory and neo-institutional theory, as well as from a structuration theory perspective and a punctuated-equilibrium theory. The structural dimension thus focuses on organisational factors (including actual infrastructure and physical features) and attempts to explain outcomes mainly from a structural and organisational perspective, linking to other dimensions.

Institutional Theory

Institutions can be defined as "The beliefs, paradigms, codes, cultures, and knowledge that support rules and routines," a description that differs little from classic organisation theory (March and Olsen 1976, 71). "The framework outlined by Lynn (2001) identified the institutional level of governance as a significant arena in which the mode of public sector organisation was pertinent to understanding change" (Osborne 2005, 59). Henceforth, "The institutional level of the public service includes the infrastructure of government and its bureaucracy (Christensen et al. 2002), political systems of government including rule-making apparatus and routines of political behaviour (March and Olsen 1989)" (Osborne 2005, 59). These constitute prime institutional areas for management. "The number and variety of structural changes grow as institutions in which we live expand and get intertwined" (Mills 1967, 13). Specifically, "In machine bureaucracy hierarchies, the techno-structure is especially influential while in adhocracies, the search for innovation is strong" (Frederickson and Smith 2003, 78). Thus the institutional theory points to the institutional features that impact upon management, and generally speaking, the structural-institutional features of organisations anchor stability. "Problems in the characterization of change, in organisational change management, are identified as a narrow focus on organisational aspects rather than examining broader social and environmental contexts that contribute to understanding change" (Sturdy and Grey 2003). Institutional theory thus explains how difficult it is for organisations to address wider issues than the structural view.

Neo-Institutionalism Theory

In the neo-institutional theory, management is not so much concerned about structure itself, but rather with the larger institutional environment that sets the institutional conditions within which institutions themselves are situated. In the case of public administration departments or agencies, these are situated within a legislated and regulated institutional environment, constrained namely by budgetary pressures and accountability calls. Thus, neo-institutional theory holds as a key tenet that management is aimed at survival in terms of legitimacy and economy. In this sense, the neo-institutional theory links the notion of management with imperatives and an impetus for new, transformational ways of adapting to this larger institutional environment. It is regarding this perspective that Savoie considers, from a neo-institutional theory point of view, that "The policy side of government and the ability of bureaucracy to be innovative and self-questioning needed more fixing than do the machine or production-like agencies" (Savoie 2005, 118). "A number of next-generation instruments might facilitate win-win outcomes; Instruments that harness market forces in order to encourage rather than inhibit commercial drive and innovation, including many economic instruments and performance standards" (Eliadis et al., 343). But "At the institutional level of governance, public service-wide influencers shape the context and character and impact the way public service are managed and operated" (Osborne 2005, 60).

As such, March and Olsen (1989) suggest institutions are so complex as to restrict predictable outcomes in the planned change programmes and the interrelated layers of institutional members, institutions and context works against consistent outcomes of change (Osborne 2005, 233). However, an interesting integrative perspective is offered by neo-institutionalist Scott (2004, 3), who considers the institutional environment as consisting of societal norms and values, historically situated and inherited imperatives and strategic choices within "bounded rationality." Neo-institutional theory illustrates situational links.

Structuration Theory

Beyond Piaget's structuralism theory (1968), where he acknowledges in a constructivist fashion that "There exists no structure without a construction, abstract or genetic," the structuration theory of Giddens (1984) takes a process perspective consistent with *in becoming* ontology, to offer a structurally, systematically integrated perspective on the main organisational features. As such, it is obvious within structuration theory that Giddens considers change as a normal evolutionary process, but that holds for principal feature the structure and, more precisely, the process of structuration as its key tenet, much like the institutionalisation process that created neo-institutionalism. For Hannan and Freeman (1977, 1984), "Structural inertia theory challenged this view, depicting a world of relatively inflexible organisations in which change is both difficult and hazardous."

Nonetheless, "The main structural challenge is the departmental model of organisation. Today, many companies are developing structures that are smaller, decentralised, and based on strategies of cooperation as well as horizontal relationships. This has happened, they say, because of the increased complexity and open-endedness of organisational goals" (Osborne 2005, 138). This is particularly the case within the public sector, where faced with increased globalisation as well as new information technology that foster greater citizenry expectations, the public service has found new grounding in structuration theory to explain a process view of both structural and systemic innovation that creates new agencies and produces new services and challenges. Structuration therefore explains the systemic linkage.

Punctuated-Equilibrium Theory

The punctuated-equilibrium theory holds for key tenets that change is indeed incremental and evolutionary in seeking to preserve a sort of organisational homeostasis, which is sometimes punctuated by periods of innovation, transformation and perhaps even revolution. In considering innovation, "Kuhn (1962) stressed the importance of punctuated equilibrium" (Clegg 2003, 548), where within structural features, innovation can be envisaged as radically new. Taking the organisation out of equilibrium can be favourably compared to finding a catalysts for change, which by its significance to the organisation and the challenge to its *raison d'être* can create an impetus for change. But moreover, it can create an imperative for innovation, taking new and extraordinary organisational measures within a structured or a systemic perspective to innovate. But Brown and Eisenhardt (1997) note "Firms engage in change according to continuous change continuum, rather than implement change as a discrete episodic event" (Osborne 2005, 219). Thus it may well be the case that equilibrium or organisational homeostasis is maintained most of the time, and that episodic changes of punctuated-disequilibrium then foster true innovation. The challenge is whether this disequilibrium happens outside the control of the organisation, or whether it happens strategically and in control. This theory explains the linkage between structure and strategy.

Strategic Dimension

Strategic dimension theories are concerned with decision making, political interests and intention. Whereas situational theories are focused on external determinants, sociocultural theories focus on the internal and social ones, and structural theories focus on institutional characteristics, the strategic theories focus on extra-organisational dynamics involving politics and strategic policy. The strategic dimension includes traditional top-down management theory, new public management and leadership theory—all in a managerial, political view. Preceding, theoretical linkages are also explained.

Management Theory

Closely aligned with classical administration and originally based on *The Principles of Scientific Management* by Frederick Taylor (1923), management and more recently strategic management have become the dominating paradigm to rationally explain strategic patterns (Mintzberg 2007). Whereas management focuses on the execution of daily activities and on implementation of policies and programs, it is also concerned with managerial power inside as outside organisations. What's more is that improvement has been a steady theme within strategic management, namely in light of expectations of efficient and effective public service delivery. Within the decision-making and game theories, strategic management also discourses on the role of intuition, on the necessity of the involvement of stakeholders and the allocation of incentives to drive the organisational strategy to objectives. Within management theories also falls strategic planning, which is aimed at intended objectives, as well as change management, which is interested with the revolutionary process. In general, management theory focuses on defining intentions and working on implementation. In this perspective, strategic analysis is the crucial step developed in order to analyse thoroughly the organisation overall politics as played by the organisational actors themselves in this context. Henceforth, management theory in general explains the linkage between strategy and structure.

New Public Management

New public management describes a wave of public sector reforms throughout mostly Western public administrations since the 1980s. The key assumption supporting NPM is that the market, in its competitive mechanisms, presents greater efficiencies, whereas the reduction of the public administration also gained political capital, in particular under Margaret Thatcher and Ronald Reagan. "While some implemented sweeping transformational changes throughout the public service as the case of New Zealand, nations such as Norway responded with a more incremental approach, focusing on management efficiency rather than 'rolling back the state'" (Osborne 2005, 56). As with management theories, NPM focuses on the top-down approach and is mainly strategic. It mostly leverages economic theories as well as private sector business models, however "Because governments are non-profit, objectives tend to be either very general, or ambiguous, so it is difficult to measure returns on investment (ROI) in order to justify management decisions" (Bontis; in Borins 1995, 147). NPM thus highlights the linkage between the strategy dimension and the systemic dimension.

Leadership Theory

A more recent body of management literature has been concerned with leadership theory. This has been coming particularly from private sector case studies of successful business entrepreneurs. Within the public management literature, there have also been some studies of leadership, most often within a larger situational or institutional context, such as Allison's (1999) *The Essence of Decision Making* as relating to John F. Kennedy's leadership or to studies of Churchill in England. However, there is a growing recognition that leadership is quintessential as well within public service, and to some extent, the emerging literature has focused on middle management leaders. Hence, "The core of this approach is the concept of persuasion that the successful manager of an innovation needs to persuade the key stakeholders that a given innovation is in their best interest" (Osborne 2005, 205). Furthermore, "The pace and character of a change is reliant on how managers broker relationships and balance competing interests in the organisation, management, administration and core business of each public service organisation" (Osborne 2005, 65). "Strategic leaders create a vision that encompasses a view of the future state of the organisation in such a way that organisational members have a clear focus of their decisions and actions and are motivated" (Osborne 2005, 103). What's more, "The real work of new leaders within the public organisations is thus strategic, that is to prepare their members within the organisations to cope with and adapt to changes of mission, environment and/or direction" (Valle 1999, 245). Leadership theory relates to the linkage with socioculture.

Systemic Dimension

The systemic dimension includes theories from the systems (approach) theory, chaos and complexity theory and the double loop (or feedback) theory, all of which understand organisational management as a systemic process, focusing upon functional elements. While the structural dimension looks at organisations as whole entities, the systemic dimension rather looks at them as a system of functional processes that interact collectively as mechanics. As with other theories, main linkages are presented.

Systems (Approach) Theory

Von Bertanlaffy's *General Systems Theory* (1968) attempted to develop an overarching meta-theory of all organic systems arising from biology, and it had great influence in cybernetics. Systems theoretical approaches were also appropriated in other fields, such as in the structural functionalist sociology of Parsons (1951), who applied the systems' principles within sociology. But before the system approach theory became mainstream within management, there first was an acknowledgment of the systemic view of organisation that arose as a process orientation within organisations studies, most notably portrayed in Giddens' *Structuration Theory* (1984). Indeed, in organisation theories at large, *Structuration Theory* was certainly the first contemporary attempt at the systematisation of the process view of organisations, along with advances in new technologies. Specifically for management, that meant interactions: "Social structures are constituted by human agency, yet at the same time, are the very medium of this constitution" (Giddens 1969, 121).

However, the emerging systems approach in organisation theories shifted towards a clear focus on technologies and processes. Indeed, as a result of digitalisation and the creation of intelligent, networked organisations, today one may rarely see those with whom one is doing business on a face-to-face basis. Interaction occurs in cyberspace, through the Internet. Therefore "The convergence of computing power and telecommunications reach is providing new technological and information resources with which to pursue business opportunities, but this is only achievable if the management and organisation of enterprises are transformed to capture the potential of new technologies" (Clegg 2003, 560). As such, "It is argued that what is needed is a contingent approach rooted in open systems theory" (Scott 2004, 209). Systems obviously help explain the systemic view.

Complexity and Chaos Theory

Complexity theory has been used in the field of strategic management and organisational studies. It is sometimes referred to as complexity strategy, chaos theory or complex adaptive systems, and it has also been studied within game theory and decision-making as well as leadership simulations. Indeed, "Complexity science represents a growing body of interdisciplinary knowledge about the structure, behaviour and dynamics of change in a specific category of complex systems known as Complex Adaptive Systems; or open evolutionary systems in which the components are strongly interrelated, self-organizing and dynamic" (Sanders 2003). However, the underlying assumption behind complexity science is precisely that it can somewhat positively and scientifically arrange itself around complexity, as if it could be isolated in a laboratory—a venture that is impossible. "The management of innovation requires embracing the complexity of modern organisation and its environment, what Peters called 'thriving in chaos' (Peters, 1988)" (Osborne 2005, 208). Henceforth, "Many authors contend that the complexity approach offers a synthetic way to look at management as the tension between opposing forces such as formal and informal networks, implementation and innovation" (Demers 2007, 161), which in itself remains very complex. Complexity and chaos theories explain the systemic to structural link.

Eric Dion, CD, MBA, PhD

Double Loop Theory

The management challenge is furthermore highlighted within a systems-of-systems perspective. It was Argyris in *Double Loop Theory* who brought systems thinking to the fore of organisation studies, explaining that it is necessary if the practitioners in organisations are to make informed decisions in rapidly changing, uncertain contexts, thus highlighting the systemic-situational link while developing this conception of organisational management through incomplete information. But Argyris was also concerned with interpretations and images, and specifically with internalisation. Hence, the essence of Argyris's double hermeneutical approach (1976) served to illustrate the systemic complexities within sociological and cultural systems by looking into the interactions resulting from intersubjectivity, identity, ideology and others, which are largely held implicitly in individuals in organisations, and within organisations themselves. Thus, beyond the systemic and structural perspectives, Argyris's loop brought the systems perspective to sociocultural features. Henceforth, "The innovative Public Service Organisation needs to be an open rather than closed system" (Scott 2004). In particular, retroaction helps explain the linkage between systems and socioculture.

Synergistic Dimension

Finally, the sixth dimension is that of the overall synergy or dynamic created by the organisation, which encompasses the organisational learning theory, the knowledge creation theory and the dynamic capabilities theory, all of which are quite dynamic. The assumption underlying the synergic dimension is that a higher degree of integration is crucial. Thus, "Better organized and increased coordination between the various multilateral, regional and nongovernmental actors should strengthen the synergies in the international response to crises."[146] This is akin to the Six Sigma and LEAN production management models that essentially focus on the integrated management effects of the overall process of the organisation

---

[146] European Union, Thematic Evaluation of the European Commission Support to Conflict Prevention and Peace Building—Concept Study, 2010, 40, http://ec.europa.eu/europeaid/how/evaluation/evaluation_reports/reports/2010/1277_vol1_en.pdf

taken as a whole—a process that can be quantitative and statistical, but that also includes qualitative methods. The links are explained.

Organisational Learning Theory

"Organisation learning is without a doubt the success story of the 1990. It replaces organisational culture as the approach to change that stimulates practitioners and scholars alike.... The rise to prominence of the topic of organisational learning coincides with the increased influence of the behavioural or adaptive learning perspective" (Demers 2007, 123). Both streams, however, assume a rationalist and positivist perspective in that behaviour is psychologically explained or that adaptation ensues rationalistically from learning. Hence organisational learning actually assumes a constructive epistemology. Indeed, in organisational learning, "Rules themselves change as the result of learning" (Demers 2007, 123), which virtually creates a hermeneutical spiral of sorts. "It is plausible to think that an organisation can know both more and less than the cumulated knowledge of its individual members" (Glynn et al. 1994). Thus, learning theory is coherent with an information processing view: "March and Olsen (1976) view learning as a continuous cycle between individual beliefs, individual action, organisational action, and environmental response" (Demers 2007, 128). From this perspective, organisational learning consists of the interdependence of the situated, sociocultural, structural, strategic and systemic dimensions. Furthermore, learning appears a quintessential condition to knowledge creation and management. This theory highlights the linkage from synergy to organisational structure.

Knowledge Creation Theory

"Organisational knowledge creation theory is aimed at developing a comprehensive view of knowledge that could shed light on organisational creativity, learning, innovation and change" (Nonaka and Krogh 2009, 636). In contrast with many previous management theories that tended to take a relatively positivist and rationalist stance in the previous dimensions, knowledge creation assumes in fact that knowledge is precisely constructed. It is understood as such by its main authors, as the integration of many of the dimensions we covered presciently. "Innovation enables knowledge, and knowledge is created in a spiral that goes through seemingly antithetical concepts such as order/chaos, micro/macro, part/whole, mind/body, tacit/ explicit, self/others, deduction/induction, creativity/control" (Weick 2005, 450). "Nonaka (1994) reveals that the knowledge creation process is an interplay between the behavioural and cognitive learning, and shows how each is allowing change to emerge and also making it stick" (Demers 2007, 128). From this definition of knowledge management, it clearly appears that its main assumption is the top-down approach, implying that management can strategically create knowledge and foster the "proper" conditions. "Organisational knowledge creation is important to organisation science, because it explains how new ideas come forth in innovation, not only how individuals tap into rich practices" (Nonaka and Krogh 2009, 645). "If we further raise the level of analysis, we arrive at a discussion of how so-called national systems of innovation can be built" (Nonaka, Toyama and Konno 2000, 30). Knowledge creation explicit the synergistic to the strategic linkages.

Dynamic Capabilities Theory

"Dynamic capability is defined as the firm's ability to integrate, build, and reconfigure internal and external competences, to address rapidly changing environments. The basic assumption of the dynamic capabilities framework is that today's fast changing markets force firms to respond quickly and to be innovative" (Teece, Pisano and Shuen 1997, 512). This implied dynamism presents an interesting perspective, whereas management is a constant, much like change. The dynamic capability theory perspective has focused on competition within high-velocity industry, hyper competition and, in the case of Aupperle (1996), spontaneous reconfigurations. In his highly criticised study of the Xenophon's Anabasis, Aupperle highlights that culture was the key to hyper-competitive advantage. "Ultimately it was the culture, not the strategy, qualitative and informal properties, and not well defined roles and structures that produced the Greek military success" (Aupperle 1996).

Other scholars have had similar thoughts in regards to dynamic capabilities theory. "Rather than trying to explain how order is designed into the parts of an organisation, configuration theorists try to explain how order emerges from the interaction of those parts as a whole" (Freedman 1992). Hence, "It is because configuration theorists, like the population ecologists, conceive of organisations as *Gestalts* (i.e. tightly coupled wholes) that they view change as rare and revolutionary; a process of destroying a configuration and replacing it with another" (Demers 2007, 48). In this dynamic capabilities perspective, it thus appears clearly that systems are open, yet there appears to be something more, perhaps intangible as culture or foresightedness, even technologies that combine in various, spontaneous configurations to create higher levels of competitiveness. As such, it can be said of certain specialised military units that their overall synergy is really their secret weapon. Moreover, in a system-of-systems perspective, such dynamism explains the synergistic links.

Meta-Analysis

Having theoretically established the six dimensions and considerations for synergy to emerge, we now turn from meta-theory to our meta-analysis of the phenomenon. Indeed, it appears that because synergy is based on fundamental management dimensions—the situational context, the socioculture, the organisational structure, the strategic policies, the systemic processes and the synergy dynamics—this provides the basis for a theoretical framework. What's more, meta-analysing these six dimensions in a quantitative perspective provides for very rich insights into the construction of our synergistic model. As means of verification for the overall theoretical model proposed for synergy, a final meta-analysis was conducted on the codes, concepts and categories to extract correlations. It was found that all dimensions are significant and positively correlated, although the variance of correlation ranges from low correlation (0.30–0.49) to moderate (0.50–0.69) and high (0.70–0.89), including one very high correlation (0.90–1.00). The fact that all of the population of N = 178 texts (see <u>References Dataset</u>) were selected within keyword searches for the comprehensive approach partially explains these positive correlations. Their high degree of significance to $\alpha = 0.01$ indicates that each dimension is also an independent, categorical variable for standalone analysis. In other words, each dimension is significant to explain the construction of our proposed model, as we have presented in the previous chapters of this book on synergy. Henceforth, the following tables represent the correlations and variance for the six dimensions of our theoretical model.

Table 8—Meta-Analysis of Covariance

Correlation	Situ	Soci	Struc	Strat	Sys	Syn
Situ	1,00	0,64	0,75	0,69	0,78	0,56
Soci	0,64	1,00	0,60	0,48	0,54	0,39
Struc	0,75	0,60	1,00	0,86	0,82	0,88
Strat	0,69	0,48	0,86	1,00	0,84	0,91
Sys	0,78	0,54	0,82	0,84	1,00	0,81
Syn	0,56	0,39	0,88	0,91	0,81	1,00

Table 9—Analysis of Correlations

		Situ	Soci	Struc	Strat	Sys	Syn
Situ	Pearson Correlation	1	,637**	,747**	,689**	,783**	,563**
	Sig. (bilateral)		,000	,000	,000	,000	,000
	N	178	178	178	178	178	178
Soci	Pearson Correlation	,637**	1	,602**	,482**	,538**	,390**
	Sig. (bilateral)	,000	w	,000	,000	,000	,000
	N	178	178	178	178	178	178
Struc	Pearson Correlation	,747**	,602**	1	,861**	,821**	,884**
	Sig. (bilateral)	,000	,000		,000	,000	,000
	N	178	178	178	178	178	178
Strat	Pearson Correlation	,689**	,482**	,861**	1	,835**	,914**
	Sig. (bilateral)	,000	,000	,000		,000	,000
	N	178	178	178	178	178	178
Sys	Pearson Correlation	,783**	,538**	,821**	,835**	1	,807**
	Sig. (bilateral)	,000	,000	,000	,000		,000
	N	178	178	178	178	178	178
Syn	Pearson Correlation	,563**	,390**	,884**	,914**	,807**	1
	Sig. (bilateral)	,000	,000	,000	,000	,000	
	N	178	178	178	178	178	178

** The correlation is significant to 0.01 (bilateral).

It first appears that all correlations are positive and that the sociocultural dimension is the least correlated overall, followed by the situational dimension. However, they still remain quite valid. The structural, strategic and systemic dimensions appear as the most correlated, to some extent confirming that these dimensions are the core of strategic management. The synergic dimension also appears very correlated, confirming its validity and reliability as a category of management based on the selected literature reviewed. This is how the quest for synergy was established. Together, these six dimensions are positively correlated, and the meta-analysis of the preceding correlation of variance highlights these positive relationships.

The bottom-left quadrant, at the intersection of structure, strategy, systems and synergy, appears as the most correlated, indicating that these categories are strongly related together in our theoretical model. On the other hand, the societal and situational categories appear less relevant to explain the model; indeed, they seem to indicate that they are lesser considerations, such as indicated in our qualitative analysis. In essence, strategy is very highly correlated to synergy. Structure and systems are both highly correlated to synergy, whereas situation is moderately correlated and society is lowly correlated. This meta-analysis of variance from the correlations points out the core management categories, within which the practice and the literature reside with strategy, structure, systems and synergy. As these are the strongpoints of our model, weak points clearly reside in socioculture and situational context. Nonetheless, their individual significance to $\alpha = 0.01$ and their positive correlations altogether point to each dimension as valid and reliable dimension of analysis under our integrated, holistic and dynamic synergistic theoretical model. As such, this meta-analysis validates our own model.

Conclusion

This annex to our doctoral thesis is central in discussing synergy as a theory. Through the systematic grounded theorisation and content analysis of the literature, it was found that six dimensions would be required considerations to affect synergy as a theory. Indeed, synergy must first be considered as conditions to more explicitly emerge as such. There is a second consideration to foster common sociocultural comprehension surrounding this synergy. Third, an integrative structure, framework or architecture is needed in order to coordinate synergy. What's more, there is a fourth consideration to be given to the strategic, value-adding concertation management. The search for systemic efficiencies appears fifth as to leverage cooperative effects within synergy. And finally, there is a sixth consideration for collaborative dynamics that would foster this synergy. From the literature, it thus appears some of these considerations are sometimes considered, but most of the time they are considered on an individual basis and not in a single holistic, integrated and dynamic meta-theory such as we have presented herein. This is the value added of this <u>Annex A</u> in discussing synergy as potential theory and meta-theory of the comprehensive approach.

In the final meta-analysis, synergy should be understood as a crucial condition, as psychosocial cultural comprehension, as integrative structural coordination, as value-added strategy to the coalition, as efficient system of cooperation and as collaborative dynamics, which together help foster such synergy in all dimensions. Indeed, as some literature indicates,

> When collaboration is achieved, significant advantages include: a. More accurate, shared situational awareness; b. Easier identification of, and agreement about, outcomes; c. Earlier identification of emerging opportunities as an operation progresses; d. Improved capacity for mitigating undesirable consequences; e. More efficient use of resources; and f. Increased legitimacy for the campaign and its conduct overall. (CF Land Ops 2008, 5–19)

This implicitly highlights the fundamental dimensions of management required to foster greater synergy. The situational context, the socioculture, the organisational structure, the strategic policies and the systemic processes combine to form a collaborative dynamic known as *synergy,* which is composed of many numerous theories and thus constitutes a meta-theory.

Moreover, by meta-analysing our coded, conceptualised data and their categories, we further found that all six dimensions presented are quantitatively significant and positively correlated. This verification method thus confirms the high degree of validity and reliability of this research design, which started from grounded theory, evolved into content analysis, and included participation observation, as well as meta-theorisation and a final meta-analysis as its verification. Through a multidimensional analysis of the practice of synergy, it is possible to propose a theory of synergy for the comprehensive approach in the case of Canada's engagement in Afghanistan. What's more, as demonstrated previously, it appears possible to apply synergy to Canada's current engagement in Iraq and the Levant, though Canada's current mission is predominantly military. Such engagement should make leverage of synergy as crucial condition, of synergy as sociocultural comprehension, of synergy as integrative coordination structure, of synergy as coalition value-added strategy, of synergy as systemic cooperation efficiency and of synergy as collaborative dynamics, pointing out our theoretical model, which best reflects upon the comprehensive approach.

Figure 8—Synergy: A Theoretical Model

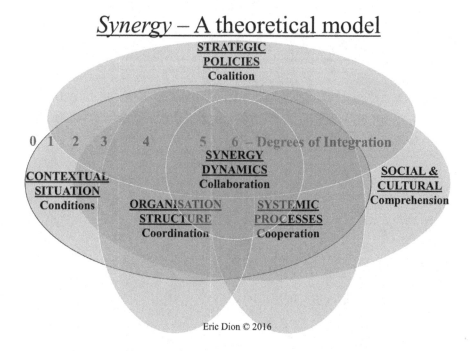

References Cited in Annex A

Allison, Graham T., and Philip Zelokow. 1999. *The Essence of Decision— Explaining the Cuban Missile Crisis*, 2nd edition. Longman.

Argyris, Chris. 1976. "Single-Loop and Double-Loop Models in Research on Decision Making." *Administrative Science Quarterly* 21: 363–375.

Aupperle, Kenneth E. 1996. "Spontaneous Organisational Reconfiguration: A Historical Example Based on Xenophon's Anabasis." *Organisation Science* 7, no. 4: 445–460.

Borins, Sandford. 1995. "A Last Word." *Canadian Public Administration* 38, no. 1: 137–138.

Borins, Sandford. 1995. "The New Public Management Is Here to Stay." *Canadian Public Administration* 38, no. 1: 122–132.

Brown, S., and K. M. Eisenhardt. 1997. "The Art of Continuous Change : Linking Complexity Theory and Time-Paced Evolution in Relentlessly Shifting Organisations." *Administrative Science Quarterly* 42, no. 1: 1–34.

Burchill, S., et al. 2005. *Theories of International Relations*, 3rd edition. Palgrave MacMillan. http://psi505.cankaya.edu.tr/uploads/files/Theories%20of%20IR.pdf.

Canada. 2008. *Canadian Forces Operational Planning Process*, Canadian Forces Joint Publication 5.0. http://publications.gc.ca/collections/collection_2010/forces/D2-252-500-2008-eng.pdf.

Corning, Peter A. 2007. *Synergy Goes to War.* Palo Alto, CA: Institute for the Study of Complex Systems. http://complexsystems.org/publications/bioeconomic-theory-of-collective-violence (accessed October 22, 2016).

Cyert, R., and J. G. March. 1963. *The Constitution of Society.* Englewood Cliffs, NJ: Cambridge University Press, Prentice-Hall.

Demers, Christiane. 2007. *Organisational Change Theories: A Synthesis.* Sage.

Dunleavy, Patrick, Helen Margetts, Simon Bastow, and Jane Tinkler. 2006. "New Public Management Is Dead—Long Live Digital-Era Governance." *Journal of Public Administration Research and Theory* 16, no. 3 (September): 467–494.

Frederickson, H. George, and Kevin B. Smith. 2003. "Public Institutional Theory." In *The Public Administration Theory Primer*, Westview Press, 67–94.

Frederickson, H. George, and Kevin B. Smith. 2003. "Theories of Political Control of Bureaucracy." In *The Public Administration Theory Primer*, Westview Press, 15–66.

Glaser, B. G., and A. L. Strauss. 1967. *The Discovery of Grounded Theory: Strategies for Qualitative Research.* Chicago: Aldine, 1999.

Giddens, A. 1984. *The Constitution of Society: Outline of the Theory of Structuration.* Cambridge: Polity, 1986.

Haas, Peter M., and Ernst B. Haas. 2002. "Pragmatic Constructivism and the Study of International Institutions." *Millennium—Journal of International Studies*, 31, no. 3 (July): 573–601.

Hildebrand, D. 2005. "Pragmatism, Neopragmatism, and Public Administration." *Administration and Society* 37, no. 3: 345–359. http://aas.sagepub.com/cgi/content/abstract/37/3/345.

Hildebrand, D. 2008. "Public Administration as Pragmatic, Democratic, and Objective." *Public Administration Review* 68, no. 2: 222–229. http:// davidhildebrand.org/index.php?page=research/abstracts.php.

Kaplan, Robert S., and D. P. Norton. 2006. *Alignment: Using the Balanced Scorecard to Create Corporate Synergies.* Harvard Business School Publishing.

Levinthal, Daniel A., and James G. March. 1993. "The Myopia of Learning." *Strategic Management Journal* 14: 95–112.

Lynn, Jr., Laurence E., Carolyn J. Heinrich, and Carolyn J. Hill. 2001. "Studying Governance and Public Management: Challenges and Prospects." *Journal of Public Administration Research and Theory* 10, no. 2: 233–261.

Lynn, L. 2001. "The Myth of the Bureaucratic Paradigm: What Traditional Public Administration Really Stood For." *Public Administration Review* 61, no. 2: 144–160.

March, James G. 1991. "Rationalité Limitée, Ambiguïté et Ingénierie des Choix." In *Décisions et Organisations*, Paris: Les Éditions d'Organisation, 133–160.

March, James, G. 2006. "Rationality, Foolishness, and Adaptative Intelligence." *Strategic Management Journal* 27: 201–214.

March J. G., and J. P. Olsen. 1984. "The New Institutionalism: Organizational Factors in Political Life." *American Political Science Review*, no. 78: 734–749.

Mills, C. Wright. 1967. *L'Imagination Sociologique.* Découverte, Collection de Poche.

Mintzberg, Henry. 2007. *Tracking Strategies: Toward a General Theory.* New York: Oxford University Press.

Nonaka, Ikujiro, and Georg von Krogh. 2009. "Tacit Knowledge and Knowledge Conversion: Controversy and Advancement in Organisational Knowledge Creation Theory." *Organisation Science* 20, no. 3: 635–655.

Nonaka, Ikujiro, and Ruoko Toyama. 2003. "The Knowledge-Creating Theory Revisited: Knowledge Creation as a Synthesizing Process." *KM Research* 1: 2–10.

Nonaka, Ikujiro, Ryoko Toyama, and Noboru Konno. 2000. "SECI, Ba and Leadership: A Unified Model of Dynamic Knowledge Creation." *Long Range Planning* 33, no. 1: 234.

Osborne, Stephen. 2005. *Managing Change and Innovation in Public Service Organisations.* Routledge.

Patton, M. Q. 2008. *Utilization-Focused Evaluation*, 4th edition. Sage Publications Inc.

Paul, R. and L. Elder. 2006. *Critical Thinking Tools for Taking Charge of Your Learning and Your Life.* New Jersey: Prentice Hall Publishing.

Piaget, Jean. 1979. "Le Structuralisme." *PUF, Que Sais-Je?* no. 1311: 5–16.

Plane, Jean-Michel. 2008. *Théorie et Management des Organisations.* Paris: Dunod.

Rouleau, Linda. 2007. *Théories des Organisations: Approches Classiques, Contemporaines et d'Avant-garde.* PUQ.

Sanders, Irene T. 2003. *What Is Complexity?* Washington Center for Complexity and Public Policy, International Journal of Complexity in Leadership and Management.

Savoie, Donald J. 1995. "Just Another Voice from the Pulpit." *Canadian Public Administration* 38, no. 1, 133–136.

Savoie, Donald J. 1995. "What Is Wrong with the New Public Management?" *Canadian Public Administration* 38, no. 1: 112–121.

Sayer, Andrew. 2000. *Realism and Social Science.* Sage Publications.

Schein, Edgar H. 1993. *Organisational Culture and Leadership: Classics of Organization Theory.* Jay Shafritz and J. Steven Ott, eds. Fort Worth: Harcourt College Publishers, 2001.

Schein, Edgar H. 2004. "The Dimensions of Culture." In *Organisational Culture and Leadership*, 3rd edition, 85–222.

Scott, Richard. 2004. "Reflections on a Half-Century of Organisation Sociology." *Annual Review of Sociology* 30: 1–21.

Teece, D., G. Pisano, and A. Shuen. 1997. "Dynamic Capabilities and Strategic Management." *Strategic Management Journal* 18, no. 7: 509–533.

Watson, Ken. 2011. "Implementing an Integrated Approach to Train SOF for the FID Mission." Joint Special Operations University Report 11-4, JSOU and NDIA SO/LIC Division Essays, July, 47–53. https://jsou.socom.mil/JSOU%20Publications/11-4_Essays_110811b.pdf.

Weick, Karl E. 2006. "The Role of Imagination in the Organizing of Knowledge." *European Journal of Information Systems* 15, no. 5: 446–451.

Weick, Karl E., Kathleen M. Suncliffe, and David Obstfeld. 2005. "Organizing and the Process of Sensemaking." *Organisation Science* 16, no. 4: 409–421.

Woodcock, Alexander E. R., Anders Christensson, and John T. Dockery. 2008. *A Systemic Approach Is Needed for Fully-Integrated Civilian-Military Policy-and Decision- Making.* Cornwallis XIII. http://www.thecornwallisgroup.org/pdf/CXIII_9_WoodcockChristenssonDockery.pdf.